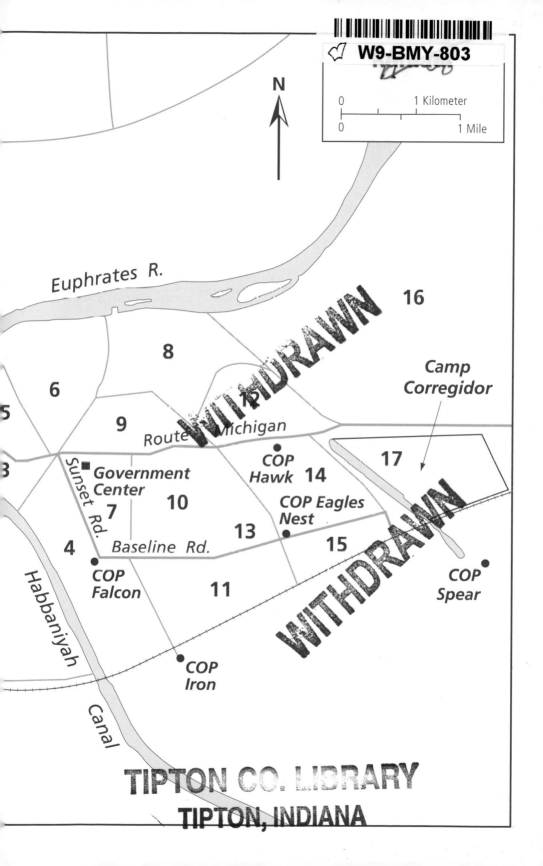

N

0   1 Kilometer

0   1 Mile

Euphrates R.

16

WITHDRAWN

Camp
Corregidor

8

6

5

12

9

Route Michigan

COP
Hawk

17

14

Government
Center

COP Eagles
Nest

10

Sunset Rd.

7

13

15

4

Baseline Rd.

COP
Falcon

COP
Spear

11

WITHDRAWN

Habbaniyah

COP
Iron

Canal

The Sheriff of RAMADI

Navy SEALS
and the
Winning of al-Anbar

by Dick Couch

NAVAL INSTITUTE PRESS
Annapolis Maryland

Other Books by Dick Couch

Fiction

SEAL Team One

Pressure Point

Silent Descent

Rising Wind

The Mercenary Option

Covert Action

Nonfiction

The Warrior Elite

The U.S. Armed Forces NBC Survival Manual

The Finishing School

Down Range

Chosen Soldier

This book is dedicated to Marc Lee,
Mike Monsoor, and Clark Schwedler,
three Navy SEAL warriors who perished in the
fight to wrest al-Anbar province from the
al-Qaeda-backed insurgents and
return it to the Anbari people.

Naval Institute Press
291 Wood Road
Annapolis, Maryland 21402

Library of Congress Cataloging–in–Publication Data

Couch, Dick, 1943–
Sheriff of Ramadi : Navy Seals and the winning of
al-Anbar / Dick Couch.
      p. cm.
Includes index.
ISBN 978-1-59114-138-9 (alk. paper)
1. Iraq War, 2003—Campaigns–Iraq–Anbar Province. I. Title.
DS79.76.C6775 2008
956.7044'345–dc22

                              2008023334

Printed in the United States of America

15 14 13 12 11 10 09 08   10 9 8 7 6 5 4 3 2
First printing

Interior design and composition by Chris Onrubia, Fineline Graphics LLC

Contents

Foreword

America's time in Iraq has been hard. Our efforts to secure our nation's interests and usher in a brighter future for a fellow people have not always met with the success we anticipated or would have liked. In the Navy, sailors speak of such times as a "stern chase," and a stern chase is a long one. Yet as our fighting men and women know so well, America has faced such trials before. What distinguishes us as Americans is not that we are subject to such challenges, but rather how we respond to them —with persistence, with clarity of purpose, and with the determination to succeed in the service of our nation.

Those in the media and the body politic have often been quick to point out the deficiencies of our efforts in Iraq. I, too, have criticized the conduct of the war. Yet the purpose of that criticism has always been to identify new pathways to security and success. In spite of our manifold sacrifices, we must never let our frustration turn into negativism and blind us to the potential for success. Our military surely has not. In combination with their Iraqi partners, our soldiers, sailors, airmen and marines have made tremendous strides in a cause some had long deemed futile.

One of the greatest of these began in the spring of 2006 in western Iraq. The Battle of Ramadi—the fight for a key stronghold in al-Anbar province, then Iraq's most dangerous area—continued into the spring of 2007. In this volume, Dick Couch has given us a superb accounting of the Navy SEALs who took part in the battle and who, along with their Army and Marine Corps comrades, returned the city of Ramadi and the whole of Anbar province back to the Iraqi people.

Before the Battle of Ramadi, al-Anbar province accounted for nearly half of U.S. military fatalities and half the deadly roadside bombs known as IEDs (or improvised explosive devices) that indiscriminately killed Americans and Iraqis alike. In Ramadi and across al-Anbar, insurgents routinely assaulted U.S. and Iraqi patrols. Gunfire and explosions were commonplace. By August of 2007, all that had changed. Ramadi's streets were patrolled not by al-Qaeda, but by Iraqi policemen—Sunni tribesmen who had helped to win back their neighborhoods from the insurgents. Days now go by without violent incident. Al-Qaeda and their surrogates occasionally slip into the city to commit acts of terrorism, but Iraqi police are in place to deal with them. Reconstruction is under way, schools have reopened, and economic progress is taking place.

There remains a long road ahead in Iraq; there will be continuing challenges and our work is not done. And yet it is beyond doubt that the gallant soldiers, Marines, and SEALs who have fought there deserve to look back on their efforts with a great sense of professional pride and accomplishment. Increasingly, the American public has come to understand that something important began to change in Iraq in late 2006 and throughout 2007. Thanks to the careful research and insightful analysis of Dick Couch, we now have a much deeper understanding of a pivotal battle that began the process of expelling al-Qaeda from its strongholds.

As Mr. Couch explains, our military expelled al-Qaeda from Ramadi not through force of arms alone. Recognizing that an insurgency is a war for the people, our fighting men and women won the people. The people of Ramadi and al-Anbar, when given a clear choice and a sense of personal security, sided with American and Iraqi security forces against al-Qaeda. The Anbari people won, Iraq won, America won, and al-Qaeda lost.

In *The Sheriff of Ramadi*, Dick Couch brings to life the brave and talented individuals who helped orchestrate this victory. These include Colonel Sean MacFarland, who commanded American and Iraqi forces during the battle and whose outreach to the tribal sheikhs of al-Anbar helped bring these influential leaders over to our side. Sheikh Sattar abu Risha led the Anbari tribes into an alliance with the Americans, and in September 2007 paid for his courage with his life. SEAL Petty Officer Mike Monsoor died in the Battle of Ramadi, selflessly giving his life to save the lives of his brother SEALs in an act of heroism that merited the Medal of Honor. The tale of these and many other extraordinary individuals make up the gripping narrative that is *The Sheriff of Ramadi*. In telling their story, Dick Couch has not only paid tribute to their bravery and sacrifice, but also provided all readers with unique insights into a pivotal battle in the war in Iraq.

Senator John McCain

Preface

A Message from the Commander

In 2006 the collapse of Ramadi seemed imminent. Into this chaos there was thrust a small element of U.S. special operations forces, mostly Navy SEALs. This SEAL task unit was given an ambiguous mission, tenuous support, and an uncertain relationship with the U.S. soldiers and Marines who were struggling mightily for control of the streets. Given operational latitude, the SEALs quickly adapted to the environment, found their unique place on the team, and became key to the ultimate liberation and stabilization of Ramadi.

Their success was a tribute to the open-minded leadership of several Army commanders and to the extraordinary courage and tenacity of the SEALs themselves. Innovative, flexible, tough, and skilled, these SEALs faced hostile fire at an unprecedented intensity and pace. Their casualty rate was high, but their valor was higher. Far from their traditional maritime environment, the SEALs in Ramadi answered every call and met every challenge. Their story is now legend.

These SEALs were among the thousands of special operations forces who were, and are, performing missions of incredible difficulty and complexity across Iraq, Afghanistan, and several other global hot spots. They run to the sound of guns, but they prefer, whenever and wherever possible, to arrive in time to prevent a crisis from occurring. They help our friends as competently as they hurt our enemies—and they understand the importance of balancing both approaches. They carry a disproportionate burden in this enduring campaign against violent extremists, and all Americans should be fiercely proud of them. Never before has such a force been assembled.

Just over twenty-one years ago, U.S. Special Operations Command was created to bring together, under a single commander and with a dedicated budget, dedicated forces from each of the military services. Since then, assigned forces have been selected, trained, and equipped to answer mission requirements that are simply beyond the capabilities of traditional military units. The standards are high and the training is difficult, and, once qualified to serve in a special operations unit, most members remain for the balance of their military careers.

Over the past few years, special operations forces have changed in many ways. Most notable is the near-total integration of special operations forces and general purpose forces in the complex battle-spaces of today's conflicts. The mutual respect is strong. Most special operations missions are now conducted with foreign counterparts who have been trained by us. Known as "combat foreign internal defense," this is the way our current battles must be waged. Again, the mutual respect with our local allies is strong. Operating away from home and at a tempo unthinkable just a decade ago, the special operations forces are stretched. The strain is manageable for now, but all leaders are concerned about the future. To this end, special operations forces have recently authorized increased manning levels to achieve a more sustainable deployment posture.

Our special operations forces are meeting the nation's highest expectations. Although many of their accomplishments and sacrifices are not made public, our special operators know they are making a real difference where it counts most. Those of us who serve with them consider it the greatest possible honor. It is my privilege to command this magnificent force.

Adm. Eric T. Olson
Commander, U.S. Special Operations Command

Acknowledgments

My sincere thanks to the officers and men of the Ramadi task units from SEAL Teams One, Three, Five, and Seven—for your service to your nation and to the people of al-Anbar, and for helping me to tell this story. Thanks for your support and for your indulgence of any oversights and omissions on my part. I can only hope that I've written your story half as well as you fought the Battle of Ramadi. You were magnificent. As this book goes to print, many of you are back on deployment—back to the war. May God watch over you and keep you safe.

Mike Monsoor, Medal of Honor recipient. Mike Monsoor leads Petty Officer Tim Dominico and Lieutenant Sean Smith in the streets of Ramadi during the battle. *AP Photo*

Introduction

Writing a book about unfolding current events is tricky business. Things change; the ideas and assumptions you make at the beginning of a project sometimes don't hold as you make your way through the effort. It becomes incrementally more difficult when you're writing about events in an active combat theater. And finally, when your subject matter is the operational activity of Navy SEALs in Iraq, well, the events you're trying to bring in focus can be complex, fast-paced, and dynamic. Writing about them often becomes, as we say in the Navy, a stern chase, and a stern chase is a tough one. This was never more the case than when I set out to document the role of the Nave SEALs in the Battle of Ramadi.

In the spring of 2006, a former Navy SEAL came to me with an interesting story. We had become friends in 2000 when I was working on *The Warrior Elite: The Forging of SEAL Class 228* (Crown, 2001). At that time he was the officer in charge of the Third Phase of Basic Underwater Demolition/SEAL training—the famous BUD/S training, or SEAL basic course. He told me of a brother SEAL who had just returned from Iraq, where he commanded the SEAL task unit (TU) in Ramadi, and of the unique and groundbreaking things the SEALs were doing there. I had just passed through Ramadi in May 2006, en route to the Army Special Forces advanced operating base at Al Asad Air Base, farther up the Euphrates River Valley. The helicopter stopped in Ramadi at the Marine base at Hurricane Point to drop off two passengers before continuing on. All I knew about Ramadi then was that it was very dangerous and a place to avoid. The gunners in the H-60 Blackhawk never removed the ammunition belts from their M240 machine guns in Ramadi, as they had at other stops along the way. When we left, the pilot didn't fly out low over the city, but spiraled up within the perimeter of the base as a precaution against small-arms fire. At a safe altitude, we then headed northwest for Al Asad. I knew we had SEALs in Ramadi, but nothing of their work there. On this particular trip, my mission was Army Special Forces. My visit to Al Asad followed the year I'd spent at Fort Bragg and Camp Mackall for the writing of *Chosen Soldier: The Making of a Special Forces Warrior* (Crown, 2007). Little did I suspect at that time that my next book would take me back to Ramadi some fifteen months later, and I would again fly into Ramadi by helo, but this time for a longer stay.

I was immediately intrigued when I began to learn of this first SEAL task unit in Ramadi. What were the SEALs doing in Ramadi? What was their mission? Al-Anbar province was a Marine area of operations. How did the SEALs fit into the battle plan for this contentious province? First, I needed to learn more about this place called Ramadi. A quick Web search gave me a range of accounts of the fighting there—from *Washington Post* articles to the numerous blogs to wikipedia.com. The information was sketchy, contradictory, and uniformly bad—bad in that by all accounts we were getting our butts kicked in al-Anbar province and especially in Ramadi. In the fall of 2006, I could find nothing in print regarding Ramadi or al-Anbar that was positive.

Al-Anbar province is the size of North Carolina and comprises the western third of the nation of Iraq. It has 10 percent of the people, nearly all of which are tribal and Sunni. There are limited resources and no oil. Ramadi is the provincial capital, with close to half the population of the province. Ramadi is to al-Anbar province what Baghdad is to Iraq; as Ramadi goes, so goes all of al-Anbar. All that had become difficult, dangerous, and frustrating in Iraq seemed to be that much worse out west in Ramadi and al-Anbar.

The articles and information I began to compile on Ramadi painted a bleak picture indeed, and wikipedia.com, the perennial Web-hit leader on Ramadi, flatly declared that Ramadi and al-Anbar were lost and that the insurgents had soundly beaten the Army and the Marines in the Battle of Ramadi. Wikipedia held this view well into June 2007. Yet I was intrigued. If this was a battle lost, what were the SEALs doing in Ramadi? They had taken their maritime commando skills into the mountains of Afghanistan, on the road to Baghdad, and into the Iraqi capital itself. Now, what were they doing out west—in Sunni tribal lands of al-Anbar in a losing cause? How had the SEAL mission changed from those early days of the conflict—when we were in hot pursuit of Taliban fighters in the Hindu Kush and the Baathist holdouts in Baghdad? The al-Qaeda-led insurgency seemed to be the more robust in Ramadi than elsewhere in Iraq. What were the SEALs doing there to meet this growing insurgent presence? The answers to these questions were not on Google or in the newspapers, and certainly there was no help from the talking heads of the major networks. I needed to go to San Diego and to the SEAL base on the Coronado amphibious base to learn more about SEAL operations in Ramadi.

In the late fall of 2006, I met with one of the returning task unit commanders, the second TU commander of the four that you will meet in this book. He had only just left Ramadi and was recently assigned to train West Coast SEALs and other Naval Special Warfare assets preparing for combat rotation. I told him of my research and the consensus of opinion, both in and out of the military, that we were losing both in Ramadi and in al-Anbar. I even had with me a copy of a pessimistic summary of a Marine Corps intelligence report that cited the deteriorating security conditions across the province. The report argued that "we haven't been defeated militarily, but we have been defeated politically—and that's where wars are won and lost." This dismal report was dated 16 August and leaked by the *Washington Post* in an article by Thomas Ricks (author of *Fiasco*) on 11 September. The report was being widely shopped around Washington by those who opposed the war. It all but conceded Ramadi and al-Anbar to the al-Qaeda-led insurgents.

"Sir, I don't know what you've been reading or where you're getting your information," this veteran Ramadi task unit commander told me, "but in Ramadi, we're winning—we're kicking some serious butt. If this country doesn't lose its nerve and quit the fight, we'll win all of al-Anbar."

This was the first *I'd* heard that we were *not* losing the battle in western Iraq. So what was the truth? From experience, I knew that sometimes warriors immersed in the daily skirmishes may have a myopic perspective on the course of the battle—the big picture. It's a can't-see-the-forest-for-the-trees thing. But this task unit commander spoke soberly and with some assurance. And he had been one of the key players in the battle.

What I came to learn was that the SEALs were locked in deadly combat, often on a daily basis, and often with some of the most dedicated and vicious of the enemy insurgents. Hard as it was, they were not only holding their own but also making a grim harvest of insurgent fighters. And we *were* making progress; it was a costly battle, but by any number of criteria, we *were* winning. As one might imagine, the SEALs were on the cutting edge of this fight in al-Anbar—kinetic operations, as the operators like to put it. They brought their guns and their shooting skills to the fight. They also brought innovative command-and-control solutions to this battle and developed some unique information and data-manage-ment applications—the all-important operations-intelligence fusion that now drive SEAL combat operations. I also came to learn that the SEAL operations in Ramadi, and by extension in all of al-Anbar, seemed to represent a best-practices approach to the marriage of conventional security forces and SOF, or special operations forces. This was indeed something new—an SOF-conventional-force fusion. And, we were winning militarily *and* politically.

After speaking with a number of SEALs who had served in Ramadi and al-Anbar, I began to think this had the makings of an important book. It appeared to me at the time that the SEAL operations across al-Anbar province were evolving into a compelling chapter in the battle history of the Navy SEALs. Furthermore, the SEAL task unit in Ramadi seemed an ideal surrogate for this story. And not that I needed additional incentive, but SEAL operations in Iraq were taking place "out west," albeit western Iraq. The informal title of that first task unit commander was the Sheriff of Ramadi. Now I was really interested. And after having spent a "tour of duty" with the Army Special Forces, I saw this as a good chance to repatriate myself back into the Naval Special Warfare community. There was certainly a story here—an important story.

———

I believe this is an important book for a number of reasons. First of all, the operations in Ramadi marked the return of the SEALs to the mission of foreign internal defense, or FID, one of helping local security forces to defend their neighborhoods and communities against insurgents. I say *return* because during the early days of Vietnam the newly formed Navy SEAL teams worked almost exclusively in an advisory role. During their involvement in that decade-long conflict, SEALs were never more effective than when they were working with the locals. In Ramadi SEALs found themselves in the middle of a very nasty insurgency. They were immediately thrust into a FID role, training and working with Iraqi army scouts. But Ramadi had no rear-area training base, nor was there an established, proscribed training curriculum. And time was short; there was a battle raging, and the insurgent opposition seemed to be growing stronger daily. Training the Iraqi army scouts proved to be an on-the-job proposition in a dangerous and dynamic operational environment. This led to the SEAL adaption of the FID mission—*combat* FID. They proved to be pioneers in this new form of foreign internal defense in a hostile, counterinsurgent environment.

Second, this book is yet another validation of this most versatile and innovative component of our special operations forces. Since their origin as the Navy frogmen of World War II, SEALs have had neither the luxury nor the burden of existing military doctrine. Most of the time, they've been given a task and simply told to do it. From the landing beaches in the western Pacific in World War II, through the jungles of Vietnam, and into the recent active theaters, our present-day SEALs, in keeping with their heritage, have been creative by necessity. They are team-centric in their training and their approach to operations; leadership is often shared from the platoon officer in charge down to the junior enlisted SEAL. In each new conflict of their short history, they've had to develop the right tactics and methods through trial and error. If one approach didn't solve the problem, they were quick to find one that would. In al-Anbar province, this current generation put their own particular spin on training Iraqi scouts in counterinsurgency and used their unique combat skill set to augment our conventional military forces in a conventional battlespace. SEALs did this in Mosul and Habbaniyah as well, but it was in Ramadi where they perfected combat FID—where they developed the tactics and procedures that will serve them in the *next* insurgency. It was also in Ramadi that they integrated their SOF skill set in a conventional-force battlespace to help break al-Qaeda's grip on al-Anbar.

Third, the operations in Ramadi represent the high-water mark in the professional development of the Navy SEALs; they were magnificent in the vicious combat operations that were to eventually rout al-Qaeda in Ramadi. When I speak with those not in the military, they seem to think that all Navy SEALs are large, ferocious men—brawny but not having much in the way of brains, much as they might be depicted by

Hollywood. Don't misunderstand, these warriors are hard men, but what sets them apart is the diverse professional skill set they bring to the battlefield. They fight hard and they fight smart. They not only trained their Iraqis in fighting insurgents in Ramadi, they also led them into battle and fought alongside them. They extended the term "brother" to the soldiers and Marines they fought alongside. When I began the project, it seemed as if the insurgents in Ramadi and al-Anbar province would win. Everything I read pointed to it. Initially, I thought I'd be documenting a gallant effort in a losing cause—a gutsy stand, but one fought from the decks of the *Titanic*. But I was reading too many mainstream media accounts of what was happening in Ramadi and al-Anbar. Along with all those journalists filing current stories about the war in western Iraq, I was wrong. As it played out, the Battle of Ramadi was won, and the Navy SEALs had a hand in it.

And finally, this book is important as it documents the battlefield courage and dedication of these special maritime warriors. I've come to believe that no group of SEALs in the history of Naval Special Warfare fought more gallantly than the Ramadi SEALs. Certainly SEALs have never fought such a continuous battle in such a lethal environment as Ramadi. There were new men in each SEAL task unit, but most were veterans going back on their second, third, and fourth combat tour. While we at home played the political blame game ad nauseam, these quiet professionals went back to the fight—again and again. They were either recovering from the last deployment or preparing for the next one. A part of this story is how these professionals felt, repeatedly going into harm's way, while most Americans are more focused on their sports team or the next episode of *American Idol*. So this book is important to me personally, for these are my brothers, a generation or two removed. Their war has become as unpopular at home as mine was, but on that score there's one fortunate difference. During Vietnam, the nation turned against the war *and* the warriors, many of whom were draftees— involuntary participants. Today, for now, it's just the war. Interesting. Most Americans, the pundits tell us, oppose this war but still support the troops, even as the gulf between our all-volunteer force and the people they serve widens. But whatever the resolution of events in Iraq, the SEALs who served in Ramadi and al-Anbar can say they won. They helped to win the west.

I began my writing career in 1989, and this is my twelfth book. As I've indicated above, I personally believe this is an important work, perhaps my most important. You're probably wondering how, with eleven books under the keel, I can make this assertion, but with your indulgence, I'm going to get a little personal. Let's go back to when I started—back to when word processors were not all that common and a Selectric typewriter, with that little spool of white correction tape, was a really big deal.

Men approaching midlife often become apprehensive and a little insecure. That comes when you begin to see the glass as more than half empty rather than over half full. For those of us who became warriors in our youth and knew the adrenaline high of active combat, sitting behind a desk in your mid-forties can be a little unfulfilling. And unless you're very unusual or living in some kind of a fantasy world, active combat, at least active combat as a special operator, is for young men. Every man deals with this in his own way; I became a writer. I decided that if I could no longer run with the young dogs, maybe I could write about it—maybe that would ease me through my midlife passage. It's a behind-the-desk skill rather than a behind-the-gun skill, but it sure beat making sales calls or running a corporate marketing program. At least that's how it was for me. Yet I certainly didn't burst upon the literary scene with a best seller. It took several books before I was able to quit my daytime job.

I began writing novels and was lucky enough to have some initial success. It was a creative endeavor and allowed me to follow my characters on some great adventures. Since my first novels were military fiction, I included lots of action. There was the thrill of combat without the danger, so much so that at times I almost felt like a fraud. Each day my characters and I would plan and execute daring special operations. I was surprised at how real it could be. I felt the responsibility and apprehension of the commanders who sent young men into battle; I felt the cold detachment of killing a man, even though he might well deserve a bullet. I felt the team leader's desperate sense of loss when one of his men was killed or badly wounded. Even behind the typewriter or word processor, it can get emotional. When I was writing the final chapter of *Rising Wind* (Naval Institute Press, 1996) my wife found me early one morning, sitting at the keyboard and bawling like a baby. My main character, a terrific fellow who had been with me in a previous novel, had just been killed. He didn't see it coming. And neither did I! I'd just lost a very close friend. This may sound like a stretch for some readers, but when I'm on my game writing fiction, I *see* the action—in color. Hell, I can even *smell* it. In many ways I'm just following along behind the men in the fight, like an observer. And when I'm really into my craft, the characters take charge; they become independent actors. These fictional warriors train, fight, experience fear, win, lose, fail, and sometimes die. I'm just there taking notes from a safe distance. And that's when I feel like a fraud.

Then I began writing nonfiction, books like *The Sheriff of Ramadi*, and things changed. Candidly, it got a lot harder. I had to leave my little fantasy world and enter the realm of real warriors—but still only as an observer. In writing novels I get to go and hang out with my imaginary friends for three or four hours a day. But a nonfiction book is a 110,000-word term paper. More to the point, my characters are actual people, and I have to try to understand the world through *their* senses. What did they see? How did they feel? What did their battlefield smell like and what was the depth of their struggle and hardship? How do they handle the loss of a teammate? I try hard to get it right, but it's not easy. Often two men in the same combat action will have divergent accounts of what took place. So I have to ask the right questions, and I have to listen very carefully. When possible, I ask the person or persons who were there to read my account of their action to make sure I'm on target. But I have an advantage that most writers don't have; I've been there. Today's special operators are better trained and far more professional than they were in my day, but a firefight is still a firefight—the adrenaline, the ambiguities, the violence, and the fear are much the same. The emotions that accompany the taking of life, or having a teammate wounded or killed, don't change.

In writing a novel, I work hard to make everything "fit." I can change scenes, shape my characters, and orchestrate events for tone and pace to build suspense in telling the story. If something doesn't seem right to me, I change it. Sometimes I try to mislead or fool the reader with a false plot. This is the make-believe world of the novelist. Not so in nonfiction. I have a duty to write it as the men in the arena experienced it—to tell their story as faithfully as I can. From my work as a novelist, I use dialogue and do what I can to position the reader close to the warrior—in the squad file, so to speak—so he or she can experience and feel the events as they happened. But it's those warriors' story, not mine. To the best of my ability, the text has to match their perception and be in keeping with the recollections of those who were there. And while writing nonfiction is more difficult and time consuming, there's an overriding benefit that makes it all worth it. I get to mingle with some of the finest young warriors in America.

The extended nature of the war in Iraq has generated some deep divisions in our nation. It's not yet over; it might not be for some time. Our war is with those who hate America and all it stands for. Amid the promise and prosperity that is America, we now live with this thing called terrorism. Terrorism, and even that misnomer, the global war on terror, have come to represent all that is evil and threatening to our way of life. Only a few decades ago, it was Communism. In retrospect, the Communists and their sponsor, the old Soviet Union, were rational enemies. Even so, terror itself is not the enemy, but rather the tactic of our current enemy, the Islamic extremists, and they are anything but rational. It's simply unfortunate that western liberal democracies and their open economic infrastructures are vulnerable to this tactic we know as terrorism.

If terror is just an enemy tactic, a useful instrument in their jihad, then what is their strategy—their plan to defeat any secular change we might want to see advanced in the Muslim world? How do they oppose the desire for self-determination that many Muslims want? In a word, it's insurgency. From the perspective of those who wish to challenge freedom, democracy (economic or political), or any form of enfranchisement or a will of the majority, insurgency is a very effective tool. Its value is that it allows for a tyranny of the minority. A society's first duty is to provide order and security for its people. Insurgents, though they may be small in number, can challenge that order. Insurgents use terror, brutality, intimidation, and murder to achieve their ends. They can strike at a time of their choosing, and are not bound by societal norms that usually govern national or local security forces. And if American forces enter that nation to promote order and help with security, you can be sure that *our* rules of engagement, which reflect *our* values, will be far more restrictive than those of our enemies. The insurgents have no such rules or restrictions. The fact that any excess that violates our humane standards of conduct becomes national and international news, while barbarity on their part is given a pass, is simply a tactical downside of a culture we choose to defend.

I wish I could say that our insurgent problems in Iraq are something new and different, but that's not the case. Our inability to control insurgents in Vietnam eventually led to our defeat there. There are those who don't like to compare Vietnam to Iraq; I'm not one of them. There are just too many similarities. After World War II and the nuclear standoff between the United States and the Soviet Union began, we entered an era of regional conflicts. Korea initially pitted United Nations/American conventional forces against North Korea and, finally, the Chinese army—waves of them. The two sides fought to a standoff and an armistice was signed. Officially, that war has never ended, and we still have 18,000 troops there.

Vietnam began like Korea. The veteran North Vietnamese Army, which had beaten the French, thought they could handle the Americans as well. General Võ Nguyên Giáp, who orchestrated the final French defeat at Dien Bien Phu, felt that if he could choose the time and place, he could win on the battlefield and force an American withdrawal. He tried that in 1968. During that year he called for an uprising of Vietcong guerrillas during Tet. He also ordered multiple divisions of North Vietnamese regulars to surround the American forces near Khe Sanh. Giáp hoped to cause a countrywide disruption in South Vietnam and bring about a Dien Bien Phu–like surrender at Khe Sanh. But he didn't count on the U.S. Marine Corps or American airpower. The Vietcong attacks were repulsed across the South and especially at Hue, where the Marines took the measure of a large VC force in some of the most intense fighting of that war. At Khe Sanh whole North Vietnamese brigades were slaughtered by Marine artillery, B-52 strikes, and American tactical airpower. By the North's own estimates, more than 52,000 Vietcong and North Vietnamese were killed around Hue and Khe Sanh alone. Seven hundred thirty-five marines died at Khe Sanh; 216 at Hue. That the American media ceded the victory to the enemy does not change the fact that the VC and the NVA took a terrible beating in the field—so much so that the North was forced to change how it waged war. Our enemies focused on insurgent warfare, and five years later they sent us home—something they could never have done by sheer force of arms. Why is this important? It codified the strategy of how to defeat superior American military power. Vietnam perfected the tools of the insurgent: Hide among the people and coerce them to support the insurgency or at least remain neutral. Conduct guerrilla-type attacks using the population for refuge and cover. *And* if there is resistance from the people, use murder and intimidation to quickly stem it.

Sad as it may be, here we are again. We have a superb military, one without peer in maneuver, expeditionary, and (God help us) nuclear warfare. In 2003 the nation and the world witnessed this superiority as the Army and the Marines rolled up the Tigris and the Euphrates to Baghdad. But we were ill-prepared for the aftermath—our role as an occupation force and countering the insurgency that followed. As occupiers, we don't do a very good job. In many cases occupation requires a strong and sometimes brutal hand with the civilian population. To our credit, we really don't want soldiers and marines to be that rigorous with the locals; it's simply not how our young warriors should conduct themselves. Occupation worked after World War II because we destroyed the armies of our enemies along with their economy and most of their infrastructure. In Iraq the economy was in shambles well before we arrived. We disbanded rather than destroyed Saddam Hussein's army, and we left the infrastructure intact—a ready-made sanctuary for insurgents. The insurgency, with its terror, ethnic animosity, improvised explosive devices (IEDs), and foreign fighters grew quickly. And we reacted too slowly—in retrospect, perhaps criminally so, but that's another story. There have been and are sure to be more books on that score. Our conventional forces are capable of counterinsurgency warfare. Indeed, it is one of the missions of the U.S. Army. But it was only after the insurgency was in full bloom that we began to adopt effective counterinsurgent tactics. Our special operations forces can be quite good at counterinsurgency when it's their operational focus. But an insurgency of this scale requires diplomatic, political, and military skill, and, as we will see in *The Sheriff of Ramadi*, close cooperation between conventional and special operations forces. Following the heady days after the fall of Baghdad, we faltered. In retrospect it was almost as if we brought a knife to a gunfight—again! Modern counterinsurgency warfare belongs to the agile. We were simply not quick enough.

Counterinsurgency warfare is not rocket science, but it's highly reliant on people. Technology and systems are important, but it's the people who count. *Our people* for sure, but, more important, also *their people.* An insurgency is a battle for the people—not the ground. We can never win and never go home unless we've empowered the people to effectively engage the insurgents—and to successfully defend their neighborhoods, communities, cities, and nation. They have to provide for their own internal security. In the case of Iraq, this means in the cities, with more modern forms of secular government, as well as in the rural areas that are secular as well as tribal. If we'd made Baghdad look like Dresden, the job of bringing some form of democracy to Iraq would have been easier—a lot easier. But we didn't. The armored columns that overran southern Iraq and pushed into Baghdad went out of their way not to lay waste to the cities and the land. In fact, during those dramatic days when our 3rd Infantry Division and the 1st Marine Expeditionary Force were on the move, the focus of the SEAL mission taskings was to seize and protect key oil-pumping and transportation facilities for future use by the Iraqi people. Within a year those same facilities that we risked lives to save became targets for insurgent terrorist tactics.

Back to Ramadi. As you will see in this book, the Army and the Marine Corps, with the help of the Navy SEALs and the Iraqi army, defeated al-Qaeda and their insurgents in Ramadi. They took the streets back, neighborhood by neighborhood. But then something highly unusual and most essential happened. The people of Ramadi, led by their tribal leaders, took ownership of the streets the American and Iraqi forces had reclaimed. The people—the tribes—sealed the victory won by our forces, and al-Qaeda was defeated. Credit the leadership of the Army and Marine commanders for recognizing and promoting this reenfranchisement. The people came over to our side, turned against al-Qaeda, and the battle was won. Whatever happens in Iraq, *this* is a template for a successful major counterinsurgency operation.

As the nation begins to come to grips with our adventure, or misadventure, in Iraq, there will be many questions about what went wrong, who's to blame, what should have been done, and finally, what we need to do next. There will be no shortage of targets for blame: Bush, Rumsfeld, the weapons of mass destruction (WMD) controversy, the dismantling of the Iraqi army, too few troops, the wrong mix of troops, the lack of cultural understanding, ineffective senior military leadership, and so on and so on. I'll leave the analysis of what went wrong and what we should have done to others, although I may be unable to resist a comment or two in the epilogue. This is a book about insurgency and how a brave group of SEALs, fighting alongside their Army and Marine Corps brothers, dealt with that insurgency in Ramadi. *The Sheriff of Ramadi* is a battlefield book. It will document how special operations forces, in this case Navy SEALs, brought their courage and their skills to the insurgent battlefield in one of the most dangerous cities in Iraq—and won. It's also a story of how these maritime warriors took their skills to the fight with the Iraqis they trained. I hope it will serve as a case study for future insurgencies, as I fear we will have many more Ramadis in our future.

This book spans the period of time from when the first full SEAL task unit was stood up in October 2005, through the Battle of Ramadi, until the redeployment of the fourth task unit in October 2007. In short, it's the story of the SEALs in Ramadi during the Battle of Ramadi. When I first learned of this task unit, and the informal moniker, "the Sheriff of Ramadi," that was applied to the first commander of this task unit, I thought, "What a great title for a book." My publisher at the time thought so as well. But this title met with a great deal of resistance from the individual task unit commanders as well as the platoon SEAL operators. They were very reluctant to have themselves portrayed or credited with anything but a supporting role in the battle. And they were very insistent—make that emphatic—that in telling the Ramadi SEAL story, I did nothing to take away from the courage and professionalism of the soldiers and marines who carried the brunt of the battle. While this book is about SEALs, I've tried to fairly represent their contributions in this battle as well as the leading role of the conventional forces. As for praising the SEALs and their efforts in the Battle of Ramadi, I'll leave that to the conventional-force commanders and soldiers who fought with them. But the title remains. There was, as you will see in later chapters, a Sheriff of Ramadi, and he stood tall amid the chaos of the battle. He just wasn't a Navy SEAL.

I've had the opportunity to observe SOF-conventional-force inter-action both stateside and in Iraq. It can be a little turfy stateside, and over there not every deployed Army or Marine conventional commander wanted a group of Navy SEALs moving about his area of operations. Yet in Ramadi, it worked, and worked well. Perhaps it was the vicious nature of this battle that forced this SOF-conventional cooperation. I happen to believe it was the professionalism of all involved, each playing their role and bringing their individual talents to focus on the enemy. It was also an issue of mutual respect. And in that vein, I hope this story will serve as an example of just how effective special operations and conventional forces can be when they work together and when they play to the strengths that each brings to the battlefield.

My other nonfiction books about SEALs and Army Special Forces were challenging, but this one was especially so. One might think that Navy SEALs returning from battle are anxious to tell their story. Not so. These are professional warriors, and they are very self-sufficient in their service. They seek approval from their teammates and understanding within their family circle and close friends, but they don't seem to need the gratitude of others. The SEALs I interviewed invariably wanted to deflect talk of their own contributions and tell me about those of others. The platoon SEALs, the ones who took to the streets of Ramadi with the Iraqis they trained, were especially generous in their praise of the soldiers and marines with whom they shared the battlespace. They also credited a great deal of their success to the work of the non-SEAL support elements within their task unit organization. The senior leadership within the SEAL platoons invariably cited the leadership of their task unit commanders for their operational success. As for the individual task unit commanders, once we got passed the sheriff thing, they wanted to talk about the conventional commanders who supported them and the selfless service of those in their commands—their SEAL operators as well as their task unit support elements. When I spoke with the conventional commanders who served in Ramadi, they had nothing but praise for "their" SEALs. What emerged, and what you are about to read, is a story of dedication, innovation, professionalism, and courage under fire. Ramadi was not the only place where this happened, but this is the story of the SEALs in Ramadi.

Regarding the mechanics of this book, as in my other nonfiction works, there are some conventions I have to observe—my ROEs, or rules of engagement. I was granted free access to the SEALs who returned from Ramadi and those preparing to go, and their cooperation was on a voluntary basis. While I was in Ramadi, the deployed task unit from SEAL Squadron Seven extended me every courtesy, for which I was, and am, more than grateful. In telling this story, I use no real names, and all photography has been altered to defeat face-recognition software. The manuscript was reviewed by the Naval Special Warfare Command staff for the appropriate handling of tactics, techniques, and procedures. This especially applied to methods of intelligence collection and intelligence exploitation, which remain highly sensitive issues. The conclusions, opinions, and any errors are mine alone.

It's an honor to tell the story of these brave and talented American warriors.

Infantry move and cover. Two soldiers from the 1-37 move cautiously through the streets of Ramadi. Army patrols and SEAL overwatch positions in Ramadi took fire on a routine basis.

The Ramadi SEALs: Evolution of the Warrior

In order to fully understand the Navy SEALs in Ramadi and the operations of the Naval Special Warfare task unit there, one has to understand their culture. These warriors are different from the Vietnam-era SEALs of my generation and from our forebears, the frogmen of World War II. They are different even from the SEALs who came of age in the pre 9/11, post–Soviet Union days when terrorism was an emerging threat and had yet to take on its current form. The Navy SEALs currently engaged in the active theaters have a marvelously diverse skill set. They can be flexible and terribly innovative in their approach to warfare. Yet they thrive in a tradition-bound culture that is, in some ways, almost tribal—not unlike that of the Iraqis of al-Anbar province. How is it that they can be both at the same time? This is a complex issue and an important one. As you will see in later chapters, these warriors in Ramadi owed much of their success to their ability to adapt and evolve in this particular battlespace. Let's first take a look at their roots—the first Navy frogman.

The forefathers of the Navy SEALs were born of necessity and in adversity. Following the attack on Pearl Harbor, in 1942 Japanese naval power was crippled at the Battle of Midway, and Japan's advance in the Pacific was finally checked in the land and sea actions around Guadalcanal. Then U.S. forces began the long drive across the Pacific to the Japanese home islands. This was to be an island-hopping campaign, and the first of those islands was Tarawa. With insufficient hydrological data, the Marines went ashore in the early morning hours of 20 November 1943. Many drowned under the weight of their gear as their landing craft beached on underwater reefs well offshore; many more were gunned down as they waded the shallow stretches between reef and beach. More than a thousand marines died on Tarawa, and more than two thousand were wounded. Given the many amphibious operations on the road to Japan, these losses simply could not be allowed to continue. Amphibious operations are, by their very nature, risky and costly, but hydrographic intelligence could minimize risk and save lives. Men were needed to go in ahead of the invasion forces to survey these landing beaches. There was a war on; these men had to be found and quickly trained for this important task. The Navy turned to a maverick lieutenant commander named Draper Kauffman. Kauffman proved to be the perfect man for the job. His arrival at Fort Pierce, Florida, in the summer of 1943 was by a curious and circuitous journey.

Draper Kauffman graduated from the Naval Academy in 1933, but owing to his vision, which had deteriorated during his four years at Annapolis, he was unable to pass the commissioning physical. Successive retesting kept him out of uniform—an American uniform. With war clouds gathering over Europe, Kauffman enlisted in the French army just in time to participate in its rout by the Germans. After a brief stint as a POW he was repatriated to England, where he promptly joined the Royal Navy, just in time for the Battle of Britain. Midway through his British naval officer training, he volunteered for bomb-disposal work. So while the Spitfire and Hurricane pilots fought the waves of German bombers over England, Sublieutenant Draper Kauffman was crawling through the rubble of London, defusing unexploded bombs. At the time he was the only American serving in the Royal Navy, and few in Britain served in a more dangerous or demanding calling.

A month before America entered the war, Kauffman was called home and commissioned in the U.S. Navy. He immediately became the nation's expert in making unexploded bombs safe, and he founded the Bomb Disposal School, training soldiers, sailors, and marines in the delicate art of explosive ordnance disposal. In the summer of 1943, in anticipation of the Pacific amphibious campaign, the Navy asked (ordered) Kauffman to solve the problem of removing obstacles from landing beaches. He was told, "Get together some men and train them to get rid of these [beach] obstacles. Your orders will allow you to go anywhere you think best to set up a training base. You can have anyone you ask for, in or out of the naval service. This is an emergency, and we don't have much time." Kauffman chose Fort Pierce, Florida.

In the summer of 1943 Fort Pierce was a mosquito-infested mangrove swamp. The new all-volunteer unit was called the Naval Combat Demolition Unit. The men set up the training headquarters in an abandoned casino. Another unit based at Fort Pierce was a veteran outfit simply called the Scouts and Raiders. Their program called for an intensive eight-week physical training regime. Kauffman asked the Scouts and Raiders if they could compress the highlights of this program into a single week. This became the new demolition unit's first week of training, or Indoctrination Week. It quickly became known as Hell Week. Kauffman and the assigned officers went through this first Hell Week with their enlisted trainees. This established a precedent that continues to this day; officers and enlisted men suffer and train side by side. The grim requirements of that first Hell Week—physical punishment, long ocean swims, dragging boats through choking mud, harassment with explosive charges, and little or no sleep—are all found in current-day SEAL training. Following Hell Week, those who survived were trained in demolitions, beach reconnaissance, and hydrographic survey work. Then, as now, they trained in boat crews of six to eight men with an officer in charge. These boat crews worked as teams, each trying to best the other. It paid to be a winner—competition was continuous in the training of frogmen then, as it is for SEALs today. Winners get a break; losers get additional push-ups or another trip back into the swamp, the surf, or some other unpleasant evolution.

Kauffman also set the tone for a special bond between officers and enlisted men. Beginning with the first class, he brought the volunteers into a room, officers on one side and the enlisted men on the other. To the enlisted he would say, "I will do everything in my power to see that no officer graduates from this school under whom I would not be happy to go into combat." To the officers he would say, "I will do everything in my power to see that no enlisted man graduates from this school whom I would not want to lead in combat." The officers and enlisted men then shared and shared alike in the miseries of Fort Pierce and NCDU training.

The first Fort Pierce graduates were too late for Tarawa, but they were to participate in virtually every subsequent amphibious operation in the Pacific and were at Normandy on Omaha and Utah beaches. The NCDUs evolved into the Underwater Demolition Teams, or UDTs, but the mission of clearing landing beaches remained essentially the same. They suffered a 52 percent casualty rate on Omaha Beach. The three-dozen odd men who graduated from Kauffman's initial training grew exponentially in number. Two years later, on the eve of the Japanese surrender, the Navy counted more than five thousand men in the UDTs, with three thousand of them poised for the invasion of the Japanese home islands.

Each landing beach was different, and each presented its own unique challenges. So these first frogmen became adept at improvisation. As the problems arose, they solved them. My particular favorite is the development of the waterproof firing assembly. From the beginning the NCDUs and UDTs were trained in the use of demolitions. Beach obstacles, from man-made steel tetrahedrons to natural coral reefs, had to be blown out of the way, and that meant the reliable priming of explosive charges—underwater explosive charges. Navy scientists and engineers tried any number of ways to make a reliable waterproof initiator for submerged explosives. None of them worked. Then a bright sailor came up with idea of using condoms and rubber cement. It was simple and cheap, and it worked every time. The UDTs in the Pacific became a huge consumer of military-issue condoms. When I went through training in 1968, we waterproofed our firing assemblies the same way. It's still done that way today.

A few years ago, a SEAL team commanding officer stated in his standing orders: "Flexibility is found in the dictionary under Naval Special Warfare." That all started with the frogmen of World War II. The conditions were ideal for innovation and spontaneity. All the men chosen for this new naval specialty were volunteers, carefully selected and screened. They were subjected to a physical regime that further cut their numbers, often dramatically. Then they trained as teams, in a competitive environment and with officers and enlisted men sharing the same miserable conditions and dangers. This produced a tightly bonded group of men who were smart, tough, and adaptable. There were procedures for handling explosives, but given the conditions under which these first demolitionists practiced their trade, they developed the procedures and wrote most of the first manuals. Finally and perhaps most important, they worked alone, with little tactical oversight. They were the first of their breed. Unlike conventional forces, there were no admirals or generals who had experience in this form of warfare. Basically, Admiral Ernest J. King, then chief of naval operations, gave the order to "do it," and fortunately there was a resourceful officer named Draper Kauffman there to get the job done. This way of doing business became a part of the NCDU/UDT culture and has carried forward to today's SEALs—to the SEALs now serving in Ramadi and al-Anbar province. Indeed, an oft-heard command within our deployed SEAL platoons is "Okay, guys, make it happen," and the job gets done.

For you readers who wish to learn more about the fascinating life and times of Draper Kauffman, I recommend *America's First Frogman: The Draper Kauffman Story* (Naval Institute Press, 2002). It's an intimate, in-depth look at the wartime exploits of this remarkable man—a courageous, self-effacing patriot with a wry sense of humor. *America's First Frogman* was written by Elizabeth Kauffman Bush, Draper's sister and President George H. W. Bush's sister-in-law. Following the war, Kauffman enjoyed a long and distinguished career, retiring with the rank of rear admiral. Along the way he was twice awarded the Navy Cross and a host of other combat decorations.

I personally had but one encounter with Admiral Kauffman; it was while he was superintendent of the Naval Academy and I was a midshipman. He advised me *against* putting in for UDT/SEAL training.

"Son, you can be a surface warfare officer or an aviator or a submariner, but not a UDT officer. That's not why you came to Annapolis, and that's not why this school trains young men like yourself."

Admiral Kauffman's advice to me in 1967 was the Navy party line for Annapolis graduates. Yet it spoke to the founding leadership of the UDTs and the recently commissioned SEAL teams. Newly minted ensigns from the Naval Academy were not allowed to go from the Academy to UDT/SEAL training because duty in the teams, at that time, was considered unsuitable for career naval officers. In fact it was discouraged. In my opinion this has both helped and hindered the development of the UDTs and SEAL teams. It turned away many bright and capable career-minded officers. But it did, in effect, attract those nonmainstream mavericks, officers not unlike Kauffman himself. Quite often the best combat leaders and innovators are men who care more about their duty than their careers. This changed in 1970 when Naval Special Warfare became a career path for naval officers and new Academy ensigns began to enter training directly from Annapolis.

Following World War II, American forces were drawn down dramatically. It had been a costly war, both in lives and treasury, and the nation wanted its servicemen home. The demobilization of the Underwater Demolition Teams followed that of the Navy and the other services.

Some doubted that there would be a need to clear landing beaches in the future. With advancements in airpower and the advent of the atomic bomb, many military planners felt that amphibious operations were a thing of the past. By 1948 there were four teams numbering just over two hundred officers and men. These four teams were the available UDT personnel going into the Korean War. Korea was a confined, regional engagement with none of the massive amphibious operations of the previous world war. Yet there were the administrative landings at P'ohang and MacArthur's dramatic invasion at Inchon. There was little need for obstacle clearance at Inchon because the North Koreans felt the thirty-foot tides there would make a landing impossible, but the UDTs did serve in a reconnaissance role and as wave guides to help steer landing craft to the right beach.

There were two new requirements imposed on the UDTs in Korea that were not part of their World War II taskings: onshore raids and mine clearance. UDT elements paddled ashore in rubber boats loaded with explosives and conducted raids on North Korean rail lines, bridges, and tunnels. These missions were the first over-the-beach operations to become a staple of today's SEAL mission requirements. Many of the procedures developed by those amphibious frogmen, like the use of scout swimmers, are still practiced. And these first crude from-the-sea ventures laid the groundwork for future shore-centric SEAL operations.

The UDTs were also asked to help with mine clearance. These were dicey operations that required UDT swimmers to dive down and attach lines to moored underwater mines. Because the water in Korea was quite chilly, they pioneered the operational use of exposure suits—in this case dry suits—for this dangerous work. For deepwater mines and to mark submerged wrecks, they used a new French diving apparatus called the aqualung. It was the first use of open-circuit diving equipment in combat. Helicopters were just coming into operational use and were used to deploy and recover swimmers in these mine-hunting operations. UDT divers also used the new aqualung to place charges on the cryptographic equipment of two sunken minesweepers in Wonsan.

In the decade following the Korean War, the evolution of the UDTs was primarily underwater. Advances in radar and sonar meant that rubber boats and even surface swimmers could be vulnerable to detection. This meant developing the capacity to approach an enemy beach or harbor without being seen or heard. This required an underwater approach. The aqualung was a huge step in taking men under the sea but had its limits as a tactical diving apparatus. There were the telltale bubbles rising to the surface, and the aqualung had limited underwater duration. While the aqualung was simple and reliable, a better tactical apparatus was needed. During World War II Dr. Christian Lambertsen developed a closed-cycle oxygen rebreather for use by the Office of Strategic Services (OSS)—the forerunner of the Central Intelligence Agency (CIA). Soon this rig, the Lambertsen Amphibious Respiratory Unit, was adapted by the UDTs. This scuba (a term Lambertsen coined) consisted of an oxygen bottle, a breathing bag, and canister of soda lime. The diver's breathing medium, pure oxygen, was recirculated within the system with oxygen added as needed and the carbon dioxide scrubbed out by the soda lime. The standard tactical rig in SEAL teams today is the Draeger LAR V rebreather, a highly refined version of Lambertsen's scuba.

Now that the UDT men had the means to swim under the sea for some duration, a method was needed to transport them from offshore, over the horizon, to a launching point off the shoreline. The British and the Italians had experimented with battery-powered undersea vehicles that were little more than low-speed, steerable torpedoes a diver had to straddle to ride. Tactically, the Italians were the most accomplished, severely damaging a British battleship in the port of Alexandria in 1941. The UDTs found several of these crude craft in storage and tested them. Smaller, sea-scooter-type units were also tested. The latter proved easier to handle, but neither were found suitable for the fifteen- or twenty-mile transit required to get combat swimmers close to an enemy coast or to penetrate an enemy harbor. But these early efforts were good training wheels for developing the first generation of battery-powered wet submersibles, mini-subs capable of delivering swimmers over extended distances. Pioneered by the UDTs, these small, water-filled fiberglass subs were called swimmer delivery vehicles. Again, the employment of the tactical rebreather and underwater transport were developed through trial and error by these Navy frogmen. The equipment was tested in simulated combat conditions, then taken back to the shop for modification as needed.

Today's SEALs regularly operate from submerged submarines, but this was unheard of sixty years ago. During World War II UDT men were launched from the decks of surfaced submarines, but never underwater. The marriage of UDT diver and submarine was first tried in the late 1940s and made an operational tool in the 1950s. Then, as now, most submarines were only equipped with escape trunks, which were used only to "lock out" men trapped underwater in a crippled sub. The locking out and recovering of submerged divers was, and still is, a highly choreographed underwater ballet. A great deal of coordination was needed between the UDT swimmers and submarine sailors. Since submarines don't hover well, these operations had to take place while the submarine was under way at low speed. The early lessons and procedures validated by the UDTs are in use today, as nuclear submarines routinely launch and recover SEALs and their mini-subs. An important mission of the Navy's newest *Virginia*-class submarines is the launch and recovery of SEALs. The protocols and procedures that drive these complex operations were pioneered by the UDTs.

Getting frogmen to the job site was one matter; picking them up was another. In World War II they were often recovered by a kind of rubber lasso. A speeding small craft with an inflatable Zodiac-type boat tied alongside would race down a line of swimmers. A rubber loop secured to the speeding boat by a bungee cord would be dropped over the swimmer's raised arm, and he would be flipped into the inflatable as it sped past. In the 1950s the UDTs began to work with helicopters. Swimmers were cast or dropped from helicopters and retrieved as the helo flew past towing a ladder across the top of the waves. This procedure is still used today, but only when the presence of a slow-moving helicopter offshore is compatible with the mission. Cast and recover by helo is still a procedural-driven business; communication between the aircrew and the swimmers is essential. The last SEAL killed in Vietnam died as a result of poor communications between SEALs and the aircrew of a helicopter during a night combat cast.

Entering the decade of the 1960s, there were still four UDTs, two on the West Coast and two on the East Coast. These teams were considered fleet support units and trained primarily in support of amphibious operations and harbor penetration/ship attack missions. But when these early frogmen were not training, they were often trying to invent new and improved ways to better accomplish their mission. This throw-the-book-away, try-something-new, adaptive mind-set was the greatest legacy of the early frogmen. Today there are still a few active-duty SEALs who served in the UDTs, but their numbers are dwindling. Like myself, they're proud to have served in SEAL teams *and* the UDTs.

Shortly after he took office, President John F. Kennedy directed that all service components develop an expanded capacity for nonnuclear warfare. He told Congress specifically, "I am directing the Secretary of Defense to expand rapidly and substantially . . . the orientation of existing forces for the conduct of non-nuclear war, paramilitary operations, and sub-limited or unconventional wars." As a result of this directive, two new teams were commissioned in January 1962: SEAL Team One on the West Coast and SEAL Team Two on the East Coast. The new teams took up residence at the naval amphibious bases at Coronado, California, and Little Creek, Virginia, respectively, where they both reside today. The acronym SEAL came from a contraction of sea-air-land and was first used by the Navy's Unconventional Activities Committee, whose recommendations led to the formation of the SEALs. The teams were drawn from UDT veterans but were tasked with mission responsibilities that included airborne and land operations as well as traditional maritime-related activity.

Almost immediately the new teams began to train for direct-action and reconnaissance missions on land, coming from or under the sea or from the air. The wily veterans from the UDTs quickly went to work. They immediately saw the need for lightweight weapons and used team operational funds to purchase AR15 rifles on the open market—a procurement that was totally nonregulation. But the new rifle, the forerunner of the M16, was the best gun for the new maritime commandos. They also began experimenting with new parachutes. The UDTs were past masters in scrounging useful equipment from military salvage depots; the new SEALs were even better. They found parachutes in the salvage yards that had passed their allotted useful life and modified them for SEAL use. They had to be steerable, capable of delivering a man into the water, and suitable for HALO (high-altitude, low-opening) use. The procurement and modification of weapons and equipment were second nature to these frogmen-turned-SEALs. Much of this activity was encouraged by their non-career-minded officers, who pretended not to notice.

Early on, UDT training was the same as SEAL training; the rigorous conditioning and the notorious Hell Week remained much the same. All graduates of the then-basic four-month course were sent to Fort Benning, Georgia, for three weeks of Army airborne training. Most returned for duty in one of the UDT teams, but a few men went straight to a SEAL team. New men and those veterans coming from the UDTs underwent an additional six weeks of training to become operationally qualified SEALs. The time for training and qualification for SEALs has grown over the years. Just as with the operational tasking of the underwater demolition and SEAL teams, the training of these men has been an evolutionary, dynamic process. There were no SEAL training manuals. All training was developed in-house or taken from Army or Marine Corps training materials. The new SEALs trained their own. Before we step into Vietnam, it might be helpful to spend a moment on their training, specifically basic training.

The World War II frogmen trained to their requirements—combat beach reconnaissance and obstacle clearance. The Navy needed tough, resilient men who could endure hardship and danger and who could handle explosives. And it needed them fast. Training was then geared to those specific requirements. Leading up to and during the Korean War, the requirements expanded to include diving and the basic weapons of the maritime amphibious raider, so training was modified to screen for men who could master these new disciplines as well. If anything, training became harder. With the commissioning of the SEAL teams, basic UDT training became basic UDT/SEAL training, which led finally to the current training program, BUD/S—Basic Underwater Demolition/SEAL training. Throughout these changes Kauffman's Hell Week remained a key part of training. Because of the seemingly continuous expansion of the SEAL mission, training continues to change with the requirements, and that has meant that basic, advanced, and predeployment training is longer and more comprehensive. Today, basic and advanced training for a Navy SEAL takes about a year. Another eighteen months of training at the team is now normal before a new SEAL makes his first operational deployment. Kauffman's men trained for only a few months before they went off to war. It now takes two and a half years to make a combat-ready SEAL.

Perhaps the single most enduring characteristic of this training is the high attrition rate. Historically, five good men have to begin the process in order to get one qualified, deployable Navy SEAL. A great deal of time, effort, study, and testing has been devoted to this subject, but little has been done over time to make it more efficient. The physical characteristics of those who make it and those who don't are strikingly similar. Those who successfully complete BUD/S training seem to stand higher in terms of leadership, self-confidence, self-discipline, self-esteem, and intelligence. It might seem that intelligence would not be a factor in the physical crucible that is modern BUD/S training, but it's a key ingredient in what makes a Navy SEAL. Most successful SEAL trainees are goal oriented. Training is long, rigorous, and painful. It takes intelligence and focus to clearly see the goal—to serve in the SEAL teams—in order to endure the hardships that lead to that goal. SEAL training, and the men who do and do not make it through this ordeal, are detailed in two of my previous works, *The Warrior Elite* and *The Finishing School* (Crown, 2004). Both deal with the mechanics of SEAL training and what it takes to become a Navy SEAL. Recently, careful attention to recruiting the right men and more-sophisticated conditioning methods have resulted in a higher percentage of candidates getting through this difficult training.

Following the commissioning of the first SEAL teams in 1962, the UDTs continued to train and deploy with the amphibious forces. Marines rehearsed beach landings, and the UDTs surveyed the landing zones and demolished beach obstacles as needed. The new SEAL teams focused on commando-style raiding while coming from the sea or through the air. Their training in unconventional and paramilitary warfare involved small-unit tactics for direct-action missions and behind-the-lines reconnaissance. While Vietnam loomed large in their future, this conflict was not the first operational use of SEALs. In the spring of 1962 (a year after the Bay of Pigs disaster), a small contingent of SEALs and UDT men locked out of a submarine off the coast of Cuba near Havana. Their mission was to conduct a beach reconnaissance in the event the Marines should ever be needed to land near the Cuban capital. The operation didn't go exactly as planned. They successfully exited the submarine and completed the reconnaissance, but then things went wrong. The team and the submarine failed to find each other. Just as the men in the water were starting to swim for Key West, their submarine surfaced nearby and quickly took them aboard.

SEALs first arrived in Vietnam in late 1962. SEAL Team One began regular deployments a year later. Early on, the SEALs worked closely with the CIA out of Da Nang, assisting the Agency in preparing agents to slip into North Vietnam on covert missions. Specifically, the SEALs trained South Vietnamese commandos in maritime infiltration techniques so they could enter the North from the sea. So their first mission in Vietnam was a true unconventional-warfare activity—training locals to fight the enemy on their own ground. But these efforts were largely unsuccessful. It soon became apparent to the CIA that there was little hope in generating a meaningful local resistance in North Vietnam. With the landing of the Marines in 1965 and the escalation of the war, the North Vietnamese proved far better at fomenting rebellion in the South than we did in the North. In retrospect, that should have told us something, but by that time the troop buildup was well under way.

With the exception of a few advisers, the SEALs began operating on their own in a direct-action role in Rung Sat Special Zone, a Vietcong-infested mangrove swamp between Saigon and the South China Sea. Fourteen- to sixteen-man SEAL platoons began combat rotations into the Rung Sat in 1965 and were soon operating from other riverine bases around the lower Mekong Delta. From 1966 through 1971 platoons from SEAL Teams One and Two conducted direct-action operations against the Vietcong. The strength of the two SEAL teams grew to close to 400 active SEALs, but there were seldom more than 120 SEALs in Vietnam at any one time.

Most often, we worked for conventional Army, Navy, or Marine ground force commanders. When I arrived "in-country," as we called Vietnam, my base commander said, "Dick, I want you go there and kill as many Vietcong as you can." To that kind of direction, there was only one response: "Aye, aye, sir." Most other SEAL platoon officers received similar guidance. The key to our operations in the Mekong region was good intelligence, usually from a local villager or a paid retainer. The SEAL petty officers of that era became quite adept at ferreting out information from the locals. For the most part, they were not trained for this; these intelligence-collection skills were learned on the job to better accomplish the mission. Good intelligence led to good missions. We were often assisted by Boat Support Unit One (West Coast) and Two (East Coast), the forerunners of today's Special Boat Teams. When we had no good targeting information, we'd often go out and sit on a canal bank or a jungle trail and wait for the Vietcong to come to us. Often we sat out all night with the bugs and leaches, only to return with nothing to show for it. Even in those early days, there was no substitute for good intelligence. During the course of the Vietnam War, we became good at small-unit tactics and operating at night in enemy-controlled territory. Quite often our boat-support sailors would take us close to the objective, but we would make the final journey to the target in sampans—moving through the night just like the Vietcong. These missions were developed and launched as unilateral direct-action operations, but we seldom went out without a local guide or a contingent of Vietnamese scouts.

Some SEAL platoons, such as mine, had a half dozen or more of these scouts—ours were called Kit Carson Scouts. The KCS, as we called them, were former Vietcong who had come over to our side by way of a sanctioned amnesty program. These scouts were our local knowledge. They were officially in the South Vietnamese Army, but we paid them in cash with bonus payments for operational success. They lived with us, and when we were in the field, they often walked on point or very close to the SEAL point man. When patrolling in hostile territory, we were always concerned with booby traps—small IEDs, before they were known as such. When one of our scouts refused to walk down a trail and recommended an alternate route to the objective, we were only too glad to take his advice.

We had little to do with the main-force North Vietnamese Army; in fact, we avoided them. Most SEAL activity in Vietnam targeted the insurgents—the Vietcong. The most successful operations were a result of local intelligence on a specific target—an arms cache, an enemy base camp, or a senior Vietcong leader. And we were always standing by for POW recovery or to recover a downed pilot. Not unlike the SEALs in Iraq and Afghanistan, we operated from relatively secure bases that were under the control of a conventional sector commander. In the final tally, forty-eight SEALs lost their lives in Vietnam and more than two hundred were wounded. Estimates of Vietcong and North Vietnamese soldiers killed by SEAL operations run as high as two thousand. The UDTs also deployed to Vietnam, but not in the numbers of SEALs. While their combat roles were mainly restricted to reconnaissance and demolition duties, they suffered twelve killed and some forty wounded. Three SEALs were awarded the Medal of Honor for their service in Vietnam.

There were, however, SEAL advisers who conducted business in classic Army Special Forces "by, with, and through" manner. One way was through the Vietnamese SEAL program, the Lien Doc Nguoi Nhia, or LDNN. Translated literally, the name meant "soldiers who fight under the sea." The LDNNs were brave South Vietnamese soldiers who, when properly trained and led, could be very effective. LDNNs were involved in two of the actions that later resulted in SEALs being awarded the Medal of Honor, and one LDNN was awarded the Navy Cross, the only non-American to receive our nation's second-highest decoration in the Vietnam War. Today he lives in the United States and is treated as a respected alumnus of our SEAL community.

Perhaps the most successful SEAL operations in Vietnam were conducted with the Provincial Reconnaissance Units—the PRUs. The PRU program was a CIA-sponsored effort that later became part of the secret Phoenix Program. The PRUs drew their fighters from rural Vietnamese villages and Nung tribesmen of Chinese origin who lived in Vietnam. These units agreed to fight on the side of the South Vietnamese government as long as they could fight as a unit and their pay was controlled by the CIA. The Agency paid, and they fought. Navy SEALs, along with Army Special Forces soldiers, served as advisers. In the case of the SEALs, there were anywhere from 60 to 120 Nungs for every SEAL adviser or pair of advisers. It was lonely duty for a SEAL, who sometimes lived day in and day out with these rough men in their home villages, with only an interpreter for communication. PRU advisers were always chosen from veteran SEALs. The PRUs operated in fourteen of the sixteen provinces in IV Corps—the southern part of South Vietnam. PRU units in I, II, and III Corps (the central and northern areas of South Vietnam) had Marine and Special Forces advisers. Because of their local knowledge and their capable advisers, the PRUs savaged the Vietcong irregulars in their areas. After their formation in 1967, the PRUs killed more than 20,000 Vietcong and NVA troops and took thousands of prisoners. Postwar North Vietnamese records confirm that the PRUs were the deadliest and most effective force fielded in South Vietnam. It was a great leverage of SEAL, Marine, and Special Forces talent. In retrospect, why didn't we do more of this by, with, and through activity and less direct action? In deference to the SEALs of my era, most of us, including this author, never thought of Vietnam in terms of an insurgency. We conducted operations as we were trained and got pretty damn good at it. But as foreign fighters on foreign soil, we could do little to stem the insurgent tide with a pure, unilateral direct action. This was a lesson that we, as a nation committed to the practice of expeditionary warfare, forgot all too quickly in our adventures in the Middle East and Southwest Asia.

During the decade of SEAL deployment rotations to Vietnam, the operational focus and training within the teams were on combat operations in Southeast Asia. Tactics, weapons, and equipment were designed and developed around direct-action operations in a jungle environment. My training and predeployment work-up at SEAL Team One was totally and exclusively built around combat in Vietnam. When I returned from deployment, I met with other platoons training to go in-country and briefed them on what worked and what didn't, just as my predecessors had briefed me. During my tour in 1970–1971, close to 10 percent of the SEALs on deployment were killed and 25 percent wounded. But no one ordered us into the field. Within certain constraints, we had a free hand in choosing where we went and what we did. With this latitude comes a great deal of responsibility. While I write this, I think a great deal about the platoon officers, platoon chiefs, and task unit commanders in Iraq who must make these life-and-death decisions on a daily basis. They have similar operational latitude in the conduct of their operations and the same heavy responsibility.

The Vietnam portion of the SEAL experience is well chronicled in Orr Kelly's fine book *Brave Men—Dark Waters* (Pocket Books, 1993). My own *SEAL Team One* (Avon, 1991; reprinted by Naval Institute Press, March 2008), while fiction, is an accurate portrait of SEAL tactics and the operations of the deployed SEAL platoons of that era. I also recommend *Teammates: SEALs at War,* by Barry Enoch (Pocket Books, 1996), and *Combat Swimmer: Memoirs of a Navy SEAL,* by Bob Gormley (Penguin, 1998).

For the first decade of the SEALs' existence, the life of a Navy special operator was one of continuous combat rotations to Vietnam. In spite of the broad unconventional-warfare portfolio handed to the SEALs, it was all about operations in Vietnam, period. In short we became very good jungle fighters and little else. We maintained minimum qualifications in diving and parachuting but seldom practiced these in an operational scenario. During the late 1970s and early 1980s, the UDTs and SEAL teams shrank to pre-Vietnam levels and operating budgets were tight. A fifth UDT was commissioned in the summer of 1968 for duty in Vietnam and decommissioned in the summer of 1971. There was talk of disbanding the SEALs or the UDTs, or consolidating them into a single entity for amphibious *and* unconventional duties.

While the SEALs endured continuous deployment rotations to Vietnam—rotations similar to those now experienced by SEALs in Afghanistan and Iraq—the UDTs continued to evolve underwater, focusing much of their time and energy on swimmer delivery operations and the complex business of operating wet mini-submersibles from nuclear parent submarines. These operations became so specialized and all-encompassing that in 1984, two of the four remaining UDTs were converted to SEAL teams and two UDTs became SEAL Delivery Vehicle (SDV) Teams. The new SDV Teams were manned by fully mission-capable SEALs, but they specialized in underwater and over-the-beach operations. With the conversion of the UDTs and the growth of the SEALs in the 1980s and 1990s, the current disposition of SEAL/SDV teams is as follows: SEAL Teams One, Three, Five, and Seven are based in Coronado, California. SEAL Teams Two, Four, Eight, and Ten and SDV Team Two are located in the Norfolk area. SDV Team One is in Hawaii. There is no SEAL Team Six.

Grenada, Panama, and the Gulf War all saw SEALs deployed in direct-action, special-reconnaissance, or search-and-rescue roles. In all of these conflicts, their work was maritime related and in support of conventional battle plans or expeditionary-warfare objectives. And in each of these conflicts, SEALs worked alone or as a diversion to main-force activity. Through the 1990s there were isolated engagements with the emerging threat we broadly categorized as terrorism. Perhaps the most engaging and sustained activity of that period were the operations mounted in support of the oil embargo imposed by the United Nations (UN) on Saddam Hussein and enforced largely by the U.S. Navy. In an effort to deter oil being smuggled out and contraband in, SEALs regularly boarded ships bound to and from Iraq. This activity came to be known as VBSS—visit, board, search, and seize—and was a key element in this maritime interdiction strategy. Saddam tried to get his oil to market by sneaking it out in tankers. SEALs, fast-roping from helicopters, would board these tankers in international waters and detain them. This activity soon became a cat-and-mouse game, with the SEALs swinging aboard at night, while the tankers ran for the safe-haven territorial waters of friendly Arab states. This challenging and largely successful SEAL mission came to an end with 9/11.

The events of 11 September 2001, the operations in Afghanistan, and the invasion of Iraq quickly drew the full attention and deployment commitments of our military, including Naval Special Warfare assets. For the SEALs, all deployments became combat deployments, and that's the way it's been for seven years. There were maritime operations associated with the initial combat operations in Iraq, but for the most part SEALs have taken their game inland, to the mountains in Afghanistan and the cities and villages of Iraq. Navy SEAL operations just prior to 9/11, in the Afghan campaign, and during the initial combat phase of the war in Iraq are chronicled in my book *Down Range: Navy SEALs in the War on Terrorism* (Crown, 2005). It's a selection of representative and important SEAL operations up through and immediately following the campaign to take Baghdad. When interviewing the SEALs as they returned from those combat deployments, what struck me most, aside from their professionalism and courage, was their adaptability. Existing doctrine provided some guidelines, but many of their operational taskings called for them to undertake unfamiliar mission profiles in difficult terrain against an intractable enemy. Yet they took to it like, well, like frogmen to water. Those few World War II frogmen still with us can be justifiably proud of this generation of warriors, as can the Vietnam-era SEALs and UDT men. I sure am. They do us all proud.

Before we get to Iraq, al-Anbar province, and the Battle of Ramadi, it will probably be helpful to discuss how SEALs deploy—the mechanics of how they go into battle and their chain of command. Prior to 2000, SEALs routinely deployed with units of the fleet and to theater commanders such as Pacific Command, European Command, Central Command (the Middle East), or Southern Command (Central/South America). While on these deployments, they were attached to a parent command, afloat or ashore, under a conventional-force command structure. SEAL *platoons* deployed with little command presence and limited logistic or operational support. For example, on the West Coast, Naval Special Warfare Group One kept two platoons with Central Command and four platoons with Pacific Command. Since 2000 SEALs have deployed *with* their own integral command, control, and support organization. This combat support package, complete with an internal intelligence and targeting capability, has dramatically enhanced SEAL and Naval Special Warfare capabilities in the operational theaters. This deployment of SEALs, SEAL battle staffs, and expanded combat support staff was put in place just in time for the heavy combat rotations that followed after 9/11. We'll get into the manning, composition, and capabilities of this new deployment package, the SEAL squadron, a little later. It is, however, interesting to note that this new SEAL expeditionary posture was the brainchild of Admiral Eric Olson, currently the commander of U.S. Special Operations Command—the first SEAL to hold this four-star position. It is with a great deal of pride and appreciation that I was able to begin this work with a preface by Admiral Olson.

A deployed SEAL squadron commander reports to his regional special operations task force commander. When this commander directs the activities of allied or coalition special operations forces, he becomes a *joint* special operations task force (JSOTF) commander. In Iraq that JSOTF commander is currently the deployed Army Special Forces group commander. The Middle East is the dedicated area of operations (AO) for the 5th Special Forces Group, but other groups and their commanders are in deployment rotation in Iraq. At any one time it could be the 10th Group, the 1st Group, or one of the other active Special Forces groups. Currently, the JSOTF commander is located at Balad Air Base, the large U.S. base northwest of Baghdad. The JSOTF commander in Iraq commands all special operations forces, or SOF, including assigned special missions units. The activity of the special missions units, who they are, and what they do is classified and beyond the scope of this book. They include Army, Navy, and Air Force tier-one SOF assets, and they are known to range across the battlespace in Iraq. These "special" special operators did operate in al-Anbar and Ramadi, but the focus of this text will be the SEAL task unit at Ramadi.

Since late 2006, the deployed SEAL squadron commander has held the title of Commander, Special Operations Task Force–West, which places him in command of all special operations activity in western Iraq—that is, al-Anbar province. We'll get to the evolution and scope of his duties in later chapters. The work of the deployed SEAL squadrons is done by the task units. These are the tips of the SEAL spears. They command the SEAL platoons and other task unit assets on the battlefield. There were several task units operating in al-Anbar at any given time, but this book will focus on those that rotated through Ramadi. The task unit commanders are the senior SEAL boot-on-the-ground. As one of the Ramadi TU commanders told me, "Never in my military career have I had so much responsibility and lives at risk as I did during those six months in Ramadi. And I probably never will again."

A final word on special operations task forces, task groups, and task units. These units provide lines of command, communication, and support, but at none of these levels do their commanding officers *own battlespace.* They control no territory. SEALs and other special operators live and work in an area or sector controlled by a conventional battlespace commander. That means they work and fight on turf that belongs to an Army or Marine Corps commander. Since they do not fall within that commander's direct chain of command, they must work closely with this conventional-force commander as they conduct their operations. On first pass, this might seem to limit or restrict the freedom of special operations units. In some sectors that may have been true, and it's an ongoing concern for these conventional battlespace commanders. But, for the most part, the SEALs assigned to the task units in Iraq thrived in this environment. In fact, they had nothing but praise for their conventional Army or Marine battlespace landlords. And they reserved their highest praise for the soldiers and marines with whom they shared this battlespace.

I've tried to stay abreast of our SEAL and special operations activity in Afghanistan and Iraq since we began this fight, and there have been issues regarding turf. Perhaps nowhere else was the cooperation between SOF and conventional forces better than in al-Anbar province, and in none was it better than in Ramadi. In the past I've been an advocate for SOF battlespace control. Unity of command is important, whether it's a fleet action, maneuver warfare, or counterinsurgency warfare. But Ramadi has changed my thinking. Perhaps this was due to the sheer size of the insurgent opposition in al-Anbar or the maturity of the Army and Marine forces at this stage of the fight—or both. There was some apprehension on the part of the conventional commanders in Ramadi about these sailors in their battlespace, but the professionalism of all parties quickly put those concerns to bed. For reasons discussed in later chapters, the conventional-force-commanded, SOF-supported arrangement worked very well in this particular full-blown insurgency in an urban environment. There may be other battles in other insurgencies where SOF command of the battlespace makes sense. This was not one of them. Like the Ramadi SEALs, I've come to have a new respect for what the Army and the Marines bring to the insurgent battlefield.

Before we get to the SEALs "out west" and the Battle of Ramadi, we need to take a look at the historical events and forces that shaped Iraq and al-Anbar province. How these factors played out in the battle and in its aftermath is both important and instructional. And without running too far ahead of our story, it's well to keep in mind that any solution we Americans try to impose on a different culture, which comprises most of the world, we had better bring that solution in line with the historical forces that drive that particular culture. It seems that whenever we've ignored these human-terrain factors, the result has indeed been a stern chase, and a long one.

Full Metal Jacket. The embattled home of the SEAL platoons that fought alongside the Army battalions at Camp Corregidor. *Courtesy of Lieutenant Steve Ruh*

The Terrain

T he cultural, historical, and physical terrain of Iraq, al-Anbar province, and the city of Ramadi could not be collectively more dissimilar from the land, culture, and history of the American warriors who came fight there. Yet it is most important that we as a nation, as well as those who fight our battles, understand these differences. If we can step back and take a look at this region from a cultural and historical perspective, it's a little easier to understand the cause and effect of our efforts there. Since this is a battlefield book, understanding the past and exploring the tortured and diverse history of this area is most helpful in sorting out the current engagement. So, before we get to the SEALs and the SEAL task unit in Ramadi, let's take a look at this battlespace from this perspective.

Even calling Iraq a nation is a stretch, since the current boundaries have been in place for less than a century. But the area in and around Iraq and the culture of the region is *very* old. We in America find great pride in ourselves if we can trace our lineage back to the *Mayflower*—a scant four centuries. The earliest inhabitants of Iraq, or Mesopotamia as it has been called, can trace their origins back almost three thousand years *before* the birth of Christ. The first of these ancient civilizations with a recorded history were the Sumerians. They were believed to have developed the first written language, formulated the first calendar based on the twelve-month cycles of the moon, and engaged in mathematics. The first Sumerian writings define history in terms of a recorded history; all else is prehistoric. The name Mesopotamia means "between the rivers" in Greek, and the fertile region between the Tigris and Euphrates has a legitimate claim as the Cradle of Civilization. When compared to Western civilization in the

New World, the Mesopotamians have a four and a half millennia head start.

A quick sprint through time saw the Sumerians give way to the Akkadians, followed by the Amorites, the Assyrians, the Chaldeans, and Neo-Babylonians. Around 539 BC, Cyrus the Great came into power, and his capital at Susa became the center of the Middle Eastern world. Cyrus was an interesting ruler in that he was the first to allow those he conquered to live in relative peace and security—as long as they paid tribute. He did not enslave his conquests, electing to pay those under his rule for their work on his palaces and public buildings, and he allowed his subjects to worship as they pleased. Iraq was conquered by the Greeks and then the Romans before the Arabs and Islam claimed the region in AD 638. They were to rule until the Mongols under Genghis Khan swarmed into the region in 1258. In 1432, the Turkmen tribal federation pushed in from the northeast to chase out the Mongols and occupy what is present-day Iraq. The Turkmen ruled until Shah Isma'il, the founder of the Iranian dynasty, drove them away and occupied Baghdad in 1508. Suleyman the Magnificent took the region into the Ottoman Empire in 1534, where it was to remain until the end of World War I.

Prior to 1918, the region we call Iraq and those who lived along the Tigris and the Euphrates had known war, conquest, grandeur, invasion, and occupation, which had left the area a mosaic of diverse religious, ethnic, and tribal elements. It is, however, important to understand that the tribal ties and affiliations predate Islam. Then the British stepped in and set in motion a series of events that led to the conditions we face in present-day Iraq.

The League of Nations granted Britain a mandate in Iraq, just as it awarded France control of Syria and Lebanon. This mandate was a spoil of World War I; the British inherited the region and its problems from the Ottoman Turks. The parceling out of these mandates was arbitrarily negotiated by the European powers and helped to form national boundaries that ignored the demographics of the region— an issue that haunts us to this very day. The term "mandate" is an interesting one. The British clearly wanted to bring Iraq or parts of Iraq into the empire—the India model as some thought of it, but words like "annexation" and "colony" were not popular in the post–World War I international community. Still, the British were able to merge the three provinces of Mosul, Baghdad, and Basra into a single state under their influence. For the first time, Iraq became a nation or political entity with this multiple-ethnic stew contained within modern, established borders—borders that cut through traditional tribal areas and religious regions. The Brits were experienced in telling others how to conduct their affairs, but Iraq presented unique challenges. Many in Britain favored direct control with an eye to protecting the Crown's interests in the Persian Gulf, which at the time were military bases, not oil. Others in the British Foreign Office, noting the rise of Arab nationalism, advised indirect control with an indigenous regime under British supervision—a supervision that many colonialists felt they could extend indefinitely. In 1920 the British suppressed a revolt, but not the Arab nationalists' cries for independence. Being royalists and wishing to continue their influence in Iraq, the British shopped around for a monarch. They settled on Faisal and offered him the Iraqi throne, subject, of course, to their guidance and oversight. Faisal I was a wily politician who wanted the throne, but wanted it presented to him by the Iraqi people. He got this in a national plebiscite and was crowned king in 1921. Orchestrating these events behind the scenes was Winston Churchill, then colonial secretary. Advising Churchill was T. E. Lawrence, who knew the Arabs well and sympathized with them. When the British crowned Faisal as head of state, a military band played "God Save the King." Iraq had no national anthem at the time.

The Faisal monarchy began a national regime with a treaty of alliance with Great Britain. This new Iraq under Faisal began the halting journey toward nationhood with constitutional assemblies, provisions for religious freedoms, enfranchisement, and domestic reforms. Without getting too far into the weeds on this semicolonial period, the British meddled, the nationalists chafed for more autonomy, and the League of Nations, which the United States elected *not* to join, observed. A further polarization was taking place among the Iraqi people. Those in the cities felt the British presence the most and were the most vocal in their calls for the abolishment of the mandate. In the rural areas, the tribal entities lived and ruled much as they always had. Over the next decade and a half, Faisal, and the son who succeeded him, presided over a constitutional monarchy that was characterized by instability. The downfall of the monarchy came in 1958. Prior to this end, there were ten general elections and more than fifty cabinets were formed. Change came often from a variety of causes—resignations, assassinations, palace intrigues, attacks by the press, tribal uprisings, and, with increasing frequency, coup d'etats.

A constitutional monarchy, such as the one the British introduced, is an interesting form of government. It's a form of democracy that, in its early stages, works best when there is a capable and popular regent on the throne. The king can act as a buffer or shock absorber to the competing political and military elements within his government. He can serve as yet another voice of the people; he can be a stabilizing presence during times of political crisis. The best example of this today is Thailand, where the coups are bloodless and the king is known to support rational government in the interest of the Thai people. Faisal tried to serve Iraq in this fashion, but Iraq is not Thailand. The Thais are 95 percent Buddhist and have a history of ethnic tolerance. Iraq is far more diverse and volatile. After Faisal the monarchy became increasingly influenced by the military and unstable and competing military factions.

In 1958 army officers took absolute power, banishing the monarchy and declaring Iraq a "republic" with General Abdul Kassem its president. In 1963 Kassem was assassinated by army officers who had the backing of the Baath Party, and General Ahmad Hassan became president. In 1979 Hassan resigned to make way for his ambitious and ruthless vice president, Saddam Hussein. Saddam ruled until we stepped in. The turbulent years from the World War I to present-day is the subject of many informative books on Iraq. I recommend *Inventing Iraq: The Failure of Nation Building and a History Denied,* by Toby Dodge (Columbia University Press, 2003). The work is short, informative, and very well written.

Many view Saddam Hussein as a thug in the mold of Hitler, Stalin, or Ceausescu—part sociopath and part fanatic, with a dose of the paranoid. I like to think of Saddam as the product of a long evolution of Middle Eastern rulers, incrementally smarter and a little more vicious than those they succeeded. Saddam understood the tribal, ethnic, and religious broth of modern Iraq; he knew when to bestow patronage and when to withhold favor. He also knew how to instill and exploit fear, terror, and loyalty. He freely used torture and seemed to go out of his way to cultivate a personal aura of brutality and unpredictability. What made him a player on the world stage was oil, both the riches to be gained by pumping it out of the ground and the ability to use potential oil wealth to play Western democracies and Communist nations to his advantage. He was ambitious and had visions of grandeur and expansion, but no more so than the Assyrian and Babylonian rulers who came before him. I believe Saddam saw himself as a modern Saladin who wanted to extend his control across the Middle East. But unlike the Salah al-Din of the twelfth century, he was unable to resist the Crusader invasion of the twenty-first century.

If the rulers of present-day Iraq, especially those now in office, seem divisive and duplicitous, it's because they are simply a product of the combative and fractious forces that shaped the region. And the colonial influences that sought to maneuver and influence these forces did little to endear the peoples of Iraq to the West. The national boundaries created by the British and the League of Nations after World War I could not have carved out a more difficult piece of real estate. These new boundaries sliced through Sunni-Shiite-Kurdish areas and tribal homelands that had no need or desire to be citizens of the same nation. Overlay that with the antisecular tenets of the Koran, and it's easy to see why stability in Iraq has been achieved only by autocrats and at the point of a gun. Sad to say, if it were not for oil and our national interests that are tied to the stability of the regional oil-producing states, we would not be there. But we are there, and, in part, our scanty understanding of the history and culture of this region allowed us to stumble into a nasty insurgency, one that took the Iraqi people perilously close to civil war. And as we will see later in this text, when care is taken to respect *their* historical and cultural conventions, our interests in the region can be advanced. And when we haven't, well, the evidence suggests that our interests are severely compromised.

I've taken you through this brief history lesson because it's important to what we want to accomplish in Iraq—and in Afghanistan and whatever comes next. As Tom Freidman is so fond of saying, we broke it and now we have to fix it. But if that fix runs counter to the historical and cultural forces that shaped the region and the people who live there, we're going to lose. I've heard people say, "They want the same things as we do—peace, security within their communities, and to take care of their families." True enough and easy to say, but hard to put into practice in an insurgent environment. If we wish to achieve an acceptable resolution in Iraq, we have to help the Iraqis (defined as those who live within the borders of present-day Iraq) get there within their frame of reference and their definition of governance, security, community, and family. We finally began to do that in Ramadi and al-Anbar, and it made all the difference.

Al-Anbar province is the heartland of Sunni tribal culture in Iraq. At its center is the infamous Sunni triangle that proved to be so contentious and dangerous after the fall of Baghdad. But for the string of cities along the Euphrates, it is a marginally habitable expanse of desert wasteland. Until 1976 the entire province of al-Anbar was known as Ramadi. There are few natural resources in al-Anbar, but there are thought to be deep pools of oil along the Anbari-Syrian border. It is a tribal region, and community life in this area is dominated by tribal elders and tribal sheikhs. This was true when the British tried to govern and while Saddam was in power, and it's true today. External forces who are willing to work within this structure may have a chance to advance their agenda. Those who put themselves in opposition with this tribal structure, like the British at the beginning of the last century and al-Qaeda at the beginning of this one, are going to have a difficult time. And understanding the tribes of al-Anbar is not easy. As one returning SEAL task unit commander put it, "If you want to understand tribal politics in al-Anbar, watch *The Sopranos* on TV." The British and, more recently, the Americans badly misread this region. When coalition forces tried to promote Baghdad-based central control over al-Anbar, the results were a disaster. Fortunately, al-Qaeda misread al-Anbar as well.

Ramadi, the capital of al-Anbar province, is a contentious city that seems to have inherited all of the tribal and regional baggage, along with the problems of a crowded city. Ramadi is known for its hard-line strains of Sunni practice and as a base for many top Sunni clerics. These religious ties in Ramadi reach into Jordan and Syria, and into Saudi Arabia. While these religious ties are important and deep-seated, they are often secondary to tribal considerations. Ramadi is also the seat of power for many Arab tribes, including the influential Dulaim and Jabir tribes. The farther west and north one travels from Baghdad, the more important these tribal entities become. Geographically, the city is the southwest point of the Sunni triangle, a region that approximates the old Baghdad province when partitioned by the British. It was here that the British under General Sir Frederick Stanley Maude first defeated the Arab nationalists in 1917, a humiliation that has dimmed with time but is still a bitter memory.

The insurgency in al-Anbar began in the summer of 2003, just a few months after the end of major combat operations. It seemed to originate with former Sunni Baathists in the Iraqi army who fled the American advance. When they went home, they took their guns with them. The focal points for this insurgency were the two major cities of al-Anbar province, Fallujah and Ramadi. Of the two, Fallujah, which is closer to Baghdad, quickly became a major refuge for insurgents, not only for Baathists in hiding but for unemployed Sunnis expelled from the government after the fall of Saddam. It seemed to be an easy transition from out-of-work government employee or ex-soldier to insurgent. And a few of these were more than simple soldiers or government supernumeraries; they were members of the Mukabarat, Saddam's secret intelligence and former members of the elite paramilitary unit, the Fedayeen Saddam. There was simply no commercial enterprise or industry to soak up these jobless Anbaris. In the wake of the power vacuum and a near bankrupt economy, foreign fighters—many of them with ties to al-Qaeda—began to make their way to Iraq. Fallujah became a focus for insurgents and anticoalition sentiment. Following the much-publicized killing and corpse mutilation of four Blackwater contractors in late March 2004, the U.S. military decided on a purge of Fallujah. On 4 April, four battalions of Marines, backed by a tank battalion and massive air support, attacked this city of 250,000. The Marines were making good progress when the interim Iraqi government intervened. A cease-fire was arranged when the tribal leaders in Fallujah agreed to rein in the insurgents. The Marines pulled back on 1 May.

In retrospect, this was probably an honest effort on the part of the tribal entities in Fallujah to control the insurgent elements in their city. The mood of the residents and their leaders at that time was one of guarded cooperation with coalition forces and, at worst, a wait-and-see attitude with the new provisional authority in Baghdad. And the tribal leadership may have been able to control the situation in Fallujah had they only to deal with disenfranchised Baathists and unemployed soldiers. But festering in Fallujah was a hard-core insurgent minority headed by the likes of Abu Musab al-Zarqawi and his lieutenants. I am not sure if their numbers and composition have ever been accurately evaluated, but this vicious and aggressive insurgent presence coalesced into a force that was later to be known as AQI (al-Qaeda in Iraq). And they quickly stamped out any cooperation that might have been in line with the coalition or provisional-authority efforts to bring stability to the city.

Throughout this book, I'm going to refer to the "insurgent elements" in Fallujah, Ramadi, and al-Anbar as AQI. It would not be until much later, after the death of al-Zarqawi, that the Mujahideen Shura Council (MSC) would proclaim al-Anbar to be the Islamic State of Iraq. The numbers and exact composition of the insurgents are a moving target.

It's safe to say that they're a mix of Anbaris—radical Sunni tribesmen, former soldiers and Baathist party regulars, hard-core Islamists, thugs, criminals, and a stateless collection of non-Anbari foreign fighters. The common linkage is an al-Qaeda- or Taliban-like vision of how things *ought* to be—anti-Western, antisecular, and in keeping with strict Islamic law, although many of the lawless elements associated with al-Qaeda are anything but religious. Keep in mind that we're talking al-Anbar here—the Iraqi version of the American Wild West. In Baghdad, Basra, Mosul, and elsewhere, opposition to central authority comes from more ethnically aligned groups—Sunni "insurgents," Shiite militias, the Mahdi Army, and the like. Therefore, when speaking of al-Anbar, I'll often refer to this ill-defined and dynamic insurgent presence simply as AQI. This term, and the composition as described above, may or may not be current when this work goes to press. Such is the moving target that is our opposition in Iraq.

Upstream along the Euphrates, at the same time as the Marines' initial assault and pullback in Fallujah, a similar but much smaller engagement was taking place in Ramadi, a city of some 450,000. Here, two companies of Marines swept into the city and engaged the handful of insurgent strongholds in the provincial capital. In Ramadi the Marines were more successful. In the course of four days of fighting, they managed to kill several hundred insurgents and drive those who remained from the city or into temporary hiding. It's hard to believe that in the spring and summer of 2004, the insurgent presence in Ramadi could be routed by this small force. And yet while tactically successful, this operation also served to foster resentment of American forces in this predominately Sunni city. Like the action that was soon to take place in Fallujah, this was a largely unilateral operation and a temporary, nonlocal, nontribal solution to a growing problem.

The combined Fallujah-Ramadi operations cost the Marines close to a hundred dead and several hundred wounded. In Fallujah it was hoped the Marine pullback would be followed by local containment of the disruptive factions within that city. But the insurgent presence intensified, and U.S. forces returned to finish what they started the previous spring. On 7 November 2004, fourteen Marine and Army battalions, along with six Iraqi army battalions (predominately Shiite in composition), surrounded Fallujah and attacked. So began what has been called the Second Battle of Fallujah. After six weeks of some of the heaviest urban fighting since Mogadishu, Somalia, the U.S.-Iraqi force fully occupied the city. It was a costly victory all around. Again, close to a hundred Marines and soldiers were killed and six hundred were wounded. Iraqi army losses were but a fraction of that. Twelve hundred insurgents were killed and close to a thousand taken prisoner. Twenty percent of the city's dwellings were destroyed, and more than two-thirds were damaged. A steady stream of refugees exited the city during the fighting, and there were many civilian casualties. The action was considered a military success in that it broke the back of the Sunni-led insurrection in Fallujah. The influence of al-Qaeda was significantly degraded as well. That was the good news. The bad news was that many insurgent leaders, including the late Abu Musab al-Zarqawi, escaped. And many of those who left Fallujah moved on to Ramadi.

Ramadi is roughly sixty miles west of Baghdad. The city sits astride the Euphrates River with road and rail access to the western border regions. Approximately 60 percent of the Iraqi-Syrian border lies in al-Anbar province, and much of the cross-border traffic passes through Ramadi. It's up the trapline, so to speak, for insurgents on the run. When American, coalition, and Iraqi security forces began military sweeps for insurgents in Baghdad, the bad guys headed up the Euphrates to Fallujah. And when the heat got turned up in Fallujah, as it did in late 2004, they continued another twenty miles upstream to Ramadi. And it's a two-way street; Ramadi is down the trapline for many foreign fighters entering Iraq from Syria and Saudi Arabia, headed for Baghdad.

With Fallujah more or less pacified, the heart of the insurgency in al-Anbar, and indeed all of Iraq, shifted to Ramadi in early 2005. The large provincial capital quickly became a sanctuary for AQI and the Mujahideen Shura Council, although there were many others. They simply overwhelmed the local police and, to a large extent, the U.S.-Iraqi military presence. Three major bases in the area hosted battalion-sized units of the Army, Marines, and the new Iraqi army. But in Ramadi there were no coalition or multinational force (MNF, i.e., American and Iraqi forces) troops present in strength. For most of 2005 and the first half of 2006, the coalition forces were confined to their bases. The only notable exception was a Marine outpost at the Ramadi Government Center. The streets were routinely contested by U.S. and Iraqi military patrols, but the insurgents controlled most of the turf.

By the end of 2005 Ramadi had become the focal point of resistance to the U.S. presence in Iraq and a very dangerous city. Some say that the Shiite-dominated government in Baghdad had little inclination to stem this rising insurgent tide in Ramadi and al-Anbar, thinking that the insurgency there served to weaken Sunni participation in the new government. But with its numerous roads and the main railway line into Syria, Ramadi increasingly became a major staging area and waypoint for insurgents moving into Baghdad from Sunni nations to the north and west. It's wrong to say generically that all terrorists are Sunni or that all Sunnis harbor terrorists, but most global terrorists, including Osama bin Laden, come from predominately Sunni nations. During 2006 hostile insurgent attacks, primarily through the use of IEDs, in Ramadi and al-Anbar accounted for half of the Americans killed and wounded in action in Iraq. This grim statistic did not escape the attention of the media. Yet, by the end of 2006, conditions in Ramadi and in all of al-Anbar had begun to change for the better—something that the media seemed to take little notice of until early 2007. The change in Ramadi began during what has been referred to as the Second Battle of Ramadi.

The Second Battle of Ramadi. Those who cover the war in the press seem to like finite engagements and packaged battles. This helps to assign winners and losers, and often to assign military and political blame. In my opinion, the term "Second Battle" is a classic case of this. In order to understand the work of the SEAL task unit in Ramadi and the dramatic turnaround in that AQI stronghold, one has to understand what took place in this so-called Second Battle, and that's not easy. Much of what I've read has this battle beginning on 17 June and ending on 15 November 2006, as if two armies suddenly fell upon each other in mid-June and disengaged in mid-November. Most post-November accounts held that the insurgents won or that, after some initial success, most of the U.S. Army and Marine objectives were not achieved—that Ramadi remained largely in the control of insurgent forces.

For the purposes of this book, I'm going to speak only to the Battle of Ramadi, as the so-called First Battle was little more than a skirmish when compared to what was to take place during the second half of 2006 and the first quarter of 2007. But 17 June is a good starting point for the battle; that's when the first new combat outpost was put in place, an action that set in motion the strategy that was to take back the city from AQI and their insurgent allies.

Throughout the spring and into the summer of 2006, the situation in Ramadi seemed to be unraveling; something had to be done to bring order to this important city. Ramadi was seen as the key to all of al-Anbar province. *The Sheriff of Ramadi* is the story of what took place and what had to be done to win back Ramadi—what happened before, during, and after the battle. In working on this book, I was continually amazed at how little the media—and even the senior military leadership, as their views were reported in the press—understood what was taking place out in al-Anbar. Well into the battle, the reports continued to tout the negative. In September a leaked military intelligence report claimed the province was lost to AQI. In late November yet another secret military intelligence report, as leaked to the *Washington Post,* stated that "the social and political situation has deteriorated to a point that U.S. and Iraqi troops are no longer capable of militarily defeating the insurgency in al-Anbar." The report went on to describe al-Qaeda as the dominate influence in the province. And, indeed, heavy fighting persisted in many sections of the city, with mounting American and Iraqi army casualties. But the new American-led counterinsurgency effort in Ramadi began to work—the investment of sweat and blood during those dark days of 2006 finally started to pay off. But what I found most compelling was that the soldiers and marines (and SEALs) on the street *knew* we were winning. The battalion and brigade commanders on the ground knew we were winning.

Tom Bowman, of National Public Radio and *All Things Considered,* has delivered commentaries on the insurgency in Ramadi going back to the summer of 2003. He has referred frequently to the difficulties encountered during the counterinsurgent operations in the summer of 2006. On 3 March 2007 his commentary was titled, "U.S. Soldiers, Iraqi Police Unite to Redeem Ramadi." Almost cautiously, a few veteran reporters began to file stories on this new, seemingly miraculous, and unexpected turnaround in Ramadi. Yet most journalists and online sources did not revise their version: of a battle not yet over, or even a battle lost. It almost seems as if only a battle lost or a battle gone badly is newsworthy. But what about a hard-fought battle won?

What happened in Ramadi that brought about this dramatic reversal? What was the role of the Navy SEALs in winning back this city? Why and how did we let it get so far out of hand that so much blood and treasury were required to retrieve this important city? And is this a template for what can be done in Baghdad and the Shiite-dominated areas to the south? Or in future insurgencies? Again, this is why I feel *The Sheriff of Ramadi* is an important work.

Our issues in Iraq are legion, yet most of them hinge on the inability of coalition forces and the new Iraqi government to bring about security. Nothing can go forward—commerce, business, politics (which may or may not entail democracy), education, community life—without internal security. Job one for any government, local or national, is order. The easiest way for the forces that oppose government, whether it's the new national government in Baghdad or any local government, is to prevent order. As I've stated earlier, insurgency allows for a tyranny of the minority. The fear of men coming in the night with guns is difficult to overcome, especially when those insurgent elements, through intimidation or local sympathy, are embedded in the population. Rooting out insurgents is difficult business for police and local security forces, and a near impossibility for an occupation force.

Our presence in Iraq is into its sixth year. If the Iraqi security forces, with whatever help we can give them, are able to prevail and to provide a secure and stable environment, the Iraqis win, we win, and the insurgents lose. If this cannot be done, then the insurgents win and those who have called this a civil war will have been right—the sectarian battle lines will be carved deeper with multinational alignment, and this insurgency may well become a regional conflict. But it's clear to me that *the Iraqis* have to meet and deal with this insurgency, and it matters not if the insurgents are AQI, Shiite militias, Sunni paramilitaries, foreign fighters, or veteran multinational al-Qaeda operatives. At best, American forces can be a catalyst and a resource for the Iraqi security forces. At worse, we are an occupying army whose presence is resented by the people we're trying to help. When reflecting on those heady days after the fall of Baghdad, it's almost bewildering to contemplate how we managed to paint ourselves into this corner.

The history of our involvement in Iraq and the rise of the insurgency is well-plowed turf. Some accounts are scholarly works, while more than a few others are written with sharp political bias. I find it convenient to see our venture in Iraq as having three distinct phases: the invasion, getting it wrong, and, finally, getting it right.

We went into Iraq in March 2003 for reasons that were compelling enough, at the time, to have the unanimous support of the U.S. Congress and the support of more than two-thirds of the American people. If this was a rush to war brought on by the neoconservatives, then we as a nation were easily stampeded. I'd like to think I know something of insurgency warfare, but I have to confess to being blinded by the notion of an economic democracy in the heart of Islam (the *real* terrorist antidote) and doing what was needed to prevent another 9/11 event. And, like most Americans, I was impressed—awed might be a better word—by the professionalism and courage of those marines and soldiers who drove up the Tigris and the Euphrates to Baghdad. It was a proud moment to see that statue of Saddam Hussein toppled on TV. Here at home, we cheered as our team seemed to have won the big game. But few of us were ready for the postgame headaches. A few informed people, in and out of government, had their reservations about this dramatic maneuver-warfare victory. Was this going to be like the streets of Paris or like the streets of Mogadishu? It began a little like the former, but soon dissolved into the latter. This was the invasion phase. We called it liberation. From the perspective of many Iraqis, it was the occupation phase. The Crusaders were back.

By the summer of 2003, insurgent elements were materializing across Iraq. On the heels of a repressive regime and with an economy on the ropes, there was lawlessness, a continued lack of services, and, for the Sunnis, the unfamiliar absence of patronage from the Baath Party, which was banished from power by the Coalition Provisional Authority. The disenfranchised Baathists were not the only ones ready to join an insurgent movement. There were Iraqi army soldiers who had lost their jobs and pensions, but retained their weapons. Before Saddam Hussein went into hiding, he emptied the prisons, which held genuine criminals as well as political prisoners. The porous borders allowed all manners of foreign jihadists to make their way into Iraq. And, finally, there was the presence of Americans. The soldiers and marines who patrolled the streets and villages were a constant reminder that there were foreign troops on Iraqi soil—again. Those same soldiers and marines, who were so magnificent on the drive to Baghdad, were unprepared for a shift to counterinsurgency warfare. Or perhaps it is more accurate to say that our military and/or political leaders were taken by surprise and failed to take action. Our troops became a conspicuous foreign presence.

Our initial attempts to deal with this insurgency might be illustrated with an analogy from our own Wild West. I call it the Tombstone model. In Tombstone Wyatt Earp and his brothers were able to draw out Ike Clanton and his kin and force a showdown. After the shootout there was continued sporadic violence, but the Earps were in control of the town and life went on. Wyatt and his brothers were able to get the insurgent Clantons into a gunfight—something the Earps were good at. In Iraq we charged our military with the task of hunting down and killing insurgents—people we labeled as terrorists. Only the insurgents didn't fight like the Clantons. They hid in the cities and towns, sniping at our patrols and planting IEDs. These insurgents, in their various forms and permutations, were much nastier than the Clantons. They didn't care how many of the local citizenry they killed or maimed. They were into chaos as much as they were into killing Americans. We responded to this lawlessness with offensives, counteroffensives, sweeps, and other standard military tactics. These measures were ineffective and often counterproductive. When an innocent Iraqi is killed in the fighting, occasionally by American military activity and frequently by insurgent activity, his extended family takes up the fight—against us or against the offending ethnic/religious/tribal faction. Either way the violence continues—even escalates. We were trying to use standard military doctrine to address a counterinsurgency issue. Killing insurgents is one small piece of the puzzle; winning the people is real prize. This was at the heart of "getting it wrong."

The responsibility for counterinsurgency rests with the U.S. Army, but the real specialists in counterinsurgency are the Army Special Forces—the Green Berets. Counterinsurgency comes under the SOF discipline of foreign internal defense, or FID. FID is part of the skill set of other SOF components, but it's the stock-in-trade of the Green Berets. Using their cross-cultural skills and language capabilities, they work *by, with, and through* the military and police organizations of friendly nations to defeat insurgents and/or foreign invaders. Throughout their long and storied existence, they have done this—in Vietnam, in El Salvador, and recently in Iraq and Afghanistan. But they've never had to contend with an insurgency of this magnitude. Even today, with their numbers on the rise, the Army Special Forces are hard-pressed to keep more than a thousand counterinsurgency specialists in Iraq. There are simply too few of them, and Iraq is not the only place where their talents are needed. An insurgency such as the one we face in Iraq requires the effective use of our deployed conventional forces in a counterinsurgency role—supported by Special Forces and our other SOF components. It's the only way.

In late 2005, throughout 2006, and into 2007 we began to get it right. That is, we began to make good use of our conventional forces, working closely with SOF and the Iraqi security forces, in a counterinsurgency role. It also meant effectively engaging the people and their local leaders. In Ramadi, this meant working with the Iraqi army, the local police, and, more important, the local tribal sheikhs. This was a big change for the

Camp Marc Lee, home of the Ramadi SEALs. Initially, the compound was called Shark Base but was later renamed in honor of Marc Lee, the first SEAL killed in Iraq. *Courtesy of Lieutenant Steve Ruh*

The team house. The home of the SEAL Ramadi task unit during the Battle of Ramadi, this three-story structure once housed Saddam's personal bodyguard detail. *Photo by Dick Couch*

Building out the camp. Erecting barriers and stringing concertina wire was something all soldiers, marines, and SEALs had to do in Ramadi and all across al-Anbar. *Courtesy of Lieutenant Steve Ruh*

SEAL Humvees awaiting duty. The task unit moved about Ramadi on foot or in Humvees. The shed and shop space at Camp Marc Lee came courtesy of the task unit's Navy Seabees. *Photo by Dick Couch*

The Habbaniyah Canal from the team house. Looking southeast from the roof of the task unit team house, across the Habbaniyah Canal to the smokestacks of the Ramadi glass factory. *Photo by Dick Couch*

The author and the terp. After first meeting in San Diego, Dick Couch and Patrick, a task unit interpreter, meet again at Camp Lee in August 2007. *Courtesy of Lieutenant Steve Ruh*

Main entrance to the team house. Memorial at the quarterdeck of the team house at Camp Marc Lee in honor of Marc Lee and Mike Monsoor. SEAL team emblems surround an aerial view of the camp. *Courtesy of Lieutenant Steve Ruh*

Job one—training Iraqi army scouts. SEALs from Team Seven at Camp Ramadi follow Iraqi soldiers as they fire at silhouette targets while moving forward. *Courtesy of Lieutenant Steve Ruh*

This is how it's done. The lead SEAL instructor shows a scout from the Iraqi 7th Brigade how to take a knee and take a shot. *Photo by Dick Couch*

Graduate instruction—fire and movement. An Iraqi scout provides covering fire while a fellow soldier sprints downrange to take up a forward firing position. *Photo by Dick Couch*

[Top] The streets of Ramadi. Elements of the U.S. Army patrol in western Ramadi under the cover of an M1A2 Abrams tank. Later on, the Iraqi police would be on the streets with the Army and the Marines. *Courtesy of the U.S. Army*

[Middle] Kicking doors. Petty Officer Marc Lee opens a door in Ramadi prior to searching the premises for insurgents. *Courtesy of the U.S. Navy*

[Bottom] More door kicking. Forced armed entry was sometimes the only way to gain access to a building in Ramadi. Often two boots were needed. *Courtesy of the U.S. Army*

Clearing the second story. Two soldiers of the 1-37 race up to the second story of a building to check for insurgent presence—dangerous business for soldiers and for SEALs. *Courtesy of Captain Mike Bajema*

Home of the Bulldogs. All is quiet now, but this combat outpost, COP Falcon, in western Ramadi saw some of the fiercest fighting during the battle. *Courtesy of Lieutenant Steve Ruh*

Bulldog leader. Captain Mike Bajema stands behind a .50-caliber machine gun at his place of business, the turret of an M1A2 Abrams main battle tank. *Courtesy of the U.S. Army*

Devastation along Route Michigan. Much of Ramadi along the main corridors and roads was destroyed in the fighting. *Courtesy of Lieutenant Steve Ruh*

The Saddam Mosque. The windows were shot out and the exterior was still pitted with bullet strikes, but the Saddam Mosque along Route Michigan survived the battle. *Courtesy of Lieutenant Steve Ruh*

Reliving the battle. The author stands with Lieutenant Ned Hurt on the roof of the Full Metal Jacket building, talking about the role of the Corregidor SEALs during the battle. Hurt had two combat tours in Ramadi. *Courtesy of Lieutenant Steve Ruh*

[Top] Army SEAL. A Navy SEAL at Camp Corregidor is wearing Army battle dress and displaying the famous ace-of-spades patch of the 1st Battalion, 506th Parachute Infantry Regiment—the Band of Brothers. *Courtesy of the U.S. Army*

[Bottom] They also fought. One of the many interpreters who worked with the SEALs during the battle, this "terp," seen here at Camp Corregidor, was an American citizen whose parents were born in Iraq; he spoke flawless English and Arabic. *Photo by Dick Couch*

Training the Iraqi police. SEALs at Camp Corregidor train local Sunni tribesmen who will soon take to the streets as policemen. Many were former insurgents. *Courtesy of the U.S. Navy*

Waiting their turn. Tribal police recruits, AK-47s and magazines in hand, wait to fire their weapons on a makeshift firing range near Camp Corregidor. Note the soccer goal in background. *Courtesy of the U.S. Navy*

On the firing line. SEALs at Camp Ramadi observe their Iraqi police trainees during live-fire training. Local police on the streets sealed the victory won by the American and Iraqi forces. *Courtesy of the U.S. Navy*

Proper search technique. A U.S. Army training cadre demonstrates proper search procedures to Iraqi police recruits. *Courtesy of Captain Mike Bajema*

Iraqi police on patrol. An Iraqi police vehicle cruises past COP Falcon while patrolling the streets of Ramadi. Police in pickups gradually replaced Americans in Humvees. *Photo by Dick Couch*

American Army and Iraqi police. Soldiers from the 1-37 and Iraqi police patrol the streets together. Iraqi police foot patrols gradually replaced Army patrols. *Courtesy of Captain Mike Bajema*

Engaging the locals. An Iraqi policeman speaks with one of his neighbors under the watchful eye of an American soldier and another Iraqi policeman. *Courtesy of Captain Mike Bajema*

Best of all worlds. An Iraqi soldier and an Iraqi policeman engage the local population in Ramadi. When the Iraqi security forces work with the people, the insurgents lose. *Courtesy of the U.S. Army*

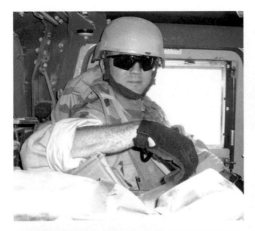

[Top Left] On patrol, after the battle. Lieutenant Steve Ruh looks across at the author in the rear seat of a Humvee at Camp Marc Lee, August 2007. *Photo by Dick Couch*

[Bottom Left] Warrior brothers, after the battle. Captain Mike Bajema (right) shares a moment with Petty Officer Ryan Job after their return from Iraq. *Courtesy of the U.S. Army*

[Top Right] Petty Officer Marc Lee. Marc Lee fought alongside his teammates from SEAL Team Three and was killed in action in the Battle of Ramadi. *Courtesy of the U.S. Navy*

[Bottom Right] Petty Officer Clark Schwedler. Clark Schwedler was killed in action near Fallujah. Here he is at Camp Shane Patton; his dog was taken home to be with his parents. *Courtesy of the U.S. Navy*

The Sheriff of Ramadi. Colonel Sean MacFarland, the Sheriff, with Sheikh Sattar Abu Risha and Captain Travis Patriquin. Patriquin and Sattar were later killed in al-Qaeda bomb attacks. *Courtesy of Andrew Lubin*

Mike Monsoor is laid to rest. As a final tribute to a fallen comrade, Mike Monsoor is laid to rest with the SEAL Trident pins of his teammates honoring his coffin.

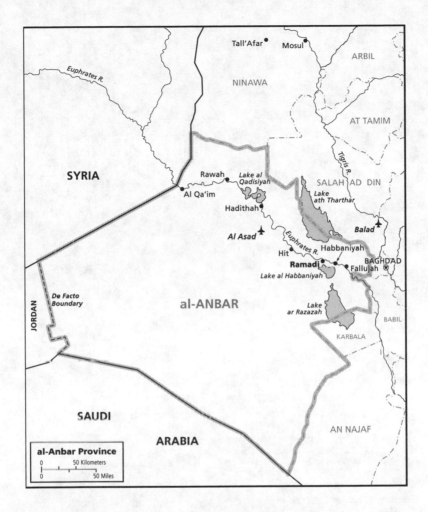

Map labels:
Tall'Afar • Mosul •
ARBIL
Euphrates R.
NINAWA
AT TAMIM
SYRIA
Rawah • Lake al Qadisiyah
Al Qa'im •
Tigris R.
SALAH AD DIN
Lake ath Tharthar
Hadithah •
Al Asad
Balad
Euphrates R.
Habbaniyah
Hit • BAGHDAD
Ramadi • Fallujah ®
Lake al Habbaniyah
De Facto Boundary
al-ANBAR
Lake ar Razazah
BABIL
JORDAN
KARBALA
SAUDI
AN NAJAF
ARABIA

al-Anbar Province
0   50 Kilometers
0   50 Miles

soldiers and marines in our conventional units. It was also a big change for the Navy SEALs assigned to the task unit in Ramadi. They were asked to operate in a manner not in keeping with their normal mission set or their training—but then, SEALs are nothing if not adaptable. In September 2005 the commander of the Naval Special Warfare Task Group–Arabian Peninsula—the senior Navy SEAL in Iraq, then located in Baghdad—elected to augment the SEAL detachment in Ramadi with a full task unit. Our story begins with the arrival of this first Ramadi task unit. This SEAL task unit, and the task units that succeeded it in Ramadi, didn't themselves win the Battle of Ramadi. But they certainly had a hand in it, and this is their story.

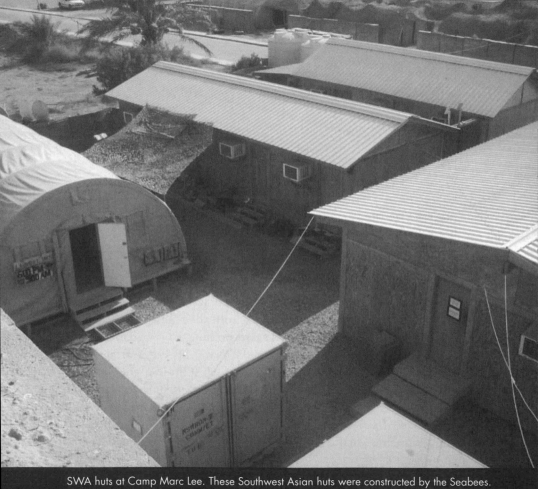

SWA huts at Camp Marc Lee. These Southwest Asian huts were constructed by the Seabees. The hut in foreground is the chow hall; the laundry tent is at the left. *Photo by Dick Couch*

The First SEAL Task Unit
in Ramadi

During the push into Afghanistan in early 2002 and the ramp-up for the invasion of Iraq a year later, the SEAL squadrons immediately abandoned their normal six-month-overseas, eighteen-month-home deployment rotation. The teams and squadrons accelerated their deployments, with shorter turnaround times to meet the Afghan and Iraqi operational requirements. Some individual SEALs would have only a month or two at home before heading back overseas. SEAL Squadron Seven, which deployed in April 2005, had yet to settle into the prewar rotation schedule, but the men did have the luxury of close to a year's predeployment preparation for this rotation. It was not until late 2006 that the deploying SEAL squadrons were able to settle back into their normal deployment posture.

"We work very hard on these deployments, and we work very hard during whatever time is given us to prepare for deployment," a squadron commander told me. "Even when the guys are stateside, they're away from home as much as a third of the time at remote training sites, getting ready for the next rotation. That said, we've been very lucky, even with the shorter wartime turnaround times. Some of the conventional units are overseas for a year and then get extended a few additional months. And depending on conditions in the active theaters, they may only get a year at home before they again have to go back to the fight for another fifteen months."

Regarding the normal six-month-overseas, eighteen-month-home rotation posture, a task unit senior chief had this to say: "Given the complexity of our operations, we need time to train and prepare for these deployments. And there are the manning and integration issues that go into getting a SEAL squadron ready for combat. But a lot of us feel that we simply have too much time out of theater. We'd be a lot happier with shorter turnaround time and longer deployments. We're professional warriors, and this is our job. So we feel a certain uneasiness in being back here while our brothers in the Army and Marine Corps are in harm's way. If anyone should be spending extended time in the battlespace, it should be us."

Indeed, I spoke with several SEALs who on their return would imme-diately seek to "move up" to a team or squadron that was closer to deployment rotation than their current team. Depending on requirements and the all-important reputation of the individual operator, many SEALs were able to return to the fight ahead of their normal rotation date.

Not only were deployment rotations compressed following 9/11, but the deploying SEAL squadrons were deployed with a mixed-team composition. The SEAL Squadron Seven that deployed in April 2005 had its full complement of operators from SEAL Team Seven, along with elements from SEAL Teams Three and Five and SDV Team One. These SEAL assets were scattered across Iraq and Afghanistan. In late June of that year, a disaster struck that rocked the Naval Special Warfare community to its core. Eleven Navy SEALs and eight Army special operations airmen perished in a combat action and failed rescue attempt in the mountains of Afghanistan, the largest single-engagement loss of life in the history of the Navy SEALs. A single SEAL survived this terrible encounter. Following this tragedy, SEAL efforts became focused on operations in Iraq and on the approaches to Baghdad.

In al-Anbar province in Iraq, SEAL elements from various West Coast and East Coast teams assigned to SEAL Squadron Seven were then assigned to a hastily constructed task unit at the Marine base at Al Asad. Al Asad was a former Iraqi air force base some fifty miles west-northwest of Ramadi up the Euphrates River—about as far from Ramadi as Ramadi is from Baghdad. This task unit had responsibilities from Ramadi out to the Syrian border, with an area of operations covering most of central and western al-Anbar province. The first permanent Naval Special Warfare presence in Ramadi was a detachment from this Squadron Seven. This detachment amounted to a partial-platoon element and a detachment support package attached to the SEAL task unit in Habbaniyah. Habbaniyah, a small city on the Euphrates between Ramadi and Fallujah, was major training base for the new

Iraqi army. Squadron Seven had a full task unit located there and was one of the first SEAL TUs to begin training Iraqi soldiers on a regular basis. Because Ramadi was the largest city and the provincial capital in al-Anbar, a SEAL detachment out of Habbaniyah was detailed to Ramadi to establish a presence there.

"When we got there, things were pretty basic," said Lieutenant Adam Wilson. Wilson was on his second combat rotation with Squadron Seven in Iraq. He commanded the Ramadi detachment. "We moved into a small compound being shared by a few SEALs from Teams Three and Five along with a Special Forces ODA [Operational Detachment, Alpha, or A-Team]. Our building or team house was one of a series of three guardhouses along the banks of the Euphrates River. As I got the story, these buildings were used by detachments of Saddam's special bodyguards that provided for his security when he was in Ramadi. The three houses were on a strip of land that was outside the wall that ringed the main base—Camp Ramadi. We had the camp wall on one side and the Euphrates River on the other. The houses themselves were impressive from the outside. Ours was of heavy concrete-type construction with stone pillars out front. Inside it was a barren patchwork of small rooms with tall ceilings—maybe four thousand square feet on two floors. Most of the fixtures had been stripped when it was abandon by Saddam's soldiers. Yet, as a small detachment, it served our needs. Of the three structures, ours was the farthest up the Euphrates and was called Shark Base. The name, as I understand it, came from one of the ODAs who preceded us. They were a scuba-qualified team and that was what they named their camp. The chief drawback of the building and the strip of land that was our little base was that it was outside the wire. We had some security from the guard towers that protected the main camp, but we were pretty exposed on the water side. Access from the Shark Base compound to the much larger Camp Ramadi was through a breach in the wall. Across the Euphrates was Camp Blue Diamond and the Marine base at Hurricane Point. So while we weren't inside Camp Ramadi proper, we were pretty secure, or secure enough at that stage of the insurgency.

"And we lived reasonably well," Wilson continued. "We had a flush toilet, generator power, running water, and a small kitchen. We inherited a cook who had worked for the ODA there, and he cooked one meal a day for us; the rest of the meals were snacks or MREs [meals ready to eat]. We set up a small tactical operations center, or TOC, with tables for our computers, and that was about it. Nothing fancy, but we could eat, sleep, collect intelligence, and plan operations."

I asked him what kinds of things the SEALs were doing there in early 2005.

"Our contributions were probably more in targeting and target analysis than actual combat operations. Once our small intelligence component got stood up, it quickly became very productive. They developed far more targets than we or the guys in Habbaniyah could cover. We passed most of these targets off to the conventional forces. Sometimes they would react to them but usually not; they had their own issues and intelligence sources. Even back then, there were more targets than there were assets to deal with them. Still, it was the beginning of our reputation as target generators. SEAL detachments and task units out in al-Anbar were becoming known for their intel and targeting capabilities. We were learning a great deal about the insurgents and the growing insurgency in our battlespace."

Intelligence-collection methodology, targeting, and the management of intelligence resources will be handled with care and, in some cases, in a purposely vague manner in this book. Since the early days in Afghanistan and following the push into Baghdad, SEALs had placed a high priority on intelligence collection and the rapid exploitation of intelligence data. Even the early detachments and task units had productive intelligence and targeting cells with relatively sophisticated database management and interrogation capabilities. This was far different from the presquadron days, before 2000, when SEAL platoons deployed with little internal intelligence support or targeting ability. These SEAL squadron and task unit intelligence components contributed to the overall theaterwide intelligence-collection effort, but their specialty was the development of timely and accurate tactical intelligence—"actionable" intelligence for SEAL operations. Throughout the course of this conflict, SEAL operational success had always been a derivative of good intelligence, from technical collectors and from human intelligence (HUMINT) sources. Human intelligence comes from getting close to the people, or close to those individuals who are close to the people, who have information. From there it's a matter of developing and managing those sources and their reporting activities. Early on, the Ramadi SEAL detachments and task units became adept at interrogation of detainees and of developing reporting sources.

As one intelligence specialist put it, "We got very good at sniffing out good tactical intelligence from any number of sources, but especially from the people. Pretty much on our own, we developed some very good in-house interrogators. Some call it interrogation, but interrogation is a harsh term. Good 'interrogation technique' is often nothing more than treating people with respect, understanding and respecting their customs, and asking the right questions. Many of us had been to the standard ten-week interrogation school and that helped a lot. But what it really comes down to is learning to read people. Where are they coming from and what can we do to make it easy for them to help us? And I'll tell you something else. An interrogation session is often an emotionally charged time, for the detainee as well as for us. Often a good strong dose of compassion makes all the difference in an interrogation."

I asked Lieutenant Wilson about the operations during his time in Ramadi.

"There were only a few of us on the operational side, and we were only set up for unilateral operations. We had not yet begun to work with soldiers from the new Iraqi army. Operationally, we'd go out only with an interpreter and maybe an informant. The Army and the Marines were out patrolling the streets, which, even back in 2005, could be a dangerous business. They asked us to set up sniper overwatches to protect them while they were on patrol, and we were glad to help—anything to make their job a little easier. Most of that work was in support of the Marines."

The business of setting up overwatch positions and sniper overwatch operations was to become an active, offensive skill set for the SEALs in Ramadi. In time it came to be a very dangerous one. Most SEAL casualties in Ramadi came directly from, or in support of, these sniper overwatch operations. The Marine Corps certainly understood and respected the SEAL sniper capabilities. Prior to the major push into Fallujah in late 2004, the Marine Corps, which has excellent snipers, put out a call for SEAL shooters to help them with that difficult urban assault. During the Battle of Fallujah, SEAL snipers established themselves as premier long-range military shooters in an urban battlespace. In military sniping it's an issue of having the right talent, the right training, and the right guns. The SEALs have all of these.

"We did a lot of targeting in Ramadi," Adam Wilson continued, "and sat a few overwatches for the conventional security forces, but we didn't do many raids. Going out into the city on a specific target is best done in conjunction with the Iraqis, and at that time, we didn't have any Iraqi soldiers working directly with us in Ramadi. If we developed something that looked promising, we'd call the task unit in Habbaniyah and they'd come over and help us."

"We were working out of Habbaniyah and training recruits for the Iraqi army there," recalled Lieutenant Ted Rolland. "Part of our duty involved training Iraqis to work in small units to serve as scouts for Iraqi battalion- and company-sized units. Habbaniyah was one of the main bases for the new Iraqi army, and we were tasked with the training of their scout elements. On occasion we'd go over to Ramadi on an operation. It was a long Humvee ride there, and we were probably at as much risk coming and going as when we were operating there."

Rolland was then the officer in charge, the OIC, of a platoon with Squadron Seven. At the time he had no idea that he would return to Ramadi in little over a year as the task unit commander with Squadron Five. "We'd go there on a specific target or set of targets, usually missions that the detachment there had worked up for us. Sometimes we had an informant or one of our scouts had information on the location of a bad guy there. At that time we had a relatively advanced program for training Iraqi army scouts at Habbaniyah, and we felt comfortable operating with them. But even then there was a high ratio of SEALs to Iraqi soldiers. Ramadi was dangerous back then, and there were certain parts that you had to stay well clear of, but it had yet to become the entrenched insurgent stronghold that we were to see later in 2006. Usually we would drive up there with our Iraqi *jundis* [*jundi* is the Arabic word for "soldier"] to the Shark Base compound in the afternoon. Once there we'd check in with Adam and his element, get an update on any local intelligence, and verify our area clearances. Then we'd go out at night, do our thing, and drive back to Habbaniyah the next morning. Even then, I was glad to get back to Habbaniyah. Each trip to Ramadi seemed to be a little more dangerous that the one before."

Throughout the summer of 2005, the insurgent activity in Ramadi was on the rise. It seemed that the influx of foreign fighters accelerated during this period as well. This violent activity was directed mainly against the marines who had been patrolling Ramadi since early 2004, and, increasingly, against the local tribal leaders. For the marines, this amounted to sniping, IEDs, and an occasional pitched street battle. For the Sunni leaders and population, insurgent violence and the threat of violence came in the form of murder and intimidation—M&I. Early on, murder and intimidation were the earmarks of al-Qaeda and their various insurgent allies. Along with the growing AQI presence, there were ethnic Sunni-on-Shiite encounters and even Sunni-on-Sunni clashes—old tribal grudges being revisited. But in Ramadi and al-Anbar, these intratribal clashes were quickly settled. The main thrust of the violence in Ramadi was a growing insurgent presence that was skillfully managed—co-opted might be a better term—by elements of AQI.

The Marine offensive that did much to clear Fallujah of insurgents in the fall of 2004 kept the majority of Sunnis away from the polls during the January 2005 parliamentary elections. This stepping away from the political process by the Sunnis in al-Anbar opened the door for the AQI to move in politically, as well as physically. That same clearing of Fallujah also flooded Ramadi with veteran insurgents and foreign fighters. By the summer of 2005, the situation in Ramadi had deteriorated to the point that many defense analysts were beginning to see Ramadi as a bellwether, saying that as Ramadi went, so went all of al-Anbar and any regional Sunni participation in the new government. Some went so far as to say that as Ramadi went, so went Iraq or at least any federal system in Iraq. With no participation in the political process, Ramadi, as well as al-Anbar as a whole, was on its way to becoming a region outside central authority—"Sunnistan," as some were then beginning to call it. The elusive Abu Musab al-Zarqawi, the most visible leader of al-Qaeda in Iraq, was most often reported as having been seen in al-Anbar. He and many of his Mujahideen Shura Council followers who were thought to have been flushed out of Fallujah had come to Ramadi, or passed through Ramadi en route to other Anbari cities.

Looking back to all that's happened in al-Anbar province to date, it might be helpful to assess the mood of the tribes in and around Ramadi in the summer and fall of 2005. The economy, which had been exploited by Saddam Hussein's excesses and crippled by the UN embargo, had not been helped by the American invasion and occupation. In fact, most Anbaris had been better off before the Americans came than after they arrived. The municipal and provincial government in Ramadi, which were of Baathist patronage, had largely been disbanded. Efforts to establish some form of control from Baghdad was viewed with distrust. The real power in al-Anbar rested with the traditional tribal leaders—the sheikhs. The prospect of elections, democracy, and a federal government dominated by the Iraqi Shiite majority did little to assuage the fears of the Anbaris and their tribal leaders. Prior to the beginning of 2005, the tribes had tacitly supported the insurgent movement against the Americans—even encouraged it. They knew of the influx of foreign fighters and al-Qaeda influence, but felt their presence benign, even useful in combating what they saw as American-Shiite influence in al-Anbar. But on the coattails of this insurgency came AQI operatives with their vision of governance based on strict Islamic law. The prospect of this form of theocracy ran counter to the tribal order in al-Anbar. The tribal leaders found themselves caught between the unwanted Western occupation forces, abetted by the Shiite-dominated leadership in Baghdad, and the brutal influence of al-Qaeda's brand of Islam. In short, al-Qaeda's aggressive religious and dictatorial social order threatened the tribal order and the preeminence of the tribal sheikhs. Yet the idle youth of al-Anbar and Ramadi rushed to swell the ranks of the insurgents to battle the American Crusaders. I suspect the emotional appeal to young Anbari men was not unlike that of American youth caught up in the opening days of our own Civil War. In the middle of all this, the tribal sheikhs stood back, waiting to see how these external forces would play out against each other. They distrusted the Americans, they resented the Shiite-dominated central government, and they feared AQI.

Perhaps the single most disruptive and intrusive element from the perspective of the tribal leaders was al-Qaeda's attempts to gain influence and control through marriage. AQI insisted that their insurgent leaders be allowed to marry into the families of the tribal leaders. This practice had served al-Qaeda well in Afghanistan and up into the Afghan-Pakistani border regions. But it was an anathema to the Anbari tribes and the tribal sheikhs. They resisted, refusing to give over their daughters in this way. Al-Qaeda responded with a campaign of M&I. Sheikhs were murdered for refusing to allow AQI leaders to marry into their families.

It was into this rising tide of violence and lawlessness that the incoming squadron, SEAL Squadron One, elected to put a full task unit into Ramadi. This SEAL squadron, with its headquarters in Baghdad, carried the title of Naval Special Warfare Task Group–Arabian Peninsula. Its primary duty was the command and control of all SEAL/Naval Special Warfare assets in Iraq—that country being just barely on the border of the Arabian Peninsula. In addition to the new task unit in Ramadi, there remained a TU in Habbaniyah, a TU in Baghdad, and a newly created SEAL detachment in Fallujah. This arrangement meant that the SEALs had to abandon the small detachment in Mosul, but their assets were now concentrated in al-Anbar province—and Baghdad.

"One our objective was to work our way out of a job in Baghdad," Sam Winters, the Squadron One commander, told me. "We felt we could be more productive and more useful out in al-Anbar—out west. But we had some responsibilities that held us in the capital. We were engaged in training the ISOF—the Iraqi Special Operations Force—which were well on their way to becoming the best counterinsurgency fighters in the new Iraqi army. It was important work, but it kept the task unit in Baghdad and primarily in a training role—not in an operational role that we felt best suited our talents. SEALs will do what they're told, but they'd much rather be out operating than training someone else. It seemed to be in the cards that going forward, we'd never abandon our role as trainers, but it appeared that out in al-Anbar we'd have a better chance to do more of both. Also in Baghdad, we had some of our SEALs assigned to PSD—personal security detail—which meant providing bodyguards for senior officials. And SEALs dislike PSD duty above all else. We're warriors. We train very hard for the fight, and when we're on deployment, we're looking for warrior's work. Don't get me wrong: our SEALs can serve as trainers and as bodyguards, and they'll do a good job. But what we really want to do is to make a difference. We felt that we could do that best out in al-Anbar province, which had a growing insurgency and a target-rich environment. The first steps to a more robust presence in al-Anbar were a full task unit in Ramadi and a detachment in Fallujah. But Ramadi was the most critical; it was right in the heart of the insurgency in al-Anbar—at that time, maybe in all of Iraq.

"Another thing that was keeping us in Baghdad was the squadron and task unit intelligence and targeting capabilities. My boss in theater, the commander, Joint Special Operations Task Force, needed what we could do in Baghdad in this regard. The real SOF training specialists, the Army Special Forces, can do the training, but they lacked our intelligence and targeting capabilities, what we call the ops-intel fusion, that we have embedded in our deployed squadron and task units. Nothing against our Special Forces brothers, but they are a little more rigid in their deployment posture; they don't have our flexibility in designing an expeditionary package tailored to both operational and intelligence requirements. We're very lucky in this regard. If we feel we need additional assets or specific talents on deployment, our stateside support elements find them for us. The Office of Naval Intelligence, for example, provides our squadrons with intel specialists with theater-specific qualifications. We're a special operations component and part of SOF, but our Navy supports us in ways that are far more comprehensive than our Army counterpart, a Special Forces battalion, is supported by Big Army. That support, once a requirement is identified, is very responsive, even when we're deployed. That ops-intel fusion and our Navy's timely response to our needs are key components that we bring to the battlespace. And it kept us in Baghdad a little longer that we'd have liked."

This might be a good time to take a look at the origins of the value-added capabilities that deploy with our operational SEALs. Specific individual talent can come from just about anywhere, but there are dedicated sources for these very important non-SEAL squadron and task unit members.

As mentioned above, there is a critical element of the deploying SEAL squadrons provided by the Office of Naval Intelligence. Within ONI there is a dedicated SEAL-support division called Trident. Trident was founded by Pete Wikul, a veteran SEAL captain. Wikul is the longest-serving Navy SEAL on active duty, which qualifies him for the esteemed title "the Bullfrog." He graduated with BUD/S Class 52, which makes him *almost* as old as this author. Captain Wikul reports directly to the director of naval intelligence; his job is to manage ONI support for deploying SEAL squadrons.

"In our day," Pete said, "SEALs did it all—intelligence collection, managing informants, and everything that goes with the information-gathering process. Our job at Trident is to take all that off the operators and allow them to focus on the tactics of their mission."

The ONI Trident organization is composed of active-duty personnel, reservists, and civilian contractors with a wide array of high-demand, low-density skills such as interrogation, collections management, imagery analysis, sensitive site exportation, counterintelligence, and targeted foreign languages. The deployed Trident organization also provides the squadrons and task units with a direct link, or "reach-back," capability to the Office of Naval Intelligence and its global information and intelligence affiliates. This reach-back capability is a direct, on-call, 24/7 source of data that connected the task units in Ramadi to American intelligence and information databases. Today Trident is a dynamic, growing, and evolving value-added element of the deploying squadrons.

The SEAL squadrons are also able to draw on the invaluable help and expertise found in our naval ratings: masters-at-arms, operations specialists, gunner's mates, storekeepers, administrative personnel, and of course, the construction-battalion, or Seabee, ratings—the builders, electricians, and mechanics. This naval service talent is found in various support units attached to the Naval Special Warfare groups on each coast. One such unit is the Combat Services Support Detachment, the collection point for Special Warfare Seabees and construction ratings. The other is the Logistics Support Unit, which manages the non-Seabee squadron augmentees. And finally there are the group Operational Support Teams that help the deploying squadrons with operational and operational-support requirements. The active-duty personnel and reservists assigned to the squadrons from these various support organizations are grouped under the broad title of IAs—individual augmentees. Most in the military, including more than a few SEALs of my generation, think of SEAL deployments as simply a bunch of SEALs or a platoon of SEALs going off to war. The impact and operational reach of today's SEALs are made possible by the work and dedication of these non-SEALs, the squadron and task unit IAs.

To understand the makeup and capability of a Naval Special Warfare task unit, in Ramadi or elsewhere in al-Anbar, it's good to start with the SEAL squadron deployment package. We touched on this at the end of chapter 1, but this is a more detailed breakdown. Naval Special Warfare Group One in Coronado is the command element for the four West Coast SEAL teams—SEAL Teams One, Three, Five, and Seven. Group One, along with the other West Coast NSW components, has the responsibility to support the Pacific and Central Commands. On the East Coast, Group Two has similar responsibilities for the European and Southern Commands, with NSW assets that include SEAL Teams Two, Four, Eight, and Ten. These SEAL and NSW assets and the assigned area responsibilities can and have been reallocated and modified to meet the current wartime requirements. There are emerging issues in Africa that now have to be addressed by these two groups. Immediately following 9/11, the deployment packages were altered and greatly accelerated to support the operations in Afghanistan and the initial push into Iraq. Currently, that surge has eased somewhat, as it relates to SEAL deployment rotations. With the growing insurgency and focus on Iraq, Group One and the West Coast deploying squadrons have taken center stage for Naval Special Warfare deployments there. In order to meet these requirements in Iraq, and during the Battle of Ramadi, the West Coast squadrons were augmented with assets from Naval Special Warfare Group Two and the East Coast SEAL teams.

The Naval Special Warfare squadron is built around a Navy SEAL team. As previously mentioned, in normal times, SEALs train for eighteen months and deploy for six. During the final six months of their training work-up, the SEAL team is designated as a SEAL squadron; the SEAL team commanding officer becomes the squadron commander. During this transformation, the fledgling squadron takes on personnel that eventually may double or even triple the size of the original SEAL team. At this point a wiring diagram might be helpful to describe the squadron organization, but after watching Group One squadrons leave Coronado for the past several years, it has become clear no two are alike in size or composition. Personnel-wise, the team-to-squadron transformation can increase the basic SEAL team manning levels of some 115 to 120 SEALs and permanently assigned team support personnel to as many as 300 or more in the fully manned squadron. Their composition and final predeployment training are driven by battlespace requirements. Typically, a Naval Special Warfare squadron will have a headquarters element, three SEAL-centric task units, and a maritime unit. The maritime unit is composed primarily of squadron Special Boat Team assets that support the three TUs as needed. For the last several years, the West Coast squadrons have gone out "heavy," with an additional task unit composed of assets from East Coast SEAL teams and Naval Special Warfare assets. I found it interesting that competition in the East Coast teams to be one of the West Coast SEAL assignees is often spirited. The recent West Coast squadron deployments have been active, or, in the new lexicon, "kinetic," and most SEALs want to be in a task unit operating in Iraq for their overseas rotation. As professional warriors, they feel that they are serving in time of war, so they look for active combat deployment.

During combat operations in Ramadi and into the summer of 2008, the West Coast squadrons have been deploying with four SEAL-centric task units—three assigned to Central Command in Iraq and one to Pacific Command in the Philippines. Task unit composition, like squadron makeup, can vary widely. As our focus is Iraq, I'm going to bypass the Pacific Command task unit and concentrate on those in Iraq. That said, the PACOM TU is actively engaged in helping the Philippine military to combat insurgents—ones with extreme Islamic and al-Qaeda ties in the southern Philippine Islands. As much of their work is maritime in nature, they garner most of the Special Boat Team assets and combatant craft. Of the task units in Iraq, I'll focus on the one in Ramadi. Since it was stood up in early October 2005, the Ramadi task unit has been the most active of the deployed Naval Special Warfare TUs. I'll even go so far as to say that never in the history of the SEAL teams have Navy SEALs been more heavily engaged over an extended period of time than they were during the fight for Ramadi—never.

Task unit organization and staffing mirror that of the squadron, but the TUs are configured for force projection; the task units are armed with SEAL platoons. These task units are the war-fighting arm of the deployed SEAL squadrons. The Ramadi task unit, while similar to other squadron TUs in Iraqi, was unique to the requirements of the Ramadi battlespace. Just as each squadron deploys with a package that's a little different from its predecessor, so was there a variation in the composition of the task units as they rotated through Ramadi. As the mission and battlespace changed and evolved, so did the Ramadi TU's complement and mission taskings.

A generic Naval Special Warfare task unit in Iraq has a headquarters element led by a task unit commander, his senior enlisted adviser or task unit chief petty officer, and an experienced operations chief. The commander is usually a lieutenant commander or a senior lieutenant fleeted up to the rank of lieutenant commander for this important command position. The task unit chief is a senior chief or master chief petty officer. The task unit commander and his task unit chief are joined at the hip in their responsibilities for the leadership and welfare of the task unit. They are assisted by a TU operations chief, usually a chief or senior chief petty officer who was a SEAL platoon chief on his last combat rotation. At this stage of the conflict, the TU commander will have multiple tours, including a tour as the OIC of a SEAL platoon. Each of the senior enlisted leaders is a veteran with multiple combat rotations behind him. Supporting the headquarters element is a small administrative element, or N1 staff, with two or three non-SEAL petty officers.

The task unit N2 section (in other services it would be the S2 or G2 staff), or intelligence element, is a critical component within the task unit. Within this N2 shop there will most usually be an intelligence cell and a targeting cell. Personnel-wise, these two vital components may have anywhere from twelve to twenty intelligence specialists and support personnel and two or more officers. The N2 is also responsible for a task element known as the Advanced Special Operations unit, whose missions and methods are classified. The ASO component will have a variety of specialists, including veteran SEAL operators. Their responsibilities range from the analytical to the operational. We will touch on their important work in later chapters. Other personnel assigned to the N2 shop range from interrogation specialists to linguists to civil-affairs officers. The collective job of the N2 section is to comb through the myriad of available intelligence information that passes through military channels for information that may relate to task unit mission requirements. They also manage the ongoing human and technical collection efforts so important to the TU's targeting cell. Every SEAL I spoke with, from the TU commanders to the platoon operators—the shooters—could not say enough about the importance of their intelligence and targeting cells. Indeed, the SEAL assault elements and their Iraqi scouts seldom went into the field without knowing exactly where they were going and exactly who they were looking for, as well as the risk parameters going in, on target, and coming back out. They also had a wealth of imagery on the battlespace. The intelligence product generated by these task unit N2 sections was a valuable resource for the local battlespace commanders as well. In the case of the Ramadi task unit, the intel and targeting cells became a go-to intelligence component for many of the Army and Marine battalion battle staffs.

The N3 (operations) section is headed by an experienced SEAL lieutenant who may also function as the task unit second in command. There are five to seven TOC watch standers and other assigned operations-support personnel assigned to the N3. They stand watch in the task unit tactical operations center, monitoring radio traffic and answering phones. They also provide coordination and communications support when operational task unit elements are in the field. The N3 also coordinates air operations and operational-support requirements, and deconflicts battlespace clearance issues. Currently, deploying task units have a master-at-arms detachment of three to five sailors that usually fall under the N3's duties. These sailors' duties include the management of detainees who are brought in for questioning and disposition. The SEAL platoons, which we'll get to shortly, are also part of the N3.

The task unit N4, or supply section, is comprised of a five- to seven-man element from the supply and construction battalion ratings and usually a gunner's mate to manage ordnance storage and weapons-related issues.

As we will see later in this chapter, the first task unit in Ramadi arrived with a robust complement of Seabees, which were essential to standing up the task unit. There is no task unit N5, or plans section, but the N6, or mobile communications, detachment is a critical TU element. It works closely with the assault elements on communications planning and manages the secure communication links within the task unit, with the local conventional forces, and with the task group headquarters. The N6 also supplies the task unit and assault elements with IT support. The N8 section is a one- to three-person medical department that supports the TU personnel and the SEAL platoon corpsmen.

Associated with squadron deployment and the task unit manning are certain assigned specialties that are essential. We'll talk more about those when we get to individual TU operations, but I'll mention one of them here. It's the eight- to ten-man explosive ordnance disposal (EOD) team that now accompanies every squadron deployment. In a perfect world, each SEAL platoon will have two EOD technicians. These brave sailors are on virtually every combat operation conducted by the TU assault elements. Since IEDs and booby traps are never far from anyone's thoughts, these men are often in the van of the patrol file. They also help with training the Iraqis in basic IED detection and avoidance measures.

And, finally, within the task unit are the SEAL operators—the shooters. SEALs train for deployment and rotate overseas with the squadrons and task units as SEAL platoons. A platoon is normally comprised of two officers and fourteen enlisted men—sometimes a few more, often a few less. Platoon size and composition may vary for training purposes, but not by much. And all SEAL platoons—East Coast or West Coast, squadron to squadron—train to a standard; they all shoot, move, and communicate from the same sheet of music. While the current business at hand is land warfare and urban combat in Iraq, their predeployment workup includes parachuting, over-the-beach operations, and attack-swimmer training and recertification. Tactically, they train in squad elements—one officer and seven enlisted SEALs—but there are mission profiles and training exercises that call for them to operate as a full platoon or in fire teams of four or fewer. Individual specialties within the platoon include communicators, medical corpsmen, snipers, breachers, and CAS (close air support) controllers, as well as little-used skills such as jumpmasters and dive supervisors. While these specialties are certified by approved schools and qualification courses, a significant portion of SEAL predeployment training is devoted to cross-training in these specialties, some more than others. For example, in a SEAL platoon, everyone is a medic because the platoon corpsmen train their platoon mates in battlefield medical procedures.

A task unit commander will normally have two platoons of SEALs to conduct his offensive operations and indigenous training activity. Two platoons is the norm, but even that standard may change because of requirements. In this book I often refer to SEAL detachments, which in most cases is a platoon or less with a support element that may be downsized from that found in a task unit. A task unit commander will try to keep his platoons intact and the squads and fire teams operating as they did in predeployment training, but the battlespace may dictate otherwise. So the platoons and squads may be mixed and matched to conform to operational requirements. Special skills may have to be grouped or emphasized for a particular mission set. Snipers and corpsmen are always in demand, and no one wants to go into the battlespace without at least one EOD tech. But somehow it all works. They become like accomplished jazz musicians who know the basics and can improvise, stepping in and out of the flow of the melody. SEALs are trained to complement a platoon mate's skills and to function with another SEAL or special operator they may not have trained with or even know. The SEAL assault elements that we're going to talk about in the Ramadi task unit will be platoon SEALs, but for the most part they will operate in configurations other than a strict platoon alignment. And the nonplatoon SEALs, including individual augmentees from the task unit and occasionally from the squadron, will occasionally go into the field with the platoon SEALs.

One of the intangibles, certainly for all Navy SEALs, but especially for every member of the task unit, is reputation. In the teams, reputation is everything. A SEAL's reputation follows him from the training commands into the SEAL teams and on into operational deployment. It's a small community and everyone knows everyone else—or has a close friend who does. Everyone knows who's quick, steady, focused, professional, and, above all, a team player. They also know if a teammate is a whiner or in any way unreliable. New men have to prove their worth; veterans who have proved themselves operationally on one deployment are expected to perform at a higher level on the next. And on that rare occasion when a SEAL operator fails to measure up, he may or may not be given a second chance with another platoon. The SEAL teams have their prodigals; sometimes they can be returned to grace, but the expectations are high. It's life and death. Sometimes the steady hand of platoon chief or a platoon leading petty officer can salvage the reputation of a SEAL who hasn't measured up. That's the nature of this brotherhood.

The non-SEALs in the task unit may not have reputations in that they may not have a history with the teams. But when an intelligence specialist or an administrator or a logistics rep demonstrates, through his or her ability and hard work, to be a task unit asset, they are embraced as a brother or sister warrior. If the non-SEALs perform well, their reputations can be made quickly and they are afforded respect by everyone. The SEAL shooters I spoke to, in Ramadi and elsewhere, were always ready to tell me about the contributions of their non-SEAL teammates. And, as just mentioned, there are female members of the squadron. They are a minority—from my experience perhaps no more than a dozen. Not all task units are authorized to have female members; it depends on the conditions of the battlespace. The task units in Ramadi had no permanently assigned females. I saw them only in the task group headquarters. During my time in Iraq, that was at the squadron base in Fallujah.

––––––––––––

In October 2006, Lieutenant Commander Jake Hanson arrived in Ramadi with his task unit from SEAL Squadron One. This task unit looked much like the one described above, with some variations, and numbered some 109 souls. This task unit was an augmenting TU from SEAL Team Two, so it was "East Coast" in its makeup. As with many task units in the ever-changing combat environment in Iraq, the assignment to Ramadi was known to the men only a few weeks before they left for deployment. At one time, it was thought this task unit was to be the one assigned to Pacific Command for duty in the Philippines, so a great deal of equipment had to be changed from a maritime, tropical load-out to one geared to a desert and urban environment. And even when their deployment destination was known, their mission in Ramadi was still unclear.

"We knew the deploying squadrons were now being heavily tasked with training Iraqis," Jake Hanson said, "and that all of the task units would be involved with training in one form or another. We also knew that Ramadi was becoming a hotly contested area. Even after we learned we'd be going to Ramadi, we didn't know if our duties would be training or operational, or both. It wasn't until the eve of our deployment that I was told we would be training Iraqi scouts. Exactly who these scouts were and what kind of training we were expected to provide, I had no idea. I did know that we had a task unit in Habbaniyah and that their primary duty was the training of Iraqis soldiers. I also knew that the name for an Iraqi soldier was a *jundi*. Past that, I had excellent platoon officers and senior petty officers. So I knew we could figure it out once we got on the ground. And that's exactly what we did."

Like seemingly all task unit commanders, Jake Hanson had an unusual background. After graduating from Virginia Commonwealth University on a baseball scholarship, he decided to join the Navy. He wanted to be a SEAL and an officer, but the SEALs get most of their new officers by way of the Naval Academy and the Naval Reserve Officers' Training Corps. So in 1993 he enlisted in the Navy for SEAL training and graduated with BUD/S Class 189. He made five deployments before the Navy sent him to Officer Candidate School to become an officer—a SEAL officer. Prior to taking command of the task unit in Ramadi, he'd had a combat tour in Afghanistan with the British Special Air Service.

"I knew there would be challenges for us in Ramadi," recalled Hanson, "and they began the day we got there. The guys from Squadron Seven had done all they could to get ready for us, but our task unit was five times the size of their detachment. We arrived with our combat gear and our Humvees, and not much else. Before we could begin to train the Iraqis, we had to find a place for everyone to eat and sleep. This happens to SEALs a lot more than it should; our operational appetite always seems to run ahead of our support and supply requirements."

"If it hadn't been for the Seabees, I'm not sure how we'd have made it," one of the SEAL platoon chiefs told me. "Well, we'd have made it," he reasoned, "but I'm not sure how much training or operational work we'd have been able to do. We quickly overwhelmed the team house there at Shark Base. We put our tactical operations center in the main living area and the intel shop moved into the kitchen. There were a few empty bunks upstairs, but not nearly enough. Our Seabees found us some tents to live in and got the Army over at Camp Ramadi proper to feed us. Twice a day we would send a couple guys and a vehicle over to the base to get chow. We had these insulated carrying trays to ferry the chow back to the team house. They kept the hot food warm and the cold food cool. We lived in tents and used Porta-Pottis. As for showers, well, we didn't take all that many early on. There was one shower in the team house, but that's a lot of guys for a single shower. The Seabees fixed up a shower tent, then built a wooden floor to the shower tent, and finally a real shower facility. Again, those Seabees kept us up and running and allowed us to get on with our work, which was training Iraqi soldiers."

The situation the task unit found itself in on arrival in Ramadi was unfortunately not unique. SEALs often arrive in a new area operationally ready for duty, but logistically deficient. Fortunately, this first Ramadi task unit had the talent to overcome the lack of basic services they encountered at Shark Base. As it was a new task unit, it had deployed with a well-staffed contingent of Seabees, including a very talented and aggressive chief petty officer.

"I've done this before," Chief Del Dixon told me, "and you learn a few things along the way. You always prepare for the worst, like you're going to have to set up shop alone in the middle of the desert, and then you'll never get surprised. I had great people with me in Ramadi on this trip. My leading petty officer was an electrician by trade and a superb builder and welder. I had two active-duty mechanics from the [Naval Special Warfare] Group Two motor pool and nine hardworking Seabees, most of them reservists recalled to active duty for this deployment. This was a very good crew with a broad range of experience. My reserve guys brought a lot of know-how from their civilian jobs. I had this one reservist who was a facilities manager for a church and school. He could fix anything, including anything on wheels. We found these two Russian two-and-a-half-ton stake trucks at Camp Ramadi when we arrived, and we were short on haulers. He got them running. Don't ask me how, but he did it."

Chief Dixon is a short, stocky, energetic chief petty officer, attached to the Combat Services Support Detachment. In addition to his sixteen years of military construction experience, he also brings the Navy Seabee can-do attitude and work ethic to the task unit. These talented full-time and part-time sailors may clock in and clock out at some stateside military base or their civilian job sites, but on deployment, they work around the clock, day in and day out. This was not the first time Chief Dixon found himself in this kind of situation. He'd built special operations camps in Afghanistan in remote areas along the

Pakistani border and guard towers at Guantánamo Bay, so he was no stranger to construction challenges.

"We brought what we thought we'd need and then some. We have standard material lists, but there's no substitute for experience. Our load-out this trip included two seven-thousand-kilowatt generators, electrical and plumbing supplies, glues, epoxies, cordless nailers, ladders, table saws, and every hand tool known to man. The mechanics came equipped to repair anything on wheels. It was a chore, but we were able to get it all aboard helos or truck convoys up to Camp Ramadi, then over to Shark Base. What we didn't have was money to buy materials; the funding budgeted for building out and sustaining the camp never arrived—not a penny. But we anticipated this as well. My storekeeper brought lots of needed and hard-to-find items for trade. And we had another bit of luck. My leading petty officer and I are from Pennsylvania, and the 228th Brigade, the parent command of the command element in charge of Camp Ramadi, was also from Pennsylvania. We made friends with their engineers and supply types, and brought them over to our range to shoot AK-47s and other weapons not in their inventory. They ran convoys all over Iraq and were able to help us find building materials and consumables. Hey, we're Seabees. They give us nothing to work with, and we'll still make it happen."

Because they were "outside the wire," the civilian contractors that serviced the needs of Camp Ramadi were not available to those encamped on Shark Base. Chief Dixon and his crew had to see to critical needs such as power and water, as well as more mundane chores such as emptying the Porta-Pottis and making chow runs over to Camp Ramadi. Yet even with the scarcity of materials and the lack of funds, they managed to complete the following projects in support of the SEAL mission in Ramadi:

- Constructed a 28′ x 48′ galley and mess hall complex.
- Built segregated, permanent, air-conditioned quarters for the task unit interpreters.
- Constructed a 28′ x 48′ mission-planning building with spaces for the SEAL two platoons.
- Built out the tactical operations center in the team house with a dedicated power source.
- Constructed a 24′ x 60′ vehicle repair/woodworking/electrical shop.

- Erected twenty berthing tents with wooden floors.
- Constructed a 20' x 32' laundry and shower facility.
- Acquired six additional Porta-Pottis.
- Set up electrical distribution for the camp and installed commercial-grade heat pumps.
- Installed WiFi capability for the camp.
- Built a 20' x 30' steel fabrication and plumbing shop.
- Constructed a 30' x 100' multipurpose Humvee shed.
- Installed a one-inch water line into Shark Base from Camp Ramadi, and built a self-sustaining water system.
- Designed and fabricated blast protection for turret gunners by using surplus Humvee ballistic windshields welded in steel frames around the vehicle turrets.

The task unit Seabee contingent was busy off Shark Base as well. In addition to the improvements made in support of the SEAL camp, they also:

- Installed electrical improvements at a Marine observation post in Ramadi.
- Constructed a six-room soundproof interrogation facility for the al-Ramadi Detention Facility (ARDEF).
- Constructed a 16' x 32' berthing facility for the Army supply yard at Camp Ramadi.
- Supported the Seabee battalion at Camp Ramadi with tents, generators, and air-conditioning units during their interim stay in Ramadi.
- Built a small training compound for the SEALs to train Iraqi soldiers at Camp Ramadi.

The task unit Seabee contingent arrived at Shark Base with generators, tools, and talent, but little in the way of operational funding. It stands to reason that they traded some of their time and expertise for building materials, but *that much material?* The mantra of the Seabees in the South Pacific during World War II was "We've done so much with so little for so long, we can do almost anything with nothing." I never asked Chief Dixon where he got his materials, and he didn't volunteer that information. He just made all these things happen. He took care of his task unit.

"Security was an issue from the day we arrived," Lieutenant Commander Hanson recalled. "Over a six-month period we took about two hundred mortar rounds in the camp. One of them shredded one of our tents. Fortunately, no one was in it, but it scared the dickens out of one of our intelligence specialists who was only thirty feet from the blast. The Seabees brought in HESCO barriers [HESCO is a commercial acronym for wire-and-fabric-bound cages that can be placed just about anywhere and filled with sand and rocks] and concrete T-barriers, and put them between and around our tents. These gave us some measure of protection from the mortars—unless, of course, you took a direct hit. And we were always taking small-arms fire and an occasional rocket. One 120-millimeter rocket hit a building near the Shark Base team house. We had some protection from the military bases located directly across the river from us, but we were still in range of indirect fire from the city, mostly from the Ta'meem District."

"Among the first of the construction projects, along with the mess hall, were the interpreter's quarters," said Senior Chief Stan Lester. Lester was in charge of managing the interpreters and of the detainee interrogation efforts. "These were all standard Southwest Asia [SWA— pronounced *swaa*] huts. Interpreters were a critical asset and we had to take care of those guys, so some of the first huts constructed went to them. We had to get them some decent housing or they'd have abandoned us. Still, we had some terrific interpreters, and they were an invaluable resource. We had a few Arabic speakers with the task unit, but no native speakers. We depended on contract interpreters with native ability. Initially, we began with two of them, and at one time we were up to eleven. Things got a lot better when we were able to build an interrogation facility inside Camp Ramadi at the ARDEF, where our interrogators and interpreters could work with detainees. A key element of our intelligence-gathering effort is our ability to process and interrogate detainees. We can't do that without interpreters— good interpreters. Here again, our Seabees came through. I don't know what the hell we'd have done without Del Dixon and his crew. They did it all."

"When we got there and finally settled into the routine at Shark Base," said Petty Officer Randy Fellers, "we began our primary mission, which was to train Iraqis." Fellers was one of the lead task unit members assigned to oversee the Iraqi scout training program. "The detachment from Squadron Seven didn't conduct training for the *jundis,* and we were given very little direction. We were told to train up a group of soldiers from the Iraqi army brigade at Camp Ramadi into a self-sufficient assault element. Of course, we had no idea who these soldiers were and just what their current level of training and experience was. Fortunately, Camp Ramadi had some reasonably good shooting ranges and training areas, and on the main camp, things were pretty secure. We could meet with our *jundis* and put them through drills without having to worry about taking fire—live fire. The guys from the last detachment took us around and showed us what we had to work with—the ranges we could use and what parts of the base we could use for training. They also introduced us to the Army and Marine military transition teams. The training of the two Iraqi brigades assigned to Ramadi rested with the military transition teams, or MiTTs as they were called. In some ways, we were an extension of the MiTTs working with the brigade at Camp Ramadi.

"We knew that the guys in Habbaniyah had been training *jundis* for a while, but most of us had never been in a pure training situation like this. The skill-base part of it was easy in that we know our business and we knew how to teach it—at least to Western soldiers. We had lesson plans in our databases. But there were other issues we needed to get our arms around. One of them was the standard to which we were expected to train these guys. Just what did they need to know to fight in the streets of Ramadi? Basically, when were they good to go? Or not good to go? And even little things, like how much time did they have to train each day? We're SEALs, and we can work 24/7 if need be. Iraqis don't really operate that way. And when we began, we really didn't understand what motivated them. The soldiers we had to train were mostly Shia and mostly from Baghdad. What did *they* think about being told what to do by a bunch of Navy SEALs who didn't speak their language? What did they think about taking what we taught them and fighting insurgents who were their own countrymen? And did it matter that, at least in Ramadi, the people *and* the insurgents were mostly Sunni? Another thing we had to wrestle with was the temperament of the Iraqis. To be real honest, they were just simply different from us. Later on we began to understand them better, but there was always a culture gap. Each group we trained was a little different, with different needs and motivations."

Lieutenant Dan Eaton echoed these sentiments. "Not only did we have to try to understand the people we were to train, but we had to make a 180-degree shift in our own thinking. In preparing for deployment, we simply had no idea that our primary duties would make us a training cadre for Iraqi soldiers. "Eaton, a platoon OIC from SDV Team One, was assigned to the task unit just prior to deployment. He was a well-traveled SEAL, and a former surface-warfare officer and salvage diver. His previous assignments included tours at SEAL Teams Eight and Ten. Jake Hanson made him his assistant task unit commander and operations officer. He told me Eaton was the smartest officer he'd ever served with.

"Our platoon SEALs, like all SEALs, had trained and prepared for direct-action operations," Eaton said of the squadron's predeployment work-up. "This led to a mind-set on the part of the operators that if it wasn't DA, or direct action, it wasn't worth doing. When we were assigned to training duty, it led to a big mismatch between the expectation and the reality. Yet there it was; we were trainers. And if we were going to get into the battlespace, it would be with the Iraqis we trained. Once that sunk in, the guys became a little more diligent about their training responsibilities."

Initially, the SEALs were given thirty-some soldiers assigned to the 1st Brigade of the Iraqi 7th Division headquarters element based at Camp Ramadi. These soldiers were rounded up by the brigade MiTT adviser. Most of them were servants and chai-tea makers, whose duties were attending to Iraqi army officers. The enlisted soldiers were willing enough, but neither the Army advisers nor the SEALs were able to persuade any of the Iraqi officers to participate in the training. The new unit was called the special missions platoon (SMP), and it was a brigade asset of the 7th Division. It was special in name only, at least at the beginning, and the SEALs were able to recruit a few more men, making a total of just over fifty *jundis* for the SMP.

"We made our mistakes early on," Randy Fellers admitted. "It took us some time to learn about our *jundis* and how to relate to them. I think we expected more of them in the way of a basic soldier skill set and in the way of physical training. We're addicted to physical conditioning for combat; we believe its part of being a warrior and a competitive edge on the battlefield. They don't. Our efforts to put them through even a mild PT program were a failure. And I think we were looking for a little too much polish and professionalism, even in the basics of shooting and fire-and-maneuver drills. Of course, there were some skills we purposefully avoided. We didn't teach long-range shooting or sniper tactics and some of our more sophisticated anti-IED countermeasures. It finally came down to how much did they really need to know to do the job, which was to conduct a reasonable patrol in hostile territory and to make a decent assault on a house. This called for training in standard patrolling techniques and basic close-quarter combat. We taught them the basics of moving tactically in squad- and platoon-sized units and how to cross danger areas. We also taught them urban fire-and-movement drills. The close-quarter battle drills and the mechanics of safely clearing a house were a little more challenging. We drilled them on how to clear a room, and tried to get them to clear an entire house, room by room, methodically. But never did we quite break them of the habit of racing for the rear of the house. So we had to be very careful coming in behind them. In the end we set minimum standards that would get them out into the battlespace with a reasonable amount of safety and tactical proficiency. Obviously, we wanted more from them, but good enough was what it had to be. I don't know how many times we said that 'good enough is good to go.' Maybe we were just a little too fussy, or, better said, we come from a warrior culture and have had the luxury of the best military training our nation can provide.

"The other thing we were slow to realize," Fellers said, "was the disposition of our Iraqis—who they were and what motivates them. Very few of us had experience in dealing with Iraqis, and the constraints of their culture as it relates to Western military training. Early on we thought they were just lazy and unfocused. They sometimes abandon reason and resort to emotion. We knew some of them had other duties, and we were lucky to get them to show up for three or four hours a day for training. It was frustrating, and at times irritating. And don't get me wrong; these issues and problems were mostly due to *our* shortcomings and inexperience. They had a lot to learn, but in many ways, *our* learning curve was steeper than theirs. For us, even 'good enough' was an elusive and hard-won goal. All along we knew that when we got out into the streets and began to operate, these Iraqi soldiers were going to be with us. So we were training our teammates. We also knew that we had limited time to get them ready. Our job was to get them on the street as soon as possible, so that meant a lot of their learning was going to be on-the-job training."

"A lot of these guys turned out to be pretty good soldiers," recalled Jake Hanson, "and that was a credit to Randy Fellers and his training cadre. The biggest thing Randy and his guys did to win over the Iraqis was to take care of them. Most of our *jundis* were recent recruits and not treated too well in the new Iraqi army. Their chow was barely fit to eat, and their senior officers up the chain of command skimmed off their pay. It pains me to say that, but it happened. Many of them had no blankets or bedding in their barracks. We stepped in and did what we could for them, seeing to their needs and getting them paid. A couple of the platoon SEALs went to Baghdad to get a load of blankets and bedding for them. Once the *jundis* understood that we cared for them, they began to respond in training and perform better on patrol.

"One of our issues was with the Iraqi officer corps," Hanson continued. "With Saddam's army and even with the new Iraqi army, officers are from the upper or moneyed class and enlisted men are, well, they have no money and no stature. Even Iraqi sergeants have no stature. Their army has nothing close to the senior enlisted cadre in our military, in either professional knowledge or influence. Very seldom could we get one of their officers to come to our training because our training was conducted by our senior enlisted SEALs. It was considered beneath them. Their attitude was 'He's an enlisted man; what can he possibly teach me?' The fact that nearly all U.S. military training is conducted by senior enlisted cadre didn't seem to matter to them. We did have one officer with the special missions platoon who came out to train and he wasn't bad, but he was the exception. If nothing else, it was a reminder to all of us in the American military just how fortunate we are to have such professionalism in our enlisted ranks. They're the backbone of our armed forces, and certainly the driving professional force in the SEAL teams."

It's been my observation that in few militaries in the world, even the highly professional British and German forces, are the enlisted ranks given the authority or afforded the respect as in the armed forces of the United States. The commissioning of our officers comes with no class or social-privilege baggage. Perhaps nowhere in our armed forces is this more true than in our special operations forces, and nowhere is the transition from enlisted man to officer as common. Indeed, three of the first four SEAL task unit commanders in Ramadi were former enlisted SEALs. Two of the four squadron commanders I worked with on this book were former enlisted men. In the majority of the world's national military organizations, the officer ranks are class based, and the movement from sergeant to lieutenant is very rare. That's certainly the case in the new Iraqi army. The really sad part is that a class- or tribal-based military hierarchy restricts any form of merit system and seems to promote corruption. Loyalty comes before professionalism, and any form of strong or progressive leadership is left to chance. We often forget how blessed our nation is to have such a dedicated and professional standing military. One day Iraq may have such a military, but it will take time and cultural adjustment.

While well outside their original charter to train up a brigade special missions platoon, the SEAL task unit in Ramadi offered to train scouts for the Iraqi battalions stationed at Camp Ramadi. "The mission of the battalion scouts differed slightly from the brigade special missions platoon," one SEAL trainer explained. "One of the MiTT objectives for the battalions of the new Iraqi army was to get them out patrolling the streets and showing a presence in Ramadi. Our job was to work with the battalion scouts to help them better support their company and battalion movements."

Since Iraqi battalions, like American Army battalions, go by numbers, the SEALs trained scout elements from the 1-1-7, the 2-1-7, and the 3-1-7. These were scouts from the 1st, 2nd, and 3rd battalions, 1st Brigade, of the Iraqi army's 7th Division. Both the SEALs and the MiTTs had their work cut out for them. This brigade, along with its three battalions, was one of the newest and least experienced in the Iraqi army.

"The training for the battalion scouts was much the same for the special missions platoon, although we put a little more premium on patrolling and fire-and-movement drills for the battalion scouts," a SEAL trainer told me. "Their job was more one of patrolling ahead of a company or battalion formation and acting as a true scouting force. So we tried to focus their training on individual tactical movement and running a good patrol. And since they had battalion duties, they didn't seem to have as much time to train as did the SMP *jundis*. With the special missions platoon, we tried to focus on assaults and working at night—operations that didn't include main-force activity. We went out with both of them, but I think we were more comfortable operating with the SMP. All told, we trained close to 150 Iraqi scouts, a third of them SMP and the rest battalion scouts, but I'd say the majority of our outside-the-wire operations were with the special missions platoon.

"A big drawback in working with all of the Iraqi scouts was you never knew just who you were going to be training and, later on, operating with on a day-to-day basis. There was a liberal leave policy within the Iraqi army, so a lot of these guys would show up for a week or so of training and then you wouldn't see them for a week—or never. They just never came back. The turnover was a little less with the SMP. We were very proud of the fact that after we had worked with these guys for a while, the turnover and the AWOLs went way down for all the scouts. We gave them good training, and we made them a little safer out there on the streets. And we took a personal interest in their welfare; they knew we went out of our way to look out for them. Probably the biggest thing we did was to never ask them to do something that we wouldn't do ourselves. We worked as hard or harder than they did in training. And they never ceased to be surprised that we would go out into the streets on patrol with them and share the same dangers they did. This is the essence of what we came to call combat FID. Train for a few days, then go out on patrol and do it for real—with the *jundis* we trained. It was an immediate validation of our worth as trainers."

"We weren't the first to train Iraqi soldiers," Dan Eaton told me, "but maybe we were the first to operate with them on a true combined basis—a bilateral operation, with some of them and some of us. I think prior to our arrival, combined operations meant that you had a few *jundis* in the back of the truck for window dressing, but basically it was a U.S. operation, and we did all the work. Then the word came down that all SOF operations would be actual combined operations, not just a token Iraqi component along for show. So the *jundis* were out there for real, and so were we.

"Operationally," Eaton continued, "this posed some challenges for us. We'd only just started training and working with the Iraqi soldiers in Ramadi. In places like Baghdad, they had the ISOF—the Iraqi Special Operations Force. They're a very capable unit with several years of training with SOF training cadre and lots of special equipment. Even in Habbaniyah, they had been training *jundis* for some time. We began with some of the least trained Iraqi soldiers and took them into the most contentious battlespace in Iraq. It was true on-the-job training, and I'm not sure those in our chain of command ever quite understood what we were up against. Or how we were making it up as we went along."

One of the key ingredients for working with the Iraqis, both in training and on operations, were the task unit interpreters. They had to understand military jargon and the subtle differences as this jargon related to both cultures. They were indispensable, both in training and on operations. Senior Chief Stan Lester looked after these essential members of the task unit, but everyone in the TU took an interest in the welfare of the interpreters. I got to know only one of them. His name is Patrick, and I met him on his home leave in San Diego. We met again when I was in Ramadi. He had been there since September 2005 and planned to stay, in his words, "until we win this thing." Patrick is fifty-six and was born in Baghdad. He came to America with his family when he was in his early teens. He had enlisted in the Navy and served a tour in uniform as a hospital corpsman. Patrick was hired as a military interpreter soon after the invasion of Iraq. He has that zest for America and all things American that's often found in our naturalized citizens.

"I hate what the insurgents are doing to my country—my country America and my former country, Iraq. The insurgents we are fighting in Ramadi are enemies of America and they are enemies of the people of Iraq." I asked Patrick if he was Shiite or Sunni. "Neither," he told me. "My family in Iraq were Christians and had been for generations. But many years ago Iraq became a place where we no longer felt comfortable."

Patrick is slender and has a mild soul with a sunny disposition. He's engaging and is well liked by Americans and Iraqis. I asked him what the *jundis* think about Americans, and, specifically, their SEAL trainers.

"They like and admire the SEALs, and they think there are no finer warriors in the U.S. military. I believe this as well. There are a great many terps [a term *he* uses in referring to himself as an interpreter] in Iraq, and I enjoy a great deal of respect as one of the terps who works with the SEALs. I train with them and I go on operations with them. As for the Iraqis, I am asked two questions—always the same two questions over and over again—by the *jundis* and the Iraqi civilians. The first is 'How long will you stay?' Not 'How long are you here?' but 'How long *will* you stay?' They all know about Vietnam and the promises that we made to the Iraqis during the first Gulf war. They're all afraid we will leave. I tell them we will not leave; that we will be here for as long as it takes for them to have their freedom. I'm not sure they believe me, but that is what I tell them. I hope we do not let them down."

"And the second?" I prompted him.

"They ask me why we are here. 'I live here,' a *jundi* will tell me, 'and I have to fight and maybe die for my country, but why are you here? This is not your country—you do not have to fight and die for Iraq.' I tell them that we already have our freedom, and that we cannot fully enjoy our freedom unless the Iraqis have theirs as well. So we are willing to come here and help them to be free. Freedom is that important, and we will fight and die for *their* freedom. I also tell them there are four things we will not do. And they are very important things." He ticked them off on his fingers; I could see that he had thought about this a great deal. "We will not tell them how to live, how to run their country, how to worship, or how to raise their families. But we will fight with them—for them."

I've given a lot of thought to Patrick's answers to these questions. When I'm asked about this second question, the why-are-we-there one, I often launch into a monologue about the danger of radical Islam or the importance of stopping al-Qaeda in Iraq or about the need for regional stability—or some other reason. I think I like Patrick's answer better. As for the how-long-will-we-stay question, well, I was just glad none of the Iraqis I met there asked me that one.

The men of this first Ramadi task unit had three issues before them that commanded their attention. One was getting the Shark Base camp built out and able to support the work and operations of a full task unit. The second was organizing the training for the Iraqi scouts at Camp Ramadi. The third was learning the AO, or area of operations, and getting familiar with the terrain where they, and their Iraqi scout trainees, would be conducting operations. In the fall of 2005, there were some semicontested areas that were under nominal coalition control, but most of the city was controlled by the insurgents. In Ramadi those coalition forces were American and Iraqi. The Ramadi area of operations was designated AO Topeka, which encompassed the city of Ramadi and an expanse of territory west of Ramadi. Al-Anbar province was the responsibility of the Marine Corps and the commander of the Marine Expeditionary Force (MEF) in Fallujah. AO Topeka was under the command of an Army brigade commander who reported to the MEF commander. The four Army battalions and the single Marine battalion assigned to the brigade had sector responsibilities in and around Ramadi. The Iraqi battalions had similar responsibilities in these sectors, and worked with the Army and Marine battalions. The Marines were responsible for the Hay Al Dhobot and Thaylat districts, areas to the east of their base at Hurricane Point. The Marines also garrisoned an outpost near the bombed-out Government Center in the Qatana District. The Army and Iraqi battalions had the rest of Ramadi. The areas west of the Habbaniyah Canal and north of the Euphrates River and Route Michigan were disputed and not entirely under insurgent control. The districts east of Thaylat and south of Route Michigan were very dangerous—pure Indian country. If Army, Marine, or Iraqi patrols ventured into that area, they were guaranteed to be attacked—either by small-arms fire, rocket-propelled grenades (RPGs), IEDs, or all of the above. The insurgents were not only well armed but capable of coordinated attacks, which meant they could initiate an attack from one direction designed to bring about a defensive maneuver that would set up an ambush coming from another direction.

"There were some places that you simply could not go," one of the task unit SEALs told me, "or you'd at least better have a good reason for going. Or go at night. We still owned the night, but in some districts they knew and owned the ground so completely that it was still very dangerous at night. You don't need a set of NODs [night-observation devices] to trigger an IED at night. In some of those districts, the IED triggermen were on duty 24/7."

"We immediately began to go out into the Ta'meem and 5-Kilo districts and into the areas to the north of the river to get a feel for the area," Jake Hanson said of their initial operations. "We'd go out with Army patrols or on our own with Army Humvee drivers. We had good Humvee drivers, some with a lot of experience driving in combat, but we had yet to learn the streets in Ramadi, and that took time. The Army guys helped us with that. Some of those young Army specialists were absolutely fantastic. A few of them were barely twenty years old, but they really knew their stuff and were very courageous. They taught us what to look for and how to drive the streets of Ramadi. It was hard to find an Army Humvee driver who hadn't been hit by an IED at least once—some of them multiple times. We were very grateful for their help.

"Our first operations with the scouts were patrols out into the 5-Kilo District and then into the Ta'meem District. We went up north a few times and into the Hay Al Dhobot, but I'd say 90 percent of our patrols were in the 5-Kilo and Ta'meem. The first scouts we took on these patrols were *jundis* from the special missions platoon. Our objective was to get them to move tactically as a unit, and they were pretty well chaperoned. Initially, there'd be six or eight of them and ten to fifteen of us—counting the EOD guys and maybe one or two soldiers or marines. We went out first at night, and later in the daytime. The ground was contested, but nothing like the south-central parts of Ramadi. The Army kept a few strong points manned in the Ta'meem and 5-Kilo and a roving quick-reaction force in those districts, so help was never too far away."

"It didn't take the scouts too long to become proficient at working the streets. We'd patrol a while, set up in a neighborhood, and try to make friends with the people. The scouts got pretty good at knocking on doors and chatting up the locals. By this time the intel guys were starting to develop some targets, so we began setting up assaults with the scouts taking the lead. We'd build a target package, set up the operation, line up our mission approvals and clearances, and get ready to move out. Usually, we'd fully brief the Americans on the operation at Shark Base while a couple of the guys would go over to pick up the *jundis*. They lived within the perimeter of Camp Ramadi proper, with two of the Iraqi battalions who were just over the camp perimeter wall from Shark Base—an area of the main base we informally called Camp Ali. We'd then brief our Iraqi contingent on the operation just before we rolled out, or as was the case much of the time, before we patrolled out on foot. We hated leaving camp in Humvees, as there were just too many guys out there with cell phones. They could see us coming and alert the insurgents for an ambush. A patrol had a better chance of getting into the city unnoticed on foot—at least into the Ta'meem or 5-Kilo, which were next to the perimeter of Camp Ramadi.

"Sometimes, if we were looking for a specific individual, we'd set in an overwatch to lie up and wait for him to show himself. There were no guarantees when you were looking for a single Iraqi in a city of 400,000. Overwatches were risky in that you were sometimes spotted getting into the overwatch position and that the target individual might be alerted to your presence. When everything worked right, we sent in an overwatch, usually with two SEALs and four *jundis*, and they would wait for daylight. When they could confirm our target was there or saw him return to the house, they'd call it in, and we'd move on the target in force. We did very little shooting from overwatches, unlike later on during the battle for the city. For us an overwatch was usually to trigger an assault by alerting a standby force of the location of a bad guy."

"We tried to work smart and teach our Iraqi scouts to work smart," Dan Eaton said of the task unit operations. "That meant we tried to leverage our ability to move about the city and to use some of our intelligence capabilities to best advantage. When possible, we also wanted to use the capabilities of the Army, Marine, and Iraqi army patrols out in the sectors where we were working. Not too long after we began going out into the streets, we had an SR [special reconnaissance] team of two SEALs and eight Iraqis watching a house. This was the home of a suspected AQI organizer. We also knew there were Army and Iraqi patrols in the area. Late that afternoon, the SR team saw our target individual and one of his lieutenants enter the house. And we thought there may be other insurgents inside as well. Rather than call back for a force of SEALs and scouts, which would have taken awhile, the SR element called in the location and routed an Army patrol to the home. The Army patrol responded much quicker than any SEAL-scouts force from Camp Ramadi. Forty minutes after the insurgent leader had entered his home, the Army and their Iraqi *jundis* had him in custody, along with a half a dozen other insurgents. And our scouts got credit for their part in this roundup of insurgents.

"On yet another SR mission, we had intelligence that a restaurant was being used as a meeting place for insurgents, but there were a lot of other Iraqis coming and going there as well. We needed an OP [observation post] that was close to the restaurant but not too close—a secure perch from which we could observe the target for several days and still be safe from informers. We found this three-story house that was several hundred yards from the restaurant entrance. It was perfect. We sent one of our interpreters to speak with the residents and to make arrangements to use one of their upper-floor rooms for a few days. We paid them well, but the key was that after being coached by the terp and our scouts, we were very polite and respectful of their customs. There are certain things that an American can do, without thinking, to give offense in an Arab household. When they saw that we took care to show this kind of respect, they responded by making us tea and offering us cakes and treats. It was all very civilized. We set up for three days, and with a camera and long-range lens we photographed everyone who came and went from the restaurant. Back at the task unit, the intel guys pored over the images and identified eight members of a cell of ten known insurgents.

"A few nights later we returned to the residence and were greeted warmly by the occupants. We watched the comings and goings for another day. When we saw a number of known insurgents go in, we called in an Army unit and they took down the whole place. Out of fifty patrons, they culled out five insurgents. One of them was the insurgent cell leader and a former bodyguard of Uday Hussein. This operation earned the Iraqi battalion commander a commendation and destroyed the insurgent cell. Our follow-on intelligence indicated that this sent shock waves through other insurgent groups. They felt that one of the insurgents who was not at the restaurant was an informant and had dropped a dime on his fellow insurgent-cell members. This was a good example of our ability to gather intelligence and target insurgents. And it would never have worked had we not gained the help and cooperation of the locals."

Two events were to shape the disposition and the operations of this first Ramadi task unit. One occurred in mid-December 2005 and the other during the first week of the following January. The first was a redeployment that took nearly a full platoon of Ramadi SEAL operators, along with a portion of task unit support personnel, and sent them to Baghdad. This had the effect of cutting the task unit down to about seventy members. The intelligence and targeting elements remained intact, but about half of the SEALs were pulled out. It seems there was a need for SEALs in the capital for personnel security detail work—perhaps the *least* favorite of SEAL mission taskings.

"This hit us pretty hard," Jake Hanson said of the drawdown of his task unit. "We were just starting to get comfortable with the mission and the battlespace, and those SEALs assigned to the various scout elements were beginning to get to know their Iraqis and learn how to work with them. Then our SEAL operators got cut in half. It stretched the remaining SEAL operators thinner, especially out in the battlespace. There was one positive with this, in that we had to work more efficiently. That meant we began to go out on operations with a few more *jundis* and a few less SEALs."

"None of us were very happy about this," one of the SEALs confided to me, "but there were a number of SEALs in the platoons who honestly preferred not to work with the Iraqis—it could be frustrating. It was like doing everything in slow motion when our own training is very high-speed. Don't get me wrong, they all did their job, but some chafed a bit when it came to training and operating with the *jundis*. I think that figured into Mister Hanson's and our senior chief's decision as to who would stay in Ramadi and who would go to Baghdad." He grinned as he recalled the episode. "Some of the guys may not have liked working with the Iraqis, but I can tell you this—they liked personal security detail a whole lot less."

"And you?" I asked.

"Me? Oh, I like the *jundis* just fine. And I began to like them a whole lot more at the thought of bodyguard duty."

The second event was the attack by AQI on the Ramadi glass factory. By January 2006, the tribes in Ramadi were beginning to see that al-Qaeda and its allies were not only against the Americans and the new

Iraqi government, but that they also directly threatened the tribes and their way of life. The Ramadi glass factory was a huge facility that no longer produced glass, but was pressed into service as a tribal meeting center and a recruiting station for the Iraqi police. This was still early on in the process of the tribes turning away from AQI, but a few of the sheikhs had had enough. They began to encourage their young men to sign up for police duty. The glass factory was an industrial complex on the eastern side of the 5-Kilo District and right next to Camp Ramadi—relatively safe territory compared to the districts in central Ramadi. On 5 January, several hundred Ramadi police candidates attended a meeting at the factory. Also present were several marines and a U.S. Army officer, Lieutenant Colonel Mike McLaughlin. McLaughlin was with the 2nd Brigade Combat Team of the Pennsylvania National Guard. He was the resident expert on Ramadi tribal matters and the American brigade's efforts to engage the Sunni tribes in Ramadi. It was police recruiting drives like this that signaled the beginning of what was to become the Awakening movement in al-Anbar, which resulted in the tribes turning away from al-Qaeda. On this final day of a very successful recruiting drive, a suicide bomber with an explosive-laden vest blew himself up in the crowded factory building. The blast killed McLaughlin, along with eighty tribal police candidates. It was also a setback for the prospects of a locally recruited police force and for any organized resistance the tribes may have been able to mount at this time against AQI in Ramadi.

"He was a good officer, and he really cared for the Iraqis," Jake Hanson said of Lieutenant Colonel McLaughlin. "We were very aware of his efforts in tribal engagement, although we did little of that at our level. Tribal engagement in Ramadi was a very complex and difficult business. Mike McLaughlin was one of the few who understood the tribes and was able to work with the sheikhs. It was through the efforts of McLaughlin that the tribal police recruiting efforts got off the ground. I went with him one night to the home of a sheikh in Ramadi. We had gathered with six other tribal sheikhs to talk about what we could do for them and to ask for their help. He got on well with the tribal leaders, and they trusted him. After he was killed, four of those sheikhs at the meeting I attended were caught by al-Qaeda and beheaded. That's how AQI does business, murder and intimidation. And it worked. After that, many of the sheikhs went into hiding or fled to Syria or Jordan."

Mike McLaughlin was a true hero and a wonderful example of the dedicated reservists who return to active duty in the service of their nation. Immediately following the attack, McLaughlin deferred medical attention for himself until the other soldiers and marines with him were taken care of. He died of his wounds a short time later.

Following the setback at the glass factory and into the early part of 2006, the SEALs focused on training the Iraqi army scouts and getting them into the streets. Yet it was not all patrolling and an occasional assault. The SEALs and their scouts began to set up sniper positions in an offensive posture. These overwatch operations had the SEALs in the role of shooters, while the Iraqis tended to security and managed any dealings with the locals. But even these operations, which were carried out in residential neighborhoods, were highly restrictive. They were in areas where a relatively small number of insurgents moved within the local population.

"I was very proud of my shooters," Hanson said of his snipers. "Perhaps more for the shots they didn't take than the ones they did. During the January elections, we were out patrolling with our Iraqis, and we had snipers out as well, all in an effort to keep down the level of violence during the voting. AQI did not want the Anbaris voting. One of our sniper teams saw some armed men on a rooftop near a polling station. They were in good position and had a clear shot."

"No one was supposed to be in the area of the polling stations armed," one of the snipers said of the incident, "and we saw some men with rifles on a roof right across the street from the polls—right where they shouldn't be. We were on the lookout for insurgents trying to disrupt the voting, and these guys fit that description. We were cleared to shoot, but it just didn't look right. They were armed with AK-47s, but they didn't seem to be getting ready to fire on the voters. They weren't moving tactically or sneaking about like insurgents usually do. So we just watched them. As it turned out, they were just some Iraqis who *also* wanted to protect the voting. You have a lot of power as a sniper, and you have to make sure of what you're doing."

"On another overwatch," said one of the SEALs, "we were looking to get a senior insurgent leader and were set up where we could keep watch on his house. This was a really bad dude, and we had clearance to shoot him on sight. Well, this Iraqi who exactly fit the description comes out of the house. He was a known insurgent leader, the kind of guy who more than deserves a bullet. But the guy on the gun had the feeling that somehow it just wasn't right. We're not squeamish about this; it's all about the shot, and yet this time our shooter somehow knew it wasn't right. Long story short, we called in a patrol that managed to chase this guy through a market and collar him. As it turns out, it wasn't him—it was his brother! He was a bad guy as well, but not bad enough for an on-the-spot bullet."

"That's why the final call is always with the shooter," Jake Hanson explained. "A guy with a gun that's shooting at you or at one of our patrols is an easy call. He's earned a bullet and the shooter is there to accommodate him. But often it's a judgment call, and the sniper has to be sure. In an insurgent situation, when we're trying to win the confidence and trust of the people, killing the wrong person can have terrible consequences."

The bulk of the task unit's operations were geared around the training of the Iraqi scouts and getting them out in the battlespace. For the most part, these were patrols designed to show presence in the streets of those districts that were contested and to build our confidence of the scouts, as well as their combat skills. While the SEALs trained the scouts, the task unit's N2 element continued to develop intelligence about insurgents, their activities, and their movements about the city. This kind of precise intelligence often led to an operation to apprehend a high-value insurgent. The format for these assaults typically had an overwatch team in position to watch the suspect's house or location for a time, then call in an assault element to seize the dwelling when the overwatch could confirm he was there. These raids called for a blocking element for security and an assault team to take the structure. They were combined operations, with most of the planning done by the SEALs and with the scouts making the final assault and search of the premises. With each of these operations, the Iraqis became a little more proficient and a little more confident. And as the tour of this first task unit wore on, the knowledge and reach of the TU intelligence section became more comprehensive and efficient. This benefited the SEALs and their scouts, and also served as a target generator for the brigade conventional forces.

Toward the end of this first task unit's tour, they were asked by the Marines to help in setting up an overwatch position that, in retrospect, was a preview of the SEAL role during the Battle of Ramadi. Route Michigan ran just north of the city center and south of the Euphrates River, past an outpost known as Camp Corregidor in the eastern part of the city and on toward Baghdad. It was the primary east-west roadway from Camp Ramadi. The insurgents knew this and targeted it. In the early months of 2006, it was hard to drive Route Michigan without being attacked. There was a particularly dangerous five-way intersection near the Saddam Mosque that was a favorite location for these insurgent attacks. The SEALs were asked to help with setting up a small outpost or strongpoint to provide added security for traffic along Route Michigan. Jake Hanson had three SEAL Naval Reservists assigned to his task unit prior to deployment. As they were three extra bodies he hadn't planned to have available, they were given assignments and duties as the need arose during the course of the deployment. One of them was the Marine sniper overwatch.

"We did just about anything Jake asked of us," Jason Connally said of the deployment in general. "It didn't matter. A few months before the deployment, we'd all been civilians and we were glad to be able to come back and help. We filled several roles, including operations officer, sniper, air controller, camp boss, and trash burners. I think one of our best contributions was the strongpoint we helped set on Route Michigan near the Saddam Mosque. It was a shooting gallery for the insurgents, and just about every vehicle that moved on Michigan took fire in that area. The marines had a good location for what amounted to reinforced overwatch position, but they needed help setting it up and manning it. Chief Dixon and his construction crew help us to build it out and we manned it. And the firing on convoys, at least along that stretch of the highway, went way down."

Lieutenant (junior grade) Jason Connally had been an enlisted SEAL and left the Navy after his obligated service to go to college. He stayed in the reserves and took a commission along with his degree in education. He was teaching high school when he was recalled to active service soon after 9/11. Don East and Bud Howard, both SEAL petty officers, were recalled as well. East was a police officer and Howard a construction worker. There are SEAL reserve units located across the nation, manned by SEALs and non-SEAL support personnel. They are seldom activated as a unit in the way Army and Marine reserve units are called up. Most of these weekend warriors return to active duty as individual augmentees. The recalls are based on the need for individual skill sets and, in the case of SEALs, individual reputations. For the most part, these recalls are not involuntary; these reservists step up and make it known they are available for recall. They raise their hands. This was the case for Connally, East, and Howard.

"The objective wasn't so much to kill insurgents," Jake Hanson said of the Route Michigan overwatch, "as it was to make them think twice about shooting at our trucks and Humvees with no consequence. My reserve guys could and did a lot of things for us, but they were also very good shooters. The insurgents quickly learned that there was a price to pay for shooting at Americans or planting IEDs in that area. For close to a quarter-mile each way on Michigan, there were no serious attacks—no big IEDs. If vehicles were taking fire near that strongpoint, it was usually small-arms fire at long range. That stretch of highway became much safer.

"The great thing about those three," Hanson continued, "as well as with all my reservists, was their attitude. They all had a range of skills, some military specialties like a sniper or an air controller or a language skill, and they often had civilian experience that was useful. But what they really brought to the table was a willingness to help. I could ask them to do anything. It didn't have to be within their specialty. Officers and senior petty officers carried sandbags and loaded trucks. Usually, I never had to ask; they just did it. The reservists were an essential part of our task unit organization and capability."

There are any number of accounts of the interaction of operations and intelligence, and how one supports the other. For example, information from a detainee may be verified by an electronic intercept that is in turn corroborated by reporting source—all of which combines to fix the location of a targeted insurgent leader or a hard target, such as an IED factory. I was privileged to learn of many successes during the early days of the Ramadi SEAL task unit, but two stand out. One illustrates the effect of a timely marriage of intelligence and operational capability; the other shows the deadly and vicious nature of the enemy we face in Iraq. The first of these took place relatively early in a task unit's tour, just two months after it arrived.

While the SEALS busied themselves with developing and training their *jundi* scouts, and everyone in the task unit worked on the construction of Shark Base, the task unit's intelligence section, crammed into the kitchen of the team house, was combing its source data for insurgent targets. As the men worked the electronic and human intelligence traplines, they began to track one of the most notorious insurgent leaders in all of al-Anbar—Amir Khalaf Fanus.

The world learned of Amir Khalaf Fanus on 9 December 2005, when a press release broke the story of his capture. Fanus was a close associate of Abu Musab al-Zarqawi, and his insurgent activity had earned him the dubious title "the Butcher of Ramadi." He was a much-sought-after insurgent—someone who can be called a true terrorist. What made this story especially noteworthy was that he was turned over to the Americans in Ramadi by a local tribe. This was one of the early signs that the people of the city were tiring of the insurgents in their midst. Fanus was by far the highest-ranking member of al-Qaeda to be physically given up by Iraqi citizens. What did not get reported were the events that surrounded his delivery into the hands of the Americans—what, as Paul Harvey would say, is the rest of the story.

The task unit intelligence organization, specifically the advanced special operations section, worked closely with military intelligence and the OGAs—other governmental agencies. In military-speak OGA is often a euphemism for CIA. This is most usually true, but not always. The task unit intel analysts became convinced that Fanus was hiding out in a rural district just north of Ramadi. Jake Hanson had a lot of faith in his N2 section. Based on the analysts' information and targeting, Hanson called for a major effort into the area where Fanus was suspected of being holed up. They didn't have his precise location, but they knew the general area where he was hiding. The tip-off was that there was to be a meeting of insurgent leaders linked to Fanus, and it was this activity that drew the task unit intel specialists to isolate his general location. They had to move quickly. The joint operation that followed involved the Army, which included armor and dismounted infantry, a full platoon of SEALs, and the Iraqi special missions platoon. This combined force moved into the area and conducted a cordon-and-search operation.

"This was a big operation," reported one of the platoon SEALs, "or at least a big operation for us. It was a semirural area, so anyone moving in the open was pretty exposed—unlike in the more populated areas closer to the city. We closed off the area and began combing the area for insurgents."

The SEALs and Iraqis took down thirteen compounds and flushed out eight known insurgents—all men known to be linked to Fanus. But they did not capture Fanus. Somehow he managed to slip through the net.

"We knew he'd been there," another SEAL said, "and this guy was an evil son of a bitch. He lived up to his name, the Butcher. We found what had been his headquarters; he had fled quickly and left everything. There were photos of him personally torturing people and beheading them. There was even a video of him executing Iraqis with an AK-47. I mean, what kind of sicko keeps a video library of his executions. We really wanted this guy, but he got away." Two days later, one of the sheikhs from that area, and some of his men, drove up to the main gate of Camp Ramadi. They had Fanus bound, gagged, and stuffed in the trunk of their car.

"They pulled him out and dumped him in a heap in the dirt," Hanson said of the delivery. "He'd had the crap kicked out of him. That *they* had delivered him was significant. What we found just as important was what the local sheikh had to say to us. He said, 'I don't want you to come into my area again. If there's someone you want and he's among my tribe, you come to me and I will get him for you.' Well, my intel people were all over that one. We didn't make a big deal of it, but we began to quietly work with this sheikh. We treated him with respect and honored his position as a tribal leader. He became a good source of intelligence for us and for the task unit who followed us in Ramadi."

Following another intelligence lead in late January, a SEAL-Iraqi scout element was moving in on a residential compound in the Ta'meem District. It was reported to be an IED construction facility. The assault team was compromised close to the house, and there was a brief, sharp exchange of gunfire. When the SEALs and Iraqi scouts overran the compound, they found that it was indeed a bomb factory. Several crude IEDs were in various stages of assembly. All the insurgents had fled but one. He had been hit in the elbow by a round that had all but severed his arm. The SEAL corpsman quickly immobilized the damaged arm, applied a tourniquet, and gave the wounded man, a Sunni insurgent, a dose of painkillers. The patrol leader then radioed for a CASEVAC—a casualty evacuation. The wounded mujahid—or muj, as the SEALs call them—was rushed to the clinic at Camp Ramadi and taken into surgery. The patrol quickly searched the IED factory and made its way back to base.

The wounded muj—let's call him Ahmad—could not believe that he was being cared for in this way. He fully expected to be shot—that's what his AQI mentors had told him the Americans would do if they caught him. And here he was getting first-rate medical care, perhaps for the first time in his life. One or two of the SEALs from the patrol who captured him, on visiting the clinic to check on wounded scouts, even stopped by to see how Ahmad was getting along. Following the operation on his arm, he began to recover the use of it. A Marine reserve lance corporal who was a physical therapist in his civilian life started to work with Ahmad to rehabilitate the wounded limb. He came to the clinic during his off-duty time to conduct physical-therapy sessions. Again, Ahmad couldn't believe this treatment. It went against everything he had been told about the cruelty of the Crusaders who had invaded his land.

"This is not unusual," one of the task unit intelligence specialists told me. "Just treating a detainee or a captured insurgent with respect and courtesy destroys much of their predisposition toward us—they've been prepared for a whole different reality. This guy was just one example. We had another insurgent who was caught working in a basement in Ramadi making IEDs. During his interrogation, we learned that he was a university student from Baghdad—an engineering student, so he was very proficient in making bombs. He had been recruited by AQI to come to al-Anbar to blow up Americans. We talked with him a while, then put him in an armored Humvee and drove him around the city, showed him what his IEDs were doing to the local population—to the citizens of Ramadi. There are a lot of Anbaris in Ramadi missing arms and legs. The guy began to cry like a baby; he had no idea that the IEDs he built had killed and maimed a lot more Iraqis than Americans. After that he began to work with us against the insurgents. Often a good dose of compassion and kindness is a powerful tool. That was sure the case with the guy with the mangled arm."

As it turned out, Ahmad was so grateful that he volunteered to be an informant. As with any informant who had been a former insurgent, his initial information was carefully screened. But after a while he came to be a trusted asset, and his information led to the capture of several important insurgents and the location of two IED factories. He even recruited members of his extended family to provide information. Ahmad was never asked to be an informant; he felt an obligation to help the Americans because they had taken such good care of him.

"This story does not have a happy ending," Jake Hanson said of this informant. "Like a lot of Iraqis, Ahmad was passionate and emotional, and while that translated into a great deal of zeal in his reporting activity, it also made him visible to AQI. We have people who know how to manage informants, and a part of their job is to keep these reporting assets safe. With Ahmad, we tried to get him to restrict his reporting activity and to be careful in his movements, but he wouldn't listen. For many Iraqis, to go into hiding for a while or to stay out of sight is an unmanly thing. For Ahmad, it was all about fighting against those who betrayed him and his people, and helping the Americans who had been so good to him. So they finally got to him."

"Got to him?" I asked.

"Yeah. They dragged him out of his house and ripped off his nearly healed arm—literally. Then they took a cordless drill and drilled a couple of dozen holes in him. AQI is big on battery-operated power tools. And finally they shot him in the head and left him in front of his house—in front of his family. It was sad. He was such a lively fellow, and all he wanted to do was to repay our kindness. But it got him killed. Yet I'd like to think he didn't die for nothing. His family and his tribe know who killed him, and they know how and why. Each death has a consequence. We're bound by our rules of engagement. Beyond that, we try to use care in the use of violence whenever possible—care that's usually well beyond our ROEs. For al-Qaeda this kind of macabre violence is commonplace and routinely directed at the Anbaris and their tribal leaders. But the AQI were not doing themselves a favor in the long run. They were simply too vicious and too high-handed with the tribes. It was only a matter of time until these murder and intimidation tactics caught up with them. We didn't get to see it play out, but the guys from Team Three and Team Five who followed us into Ramadi did."

As the tour of the first SEAL task unit drew to a close in the early spring of 2006, Ramadi had become the most violent and contested city in Iraq. There were few services and little or no government presence. It was a haven for al-Qaeda and its allies, and the core districts of the city were totally in their control. Every police station in the city had been attacked and blown up. The Americans and the new Iraqi army were beginning to make their presence felt in some of the outlying districts, but central Ramadi was still firmly in insurgent hands.

This insurgent presence, this generic AQI, was a lethal stew that had been brewing in Ramadi since the fall of Saddam. After studying the groups that made their way to Ramadi, I'm still not certain just what their collective aim was, or if they had one. Certainly, they were there to rid al-Anbar province of the Crusader presence. But the foreign influences guiding this insurgency also had an Islamist agenda for the region, one that was totally at odds with the existing tribal structure. One of the main, and perhaps most deadly, of these groups was the Mujahideen Shura Council (MSC). This was a collection of al-Qaeda followers loyal to al-Zarqawi—many as fanatical as al-Zarqawi himself—who were thought to have taken refuge in Ramadi following the storming of Fallujah. The MSC in Ramadi seemed to be working to bring other insurgent groups under its standard to join in its efforts to attack Americans. The second main group, and just as violent as the MSC, was Ansar al-Sunnah. This group was a rallying standard for foreign fighters in Ramadi. It even distributed a video titled *The Lions of the Nomads in the City of Ramadi,* a propaganda piece designed to attract local insurgents to the cause. Other groups thought to be active or claiming an insurgent presence in Ramadi and al-Anbar were the Mujahideen Army, the al-Fatihin Army, and the Islamic Army in Iraq. While often in competition with each other, their collective presence threatened both the capital city and the province.

As for the coalition presence in Ramadi, there were just over five thousand Americans in one Marine and four Army battalions, and two Iraqi brigades with a combined strength of slightly more than two thousand soldiers. These forces all worked under the commander of the 2nd Brigade Combat Team of the Pennsylvania National Guard. They were confined to the major bases in the western part of the city, a few strong points along Route Michigan, and the Marine outpost near the Government Center. An Army battalion and one of the Iraqi army brigades anchored the eastern approaches to the city at Camp Corregidor. Across al-Anbar there were battalion- and brigade-sized garrisons similarly embattled by insurgent presence—they were relatively safe as long as they remained on base but vulnerable to insurgent hit-and-run tactics if they ventured out into the cities or the countryside. Of the major cities, only in Fallujah was there relative security, and that was marred by an occasional flare-up of violence.

In the middle of this struggle between the coalition forces and AQI were the people of al-Anbar—the tribes. At first they actively or passively supported the insurgent effort that opposed the presence of Americans and that of the new Iraqi, predominantly Shiite, army. But the AQI presence that the Anbaris allowed in their midst also brought strict Islamic requirements and finally the demands that threatened their way of life. The tribal sheikhs certainly resented the Americans and the "Shiite" army, but what about these domestic and foreign fighters that were beginning to assert control? These tribal leaders hold power by a system that is far from democratic—a sheikh lies somewhere between a warlord and a mafioso on the leadership scale. Yet it is a type of governance that relies on patronage and respect—what the Iraqis call *wasta*. This system of tribal order depends on a certain amount of coercion, but the type they employ is minor when compared to the murder and intimidation practiced by AQI. For the sheikhs, *wasta* demanded that they appear in public and unafraid, with a minimum of security. They became sitting ducks for the veteran AQI fighters.

In the spring of 2006, the Anbari tribal sheikhs were caught between the proverbial rock and a hard place. They handled this dilemma in typical tribal fashion. They gave some measure of compliance to both sides, but in reality they were waiting to see which of these foreign forces were going to prevail—the Americans and the "Baghdad Iraqis," or AQI.

Also in the spring of 2006, there were forces gathering that would shape the future of Ramadi and al-Anbar province—indeed, all of Iraq. One was a bottom-up, grassroots movement among the tribes of al-Anbar and the Anbari people against the strict Islamic influence of AQI. This movement was at the time neither encouraged nor recognized by the government in Baghdad. It was the beginning of the Awakening—the tribal revolt in al-Anbar.

There were other changes coming as well. The American high command had made the decision to "take back" Ramadi. There could be no progress in Ramadi or al-Anbar as long as the insurgents owned the streets of the provincial capital. Exactly how this was to be done was being discussed at the highest levels within the U.S. military and in the Iraqi government. Was there to be another Fallujah-like assault on a major Iraqi city, or was there another way? There was, however, no question of who was to do this. In the late spring of 2006, Colonel Sean MacFarland, commander of the 1st Brigade Combat Team, 1st Armored Division, relieved Colonel John Gronski as commander of AO Topeka. Shortly before MacFarland took command, the advanced elements from SEAL Squadron Three and their Ramadi task unit began to filter into Shark Base.

"There's a battle brewing," Jake Hanson told his relief, "and you have some decisions to make. The Army and the Marines and the Iraqi army are going to be committed to this fight. The role of the SEAL task unit hasn't been defined. You and your guys can continue with the *jundi* training we started and conduct special operations within the capabilities of the Iraqi scouts. Or you can jump in the middle of this thing. One way or another, the face of battle in Ramadi is going to change. Good luck."

CHAPTER 4

Soldier and SEAL take a break. A Bulldog soldier from the 1-37 takes a smoke break on patrol while covered by his SEAL brother. *Courtesy of Captain Mike Bajema*

The Second Task Unit
and the Battle for Ramadi

SEALs and SEAL component commanders are very good at operational turnover and doing what they can for those who follow them into the battlespace. Squadron One did that for Squadron Three, which relieved it in April 2006. As the task unit in Ramadi prepared for its brother SEALs from Three, there were some important changes at the squadron or task group level.

During the last few weeks of the unit's deployment, Commander Sam Winters was able to arrange for the relocation of the SEAL task group from Baghdad to Fallujah. So when Commander Cally Garrison and his squadron headquarters element arrived in Baghdad, it was only for a few days. They soon moved the Squadron Three headquarters element and task group to Fallujah. This accomplished two important things for the SEALs fighting in Iraq. First, it physically consolidated most of the Iraqi-based Navy SEAL and Naval Special Warfare assets in Iraq in al-Anbar province. Second, it put the SEAL task group commander and his headquarters near General Richard Zilmer, then commander of the 1st Marine Expeditionary Force. The 1st MEF commander was responsible for all of al-Anbar province. Militarily, he owned western Iraq and commanded the 30,000-some American troops and coalition forces scattered across al-Anbar province—everyone but the SOF units in al-Anbar. Garrison and his SEALs were still under the tactical control of the Joint Special Operations Task Force (JSOTF) commander at Balad Air Base, and he, not General Zilmer, commanded the SEALs operating in al-Anbar. But the SEAL squadron commander was now near the Marine commander who owned the al-Anbar battlespace where his SEALs operated. Garrison was still Commander, Naval Special Warfare Task Group–Arabian Peninsula, but he was now near his landlord. When the 1st MEF commander had an issue in al-Anbar that involved SEALs or SEAL support for his conventional forces, he had his SEAL component commander near at hand.

"I can't say enough about what Sam and his people did in getting us to Fallujah," Cally Garrison said. "This allowed me to be closer to my task units and to build a closer relationship with the Marine commander who owned the battlespace out west. General Zilmer was a terrific commander and very easy to work with. And it made it easier for me to get around the province to visit my units. Job one for the conventional forces in al-Anbar was to work with the Iraqi security forces and train them to fight insurgents. We had our marching orders regarding training the Iraqis and tribal engagement, but much of what we did, especially in Ramadi, was to support the conventional forces in their mission. The area of operations in and around Ramadi happened to be an Army AO, so in some ways our guys out there worked for the Army brigade commander as well as for me. And that Army brigade commander reported to the MEF commander in Fallujah.

"The move also allowed me to rebalance my task units, so we now had three full-up TUs in Fallujah, Habbaniyah, and Ramadi—each TU with two full platoons along with their intel and targeting cells. We were finally out of Baghdad. Well, mostly out of Baghdad; we still had a few responsibilities there, but most of my squadron assets in Iraq were now out in al-Anbar.

"The climate in Fallujah and Habbaniyah was still contentious, and there was plenty of work there for us, but Ramadi was especially dangerous. In April of 2006 the violence there was on the rise. I knew the task unit in Ramadi was going to have a very active tour. When we arrived, plans were well under way for the pacification or retaking of Ramadi. It wasn't clear how that was to take place, but no matter how it was to be executed, our task unit there was going to be a part of it.

"The work of the previous squadron and the superb performance of our task units allowed us to solidify our position as the lead SOF component in al-Anbar. Prior to the end of our tour, my position was redesignated and I became the commander of the Special Operations Task Force–West. As SOTF–West, all SOF components came under my tactical control. That included the SEAL task units and the Special Forces AOB [advanced operating base] at Al Asad Air Base, which directed the work of the Army Special Forces teams at Al Asad, Hit, Hadithah, and Al Qa'im.

"This came about for a couple of reasons," Garrison continued. "First of all, it made sense as SOF capability became a useful and value-added component of the conventional-force structure and the conventional battle plan for al-Anbar. The Marine and Army commanders began to rely on us and use our unique capabilities. Second, my boss, the Commander, Joint Special Operations Task Force at Balad Air Base, had come to trust the Naval Special Warfare command organization to run the show out west. But the real key to our success were the task unit commanders and the senior leadership in the SEAL platoons—the officer and enlisted leadership. They made themselves user-friendly in the eyes of their local conventional commanders. We brought a unique blend of operational and intelligence skill sets to the battlefield, and the conventional battlespace commanders came to rely on us. More important, they came to trust us. The operative interface was a SEAL task unit leader going to a conventional commander and saying, 'Sir, what can we do to help?' That kind of cooperation and quiet professionalism goes a long way. The SEALs became far more adept at operating with the conventional forces than other SOF components. Their direct-action skills in the field, and their unique intel and targeting capability, made them a valuable asset to the brigade commanders in al-Anbar. That's why the SEALs and big Army got on so well in Ramadi. Don't make too much of this, but there's always been a bit of historical friction between conventional forces and Army SOF components. We didn't have any of that baggage, and the credit for this success goes to our junior leaders and their can-do spirit.

"Our success was also due to the bottom-up approach we took regarding SOF operations in al-Anbar. As the tactical commander, I had a go/no-go say in the operations conducted by the task units and, later on, with the Special Forces teams at the advanced operating base in Al Asad. I trusted my TU and AOB commanders to make good decisions in light of what was and was not a good SOF mission. Those commanders, in their request for mission approval, had to evaluate each mission in terms of risk/reward—how it addressed our mission responsibilities and how it served our conventional forces in that battlespace. I wouldn't go so far as to call my approval a rubber stamp, but they made the decisions, and for the most part they made good ones. We looked good—I looked good as the SOTF–West commander—because I had terrific task unit commanders, and good junior officers and enlisted leaders within those task units. They performed professionally and courageously, and none more so than the task unit at Ramadi. Without a doubt, theirs was the most dangerous and difficult mission out west."

Lieutenant Commander Jack Williams brought a fully manned task unit with two full SEAL platoons and a complete task unit organization to Ramadi. This added operational punch to Jake Hanson's reduced SEAL contingent there. Prior to Squadron Three's deployment, the movement of the squadron headquarters from Baghdad to Fallujah was a work in progress. So the Squadron Three task unit assignments had not been finalized until a few weeks before its rotation into Iraq. Jack Williams and his task unit, much like his predecessor's, had learned they were coming to Ramadi only a few weeks prior to their rotation date. Until that time, he and his squadron thought they would be in Baghdad working with the Iraqi Special Operations Force. When that requirement was lifted, it paved the way for Squadron Three to flow more assets and more SEALs into al-Anbar, including a full task unit in Ramadi.

"The ISOF operated primarily in Baghdad," Jack Williams said of the assignment his task unit did not get, "and that meant working with some of the best-trained Iraqi fighters in the Iraqi security forces. We were ready to do that, but this was counterterror work. I'm one who believes we don't have a terrorist problem in Iraq—well, we may have a terrorist problem, but killing them doesn't seem to get us anywhere, even when we target and kill terrorist cell leaders. They just regenerate. I believe we have an insurgency problem in Iraq. Terrorists create terror—they strike and run. Insurgents want to control the towns and cities; they want to take over and gain control of the people. Al-Qaeda is using the insurgency in Iraq, even guiding the insurgency, as a stepping-stone to power. Terror is simply one of their tactics. I couldn't have been happier when we learned we were going out to Ramadi. It was the most dangerous city in the most dangerous province in Iraq. If we could get to Ramadi, I felt we could find a way to fight insurgents; we could find a way to make a difference. And that's what it's all about. When we got the word about Ramadi, I told my troops that this was going to be a historical deployment and that we were going to make a significant contribution to the freedom of the Iraqi people. I also told them that we were in for a fight."

Jack Williams is an imposing presence—I've often referred to him as a blunt object. He's perhaps five-ten, weighs 240, and has the upper-body physique of a weight lifter, though his sport is jujitsu, at which he is very accomplished. His hair is as closely cropped as any seaman in boot camp. Williams is a New Englander who enlisted in the Navy to become a Navy SEAL. He graduated from BUD/S with Class 177 in 1991. After two overseas rotations with the East Coast teams, the Navy decided to send him to college to become an officer. When the 9/11 attacks in New York and Washington came, he had just begun his studies at the University of San Diego. I can't imagine a more frustrated college freshman than Jack Williams. He graduated in three years with a degree in English and a 4.0 grade point average. "Why English?" I asked him. "A naval officer has to be a good writer," he told me. "Since I had to be there, it was the most useful thing I could learn." This rotation was his second to Iraq and his second as a SEAL officer.

Jack Williams reminds me of John Paul Jones. The man considered the father of our Navy once said, "I wish to have no connection with any ship that does not sail fast, for I intend to go in harm's way." Williams didn't say this, but I strongly suspect him of thinking, "Give me a hardy troop of Navy SEALs because I'm going to lead them in close combat."

Williams knew two things going into Ramadi. The first was that it was the most dangerous and contentious city in Iraq—a city fully in the grips of insurgents. The other was that there was going to be a push by the Army and Marine battalions there to take the city back from these insurgents. This meant a battle, and he was determined that his task unit would play a part in that battle. This also meant working closely with the Army, as it would have the lead in this fight. So he counseled his task unit in the importance of working closely with the Army and, again, the historical role that was ahead of them in this upcoming battle.

Military units, especially deployed military units, are a culture unto themselves. They have personalities, histories, and traditions. Special operators are no different. Often special operators are permitted to let their grooming standards slip, depending on the mission and where they are. This was especially the case in Afghanistan, where facial hair is accepted and encouraged for Afghan males. And sometimes they may add a scarf or piece of local clothing to their operational uniforms. They may never pass for locals, but it shows respect for the local culture. And they may occasionally pass for non-Americans. These conventions are appropriate when SOF forces are operating independently or with indigenous groups. In Ramadi and most of al-Anbar, SEALs operated from conventional military bases and often with conventional military forces. And sometimes these relaxed grooming and uniform standards can be an issue when SOF and conventional forces are living and working together. Jack Williams allowed none of that. When his SEALs or other task unit personnel were out of Camp Ramadi or otherwise off Shark Base, they met or exceeded the grooming standards of the soldiers and marines serving there.

"This was my third rotation in Iraq," one platoon veteran told me, "and to be honest about it, we can get a little sloppy when we're not in the field—sloppy in a macho kind of way. We're good at what we do, and sometimes we want to let it show. But the boss told us how it was going to be, and he only had to say it once. He personally set the standard for professionalism in the field and professionalism on the base, and that was it. It was correct uniforms, close haircuts, and polished boots—no exceptions. And it was a good call. I know the soldiers and marines on the base appreciated how we conducted ourselves. Jack's a great warrior and a great leader."

The Squadron Three SEALs had come to Ramadi prepared for combat—mentally, professionally, and physically. Regarding the latter, SEALs believe that their physical conditioning gives them the edge in combat. While conducting the interviews for this book in Coronado, I spent time with all the nondeployed West Coast SEAL teams. Physical conditioning is ongoing for all SEALs, but particularly so among those preparing for combat rotation. In the summer of 2007 I watched as SEALs from Team (then Squadron) One and Team Three as they prepared for deployment. Team/Squadron One was then the next to rotate into Iraq. The SEALs from Team Three, who would follow their Team One brothers in 2008, were also in predeployment training. All SEALs do their share of swimming and running, but they've developed their own training regime to prepare for combat in Iraq. It's their adaptation of cross-training modeled after the workouts posted on the Web by gymjones.com and crossfit.com. These workouts are designed to promote the strength and stamina needed in combat— SEAL combat. This means a combination of endurance, upper-body strength, and combat quickness. I watched a squad of seven SEALs from Team Three during one of their circuit-training drills—drills in which they move from one training station to the next. They exercised for thirty seconds, then took ten seconds to change stations.

- Station one: Maximum number of squat jumps in thirty seconds—touch the ground with your fingertips, then leap in the air as high as you can.
- Station two: Max number of sit-ups in thirty seconds holding a twenty-five-pound weight to your chest.
- Station three: Max number of bench jumps in thirty seconds—feet together, jump up to a locker-room-type wooden bench, then off the other side—back up, back down.
- Station four: Max number of deep squats in thirty seconds with a teammate draped across your shoulders in a fireman's carry.
- Station five: Max number of pull-ups in thirty seconds.
- Station six: Max number of ring dips in thirty seconds—on suspended gym rings, dip to bring upper arms parallel to ground.
- Station seven: Rest—while you're draped over the shoulders of the SEAL at station four.

They kept at this for about a half hour—chatting it up and encouraging each other to give it their all. When they were finished, they were sweat-soaked and completely trashed. Then they went out on the beach in the soft sand and did minute-interval wind sprints—forty seconds of running, twenty of walking, again and again. These drills were conducted in shorts, T-shirts, and boots. Other drills required them to exercise and move with a forty-pound combat load, and, again, these drills called for bursts of speed or an all-out short-term physical effort—a few seconds of rest, then another burst.

"It takes about six months of this kind of PT [physical training] to get ready for a deployment," a Team Three platoon chief told me as we watched this squad working out. "A lot of people think all we do is play beach volleyball and jog in the park, or pump iron to look good. Not so. It's hard work and it's painful work. And it doesn't get any easier as you get older. I'm forty, and I'll be going back with Team Three for my fifth rotation. I'll be out here doing what these guys are doing this afternoon with one of my platoons. It hurts—it always hurts—but it has to be done. You have to prepare to fight—physically and mentally."

The new Ramadi SEALs began their tour where their Squadron One brothers left off, working with their Iraqi army scouts. There were now close to a hundred of them who had received training from the SEALs. With their SEAL mentors now leaving, they were being passed along to another group for training and operational duty. For the outgoing

SEALs, there was the prospect of going home and the relief that comes from not living in a combat zone. For the last six months, they'd led two lives—their operational life, with its decisions, dangers, and strain, and their nonoperational life, which was mostly taken up with preparing for the former. My time in an active combat zone was quite a while back, but I still remember lifting off from our firebase in the lower Mekong Delta and thinking, "Hey, I don't have to go out tonight—or the next. My guys are all safe and we're going home!" It's a feeling to be savored. For the incoming task unit SEAL operators, there's the job ahead. For the new SEALs on their first tour, it's the prospect of going into combat for the first time. After more than two years of training, they're finally going to do it for real. For the veterans, it's taking their skills back to the fight in a new battlespace. And for all but a few of the veterans, this is the first time they will train Iraqi soldiers and take them into battle.

"We all had mixed feelings leaving Ramadi," Jake Hanson said of the final days of his tour. "There were the details of the turnover—getting the Team Three guys familiar with the base and introducing them around, especially to the Army and Marine military transition teams. We took some of them out on break-in operations with our scouts so the *jundis* would understand they'd be working with a new group of SEALs. Given the time and the operational constraints, we felt we'd done a good job with our *jundis*. The Iraqi scouts had started to bond with each other, to work as a team and to work with Americans, something not often seen in the new Iraqi army. Some of them didn't even want other Iraqis to join the battalion scouts or the special missions platoon because they didn't think the new Iraqi scout-recruits were good enough to go out in the streets with them. They had learned to trust one another, and they learned to trust the SEALs and what we were trying to teach them. Our SEALs spent a lot of time with these guys, and we showed them the character of an American warrior—hard work and attention to duty.

"Bottom line, we treated the Iraqi scouts much better than their own chain of command. Toward the end, we treated them as brothers, and they responded by giving us their best efforts. It was a respect issue—very important in dealing with Iraqis. This extended to the cadre of interpreters we worked with as well. So there were a few tears as we left and turned them over to Three. We were glad to be going home, but it was a little bittersweet leaving our scouts and terps.

"As for Jack Williams and his task unit, they came fully prepared to do business. We traded a few bullets with the bad guys on the streets of

Ramadi, but nothing like what was coming. Both Jack and I knew there was a battle coming, and they were going to be in the thick of it. The mean streets we worked during our tour were going to get a lot meaner."

The first order of business for the Squadron Three task unit in Ramadi was to get in sync with their Iraqi *jundis*. "The last task unit did a good job with the scouts," Chief Paul Wagner told me. "But we were new to them and they were new to us. We had to get to know each other. They trusted the SEALs who had just left; now they had to trust us. So we began to train them in groups of anywhere from eight to twenty with some three to five SEALs and an interpreter serving as the training cadre. Even though they'd been trained by the previous task unit, the abilities of the individual *jundis* varied greatly. A few of them really wanted to be with an elite unit; others were just looking for duty that was away from their regular army. And within the scout elements, like the rest of the Iraqi army, there's a lot of turnover as they came and went on leave from their battalion and brigade units. Some went and we never saw them again. We began most training sessions with some veteran scouts, a few new guys, and the few guys that would turn up in the middle of a training session. This turnover was always a problem and something over which we had no control."

Chief Wagner was the task unit chief and was assigned the lead responsibility for training the Iraqi scouts. Wagner grew up in Texas and attended college on a track scholarship at a small parochial school. Then an injury cost him his scholarship and his interest in college. "I was adrift and heading for trouble when I decided to join the Navy. It was the best thing that could have happened to me. If I'd stayed in school and got my degree, I'd have been no better off. This is where I belong." He graduated with Class 221 and was a SEAL well before 9/11. This was his fourth combat rotation.

"We focused on training for the first six weeks after we got to Ramadi. This meant training on the base and conducting training operations off base. On Camp Ramadi, we did range shooting, close-quarter battle, urban-combat training, and basic fire-and-maneuver drills. The only live-fire training we were comfortable with was conducted on the range. Close-quarter work in the kill house and the inside-maneuver drills were not done with live rounds, so they were just movement drills. When we were working on base, we generally worked with them two or three hours a day beginning at 4:00 PM. We also conducted mobility training with them, getting them in and out of Humvees in a tactical manner, and we worked with them using NODs [night-observation devices] and moving at night. We also gave them medical training; very few soldiers in the Iraqi army get medical training, and first aid on the battlefield is a big thing for us."

I asked one of the platoon corpsmen about this training.

"There's not a lot we could do for them, given the time constraints and the language issues, but we gave them a basic two-hour block of medical basics. First we tell them that priority one is to win the firefight—the best medicine is fire superiority. Then we show them how to do what it takes to get the guy who's hurt out of danger and to a safe place where you can treat him. From there it's a simple matter of keeping the blood inside the body—pressure bandages and tourniquets. For them, as for us, casualty evacuation on this battlefield was very quick. Win the fight, stop the blood, call for help."

"Once we got the feel for them, a baseline on what they could and couldn't do," Chief Wagner continued, "we began going out on foot patrols with them. Initially, we operated in the 5-Kilo and Ta'meem districts. These were break-in ops for us and for the scouts who were new to the Iraqi army scout units. We worked on procedures—what we Americans did and were expected to do on patrol and what was expected of them. We'd patrol for a while, then lay up at a safe place and do a quick critique, then patrol some more. On occasion, we'd do a setup on a house, and have the scouts knock on the door to question the residents—see if they had any information for us. If things didn't look right, we'd search the house, or rather the scouts would search the house. They were trained in search techniques, and in an Iraqi home, they knew what to look for better than we did. And we'd keep an eye on them. Most of our scouts are Shia and not from al-Anbar, and the Anbaris looked on the Iraqi army as foreigners. In some ways, this was like a Union army soldier searching a home in the South during the Civil War—not always a cordial encounter. Then we'd continue with the patrol. During training on the base, the ratio of SEALs to scouts might reach one to five or more. But on these outside-the-wire training patrols, we liked it a lot lower, and were seldom comfortable if there were more than two of them for every one of us. When we began going out at night on raids or overwatch operations, we liked it to be down to one of us for one of them."

"The only exception to the 'some of them and some of us' rule," one task unit training petty officer added, "was when we were out with some of the battalion scouts, and they were with one of their company formations. We'd then be along as advisers on these larger patrols. And this was good because the ultimate goal for all the scouts was to operate with only a few of us or none of us—they'd do it all on their own. But even with these larger-scale patrols in the Ta'meem or the 5-K, in the back of our minds were the times ahead when we *and* the scouts would be out conducting an operation together and in a small unit. Only we'd be in some of the more dangerous districts closer to central Ramadi. We were training these scouts with the idea that we'd be going into contested battlespace together. The better they were, the better we'd all be when things got tough. Don't get me wrong; most of the guys in the platoon would rather operate unilaterally—a brother SEAL on one side and brother SEAL on the other. But since we were going outside the wire without them, we wanted to make the *jundis* as good as possible."

"On one of our first patrols," Chief Wagner told me, "not too long after we'd drilled them on fire and movement, we were on patrol up in the 5-Kilo area, out on the edge of the city. On this operation we were moving across this field of tall reeds and got pinned down by enemy sniper fire coming from atop a nearby building. The scouts who were closest to the sniper right away got out some suppressing fire, while the others moved away from the fire and set up a firing position. Then they took up the fire while the others moved. They executed this leapfrog maneuver just as we had rehearsed it at Camp Ramadi."

Soon after the Squadron Three task unit was settled into Shark Base, Jake Williams elected to split his operational components and send a squad, and then a full platoon, to support the 1st Battalion of the 506th Infantry—the U.S. Army battalion that occupied Camp Corregidor. The move was, in part, brought about by a friendly fire incident with the Iraqi army, so a contingent of SEALs was sent to the camp to work with the Iraqi army scouts stationed there. Camp Corregidor was little more that a reinforced combat outpost on the eastern edge of Ramadi, much smaller than the Camp Ramadi–Blue Diamond–Hurricane Point complex in the northwestern portion of the city. It was also decided that the SEALs might be able to help the 1-506 (pronounced "First of the Five-oh-sixth") as they prepared to step up operations in the Al Mala'ab District, a haven for insurgent fighters. Conditions at this battalion outpost were much more austere and isolated than at Camp Ramadi and even Shark Base. The camp took rocket, mortar, and small-arms fire on a daily basis. This relocation of Delta Platoon from the task unit at Shark Base to Corregidor began a bonding of warriors between the Navy SEALs and the famous 1-506. It was Easy Company of this same 1st Battalion of the 506th Parachute Infantry Regiment, 101st Airborne Division that Stephen Ambrose and HBO chronicled in the World War II epic *Band of Brothers*.

"It was a good move tactically and operationally," said Petty Officer Tim Dominico, "but we lived like refugees over in Corregidor." Dominico was a first-tour SEAL and the primary platoon communicator. A slim six-footer, he grew up in Alabama and had worked as a smoke jumper and firefighter before joining the Navy at twenty-seven. "It was 9/11," he said. "I didn't join right away, but after a while I knew that I needed to be a little more involved in fighting our nation's enemies.

"Our quarters at Corregidor amounted to a shabby three-story brick-and-concrete complex that had been bombed out and gutted with fire. There were a few other small units occupying the building. We were assigned some space on the second floor and had to evict the rats to take ownership. It was very primitive, and you could see sections of steel rebar sticking out from the walls. We managed to get our hands on a load of plywood, so we put in some rough partitions and framed in berthing cubicles. The building was once an Iraqi agriculture administration building and at one time was in the hands of the insurgents. As I understand it, the building had taken a small JDAM [Joint Direct Attack Munition—a smart bomb] a few years back. We ran in a power cord so we had some lighting, but we were totally dependent on the Army for chow, a head, and showers. Actually, the heads were Porta-Pottis just outside the building. There was a shower tent nearby, and right before we left, they installed a single shower in our building. We had some limited space in the battalion tactical operations center where we could keep a few computers and plan operations. The camp or base was maybe two hundred by three hundred yards or so, and we were pretty cramped. We were cheek by jowl with the Army. Corregidor was little more than a big combat outpost.

"Camp Corregidor itself was only a few hundred yards from the city, south of the Sufia District and north of the Mala'ab and Zeraa districts. A wall, some razor wire, and some open space were all that separated us from the insurgents in the city to the south and east, and the insurgents moving in and out of the Sufia to the north and west. When we got there, you could see guys out planting IEDs, but our snipers soon put a stop to that. In fact, one of our guys was up in a guard tower looking to make a shot when an incoming RPG punched a hole in the tower and literally took off the stock of his rifle—it was that close! And that was one helluva shot with an RPG from about three hundred yards. We could take fire just about any time of the day and did. If you went to the chow hall or to take a crap, you wore your body armor and helmet. We'd get mortared at least twice a day, either from the Mala'ab or from out in the Sufia District. But the Army guys sucked it up and got on with their job, and so did we. As the platoon communicator, I was one of the first SEALs in Corregidor and worked there for the whole tour. It was quite an experience. Camp Corregidor was a whole different world from the relative comfort and security of Shark Base."

Few first-tour SEALs ever see as much combat as Tim Dominico was to see at Camp Corregidor. He represents a prototype of the new breed of warriors who are coming into the SEAL teams—mature, focused, intelligent, and hardworking. They're in their mid-twenties, and they bring life experience and perspective to the business of becoming a professional warrior. He quickly became a key member of his platoon, and a go-to guy in operational planning and in combat. The battalion commander of the 1-506 called him the best military communicator he'd ever worked with.

Among its duties at Camp Corregidor, the SEAL platoon was called on to train the scout elements of the Iraqi army battalions stationed near the camp. These scouts came from the three battalions of the 1st Brigade of the Iraqi army's 1st Division. This brigade had only been rotated into Ramadi in March 2006. So, by the numbers, these scouts came from the 1-1-1, the 2-1-1, and the 3-1-1 battalions. The SEALs began training the 1-1-1, the scouts from the brigade's 1st Battalion. This brigade, this battalion, and these scouts were from among the oldest and most seasoned units in the new Iraqi army. They were veterans of the fighting in Al Qa'im and had fought alongside Americans before coming to Ramadi. But the limited base facilities at Camp Corregidor made for a restricted training program.

"We had a fifty-yard firing range laid out, so we were able to test their marksmanship," said one of the SEALs from Delta Platoon at Corregidor, "which wasn't all that bad, but there were no facilities to practice combat shooting. As for patrolling, urban-battle training, and fire-and-movement drills, we had to improvise around the camp using buildings and shipping containers. It was realistic training in that you could occasionally take enemy fire in the camp. We gave them a five-day course of instruction, working with them for about two to four hours a day. But these guys knew what they were doing for the most part. They hadn't our skills, or our weapons or radios, but they'd been fighting for a while, just like most of the SEALs in our platoon. We found that about half of them could give a good account of themselves in a fight, and the other half, well, they could follow directions and do the best they could. One or two of them were genuine SEAL material—they were smart, aggressive, and courageous. We began our training with nine of them and finally ended up putting thirty-nine of our brigade's *jundis* through our little course. The drills at Corregidor were a little make-believe because we just didn't have the facilities or the room to maneuver. But we got to know them and they got to know us. I think the time we spent with them at the beginning, restrictive as it was, paid off later on when we were in combat."

I noticed a distinct difference in the comments of the SEAL trainers at Camp Ramadi and the counterparts at Camp Corregidor. From the outset, the Corregidor SEALs seemed to speak better of their scouts than those at Camp Ramadi, even though the Camp Ramadi scouts had worked with SEALs for a much longer period of time.

"SEAL platoons have personalities," Lieutenant Sean Smith told me, "and so do Iraqi brigades and battalions. Our brigade from the 1st Division was much more seasoned than the brigade from the Iraqi 7th over at Camp Ramadi. The same with their scout elements." Sean Smith was the officer in charge, or OIC, of Delta Platoon. He grew up in Houston and graduated from the Naval Academy with the Class of 1999 and with BUD/S Class 241. Smith is a tower—he's six-five, a towheaded blond, and as enthusiastic as a retriever puppy. He has the ability to be both infectious and serious at the same time. He was on his third combat rotation.

"One advantage for us was the close proximity to our scouts at Corregidor," Smith said. "They lived right across Route Michigan, so we could see them on a daily basis. At Shark Base, the guys had to drive over to the main base on Camp Ramadi to pick up their scouts. Then it was another drive to the training areas and ranges. We hadn't the facilities at Corregidor like they did, but we were physically closer to our scouts. Also at Corregidor, we had two scouts who could speak English; one of them was very fluent. He was also a good soldier. On balance, we got on well with our scouts. We had to. Most of our training was on-the-job battlefield training. As soon as we went out the front gate with them, it was game on. We first began our patrols with them at night, then we ventured out in the daytime. They caught onto how we did things on patrol right from the start. Another thing we had going for us was the small number of scouts, and there was very little turnover. We saw the same faces over and over. Often, we never knew just who was going to show up for training or for an operation, but most of them were familiar. With our scouts, like the ones over at Camp Ramadi, there was a wide range of abilities. We quickly had to learn their individual capabilities. We came to like a lot of the scouts, and a few of them we came to trust like brothers."

"Perhaps the biggest difference for us at Shark Base and Camp Ramadi," said Lieutenant Lars Beamon, "is that our scouts seemed to have more battalion and brigade responsibilities that kept them busy—different brigade, different culture." Beamon was the Charlie Platoon OIC working out of Shark Base. He is a Texan and a compact, athletic-looking officer who graduated from the Naval Academy in 1998. He turned down an appointment to West Point because he wanted Annapolis and to be a Navy SEAL. He graduated with BUD/S Class 241, along with Sean Smith. And like Smith, Lars Beamon spent a tour aboard ship before coming to BUD/S. As with all Academy midshipmen aspiring to become SEAL officers, both had wanted SEAL training out of Annapolis. Yet both seemed, at least to me, to have gained a measure of maturity and perspective from their fleet experience. It also speaks to the Naval Academy's SEAL selection process. Here were two proven SEAL combat leaders preparing for a major battle, and somehow neither had made the cut for direct assignment to SEAL training out of the Naval Academy.

"The Iraqi battalions with the Camp Ramadi brigade had broad sector responsibilities in our battlespace," Beamon continued, "and that often kept our scouts in the field with their battalions in support of battalion operations. And then there was the Camp Ramadi–Shark Base thing; it was a trek to get over to see them. We relied on the permanently assigned military transition teams for a lot of our communication and coordination. Sometimes the MiTTs had them involved in other training or operational duties. We really never knew which scouts would be available for training or for a given mission until we went over to pick them up. Fortunately, there were usually one or two familiar faces in any given group of scouts. After a while, we began to look for them. We were glad to see them, and they were glad to see us."

While the individual SEALs and SEAL platoons from Squadron Three were filtering into Shark Base to relieve their brothers from

Squadron One and engaging their Iraqi scout elements, the same kind of relief in place was taking place throughout the task unit. Nowhere was this change-out more important or done with more care than it was within the intelligence and targeting cells. Intelligence was the lifeblood of SEAL and SEAL-Iraqi scout operations.

"The guys from One took us around to meet the Ramadi brigade and battalion S2 staffs," Ensign Rick Hedberg told me. "I'm not sure who was handed off to whom, but we linked up with key members of the intel community in our battlespace. You have to understand that our task unit worked for one chain of command and the Army and Marines worked for another. That relationship was true for the operations side of the house and true for us on the information side. So most of the liaison and cooperation was generated from the bottom up. It began at the working level, and it worked very well. The intelligence staff and Advanced Special Operations section from Squadron One had established excellent working relationships with our Army and Marine counterparts. We'd like to think that our transition with Squadron One was as good or better than within the operational SEALs. The turnover of interpreters was especially important. They were an essential asset. The really good ones had bonded with the guys from the previous task unit, and we were careful to let them know that we newcomers valued them just as much as the guys who were leaving.

"In some ways our transition was more difficult than that of our SEAL operators," Hedberg continued. "The SEALs take all their years of training and experience and adapt those skills to this particular battlespace. Our portfolio *is* this battlespace, and we have to learn it very quickly. In Ramadi there was a lot to learn." Hedberg was the assistant squadron intelligence officer and the senior intel officer assigned to the Ramadi task unit. He graduated from the Naval Academy in 2006. Owing to a kidney disorder that surfaced in his senior year at Annapolis, he became classified as NPQ—not physically qualified. This prevented him from duty aboard surface ships and submarines and kept him out of naval aviation. So he put in for intelligence duty, and on completion of his training, took an assignment to SEAL Team Three. He arrived in Iraq ten months after his graduation from Annapolis. "I might be NPQ," he said, unable to mask a certain pride, "but as far as I know, I'm the first in my class to reach the combat zone.

"We spent a lot of time studying the area of operations prior to deployment, and we were in constant e-mail contact with the guys we were to relieve in Ramadi," Hedberg said, "but you had to be there and see it—and meet the intel professionals from the other units. And you have to read—*really* read. You have to read all the traffic—intelligence generated locally as well as from other in-theater and out-of-theater sources. Then there's the backlog of interrogation reports, which give you a feel for what's transpired over time in the area. You have to read military and OGA-sourced material from any number of reporting entities. It was like drinking from a fire hose. Once in Ramadi all of us in the intel shop worked twenty hours a day, reading and asking questions about what was going on. A comment you remember from a three-month-old interrogation report might jog something you just read in an intelligence summary the previous day, and that leads to developing a target folder.

"The first week I was in Ramadi, we learned that the insurgents were using the University of al-Anbar in Ramadi as a staging area and to launch mortar rounds against our bases and outposts. So we mounted a cordon-and-search type operation to sift through the students, faculty, and others on this embattled campus. In the screening of close to one thousand Anbaris, we found twelve guys with rap sheets. For me, it was a great learning experience; it taught me a lot about asking questions and dealing with the locals. It was also to first time I worked extensively with interpreters. Working through a third person adds another layer to the job and slows the process. But it still has to be done.

"While the SEALs worked with the scouts in the field, we helped the military training teams with the training of the Iraqi brigade and battalion intelligence sections. Working with their intel people was an interesting experience. We taught them about intelligence format and sharing intelligence up and down the chain of command. We also taught them about factual reporting. They come from a culture where facts can be manipulated and half-truths brought forward because this is what those in authority want to hear. We had to help them see that in a combat situation, there is no substitute for factual reporting. The truth, as we interpret it in our culture, is a little different in their culture.

"Above all, we had to sift through the continuous and often voluminous stream of reports—spot reports, intel summaries, interrogation reports, NRC data, and HUMINT reports—to find that information useful to our task unit operational components. Our priority was intelligence that led to targets that matched our capabilities in the battlespace. And targeting information that was unsuitable for our use, we passed along to those conventional components that might be able to use it. It didn't take long for us to pick up on what the previous task unit was doing and build on that intelligence production."

During May and the first part of June, the SEALs and their scouts began pushing farther out into insurgent-controlled territory. In the eastern part of the city, the Camp Corregidor SEALs began to move into the Mala'ab District, while the Shark Base SEALs crossed the Habbaniyah Canal into the Al Warar and Al Hawz districts. These first operations for both platoons were primarily cordon-and-search operations and zone-clearance operations, and often with larger Army units. Most were foot patrols. Going into June, there were sharp exchanges of gunfire on almost all of these.

"We knew a battle in the city was in the offing," Lars Beamon said of the SEALs who were training with the Iraqi scouts in June 2006, "and we had to do what we could to get them ready. Early on they wanted to run whenever they got shot at, even when we were operating in the relative security of the Ta'meem District. We had to show them that the way to handle incoming fire was to react aggressively—fire and maneuver. If we were with them, they would do this—most of the time. We knew and they knew things were going to get ugly in Ramadi, and we were going to be doing a lot more than foot patrols in the Ta'meem or the 5-Kilo. All that training from the previous task unit, and what we could give them in the two months since we arrived, was going to be put to the test."

"Each time we entered the Mala'ab, we took fire—and returned fire," Sean Smith said of the initial operations out of Camp Ramadi. "The deeper we went into the district, the stiffer the resistance became to our presence there. One of the things we brought to the table was an aggressive attitude toward the insurgents. Some of the Iraqi units felt the enemy was ten feet tall. We convinced our scouts from the 1-1-1 that we could beat these guys. I think that encouraged the whole Iraqi 1-1-1 battalion to fight strong in the Mala'ab."

In this spring and early summer of 2006, the American and Iraqi forces were dug in at Camp Ramadi, Camp Blue Diamond, and Hurricane Point on the banks of the Euphrates on the northwest side of Ramadi. Camp Corregidor, manned by the 1st Battalion of the 506th and Delta Platoon, was a besieged outpost on the eastern side of the city. These bases supported a number of smaller strongpoints scattered across Ramadi, including a very brave and embattled company of marines at the Government Center outpost in central Ramadi. All were under the threat of continual attack, and most took fire on a daily basis. The marines at the Government Center fought off continuous attacks. The influence of the insurgent elements in Ramadi, and the violence they brought to the city, had all but confined the Army and the Marines to their bases. Most patrols were made in force and usually resulted in contact. The insurgent grip on the city and the province also threatened the traditional authority of the Anbari tribal leaders. At this juncture, there were really few options left for the Americans and their Iraqi army allies in Ramadi. It was becoming increasingly evident that they either had to drive the insurgents from the city or be forced to hunker down on their bases and in their bunkers, and watch the insurgent presence continue to escalate. It was unclear just exactly how they would rid the provincial capital of these insurgents, but they now realized that only a major effort would drive them out.

In May 2006, there was a change in the American military leadership in Ramadi. The very capable and well-respected Colonel John Gronski of the 2nd Brigade Combat Team of the 28th Infantry Division, Pennsylvania National Guard, was relieved by Colonel Sean MacFarland of the 1st Brigade Combat Team, 1st Armored Division. John Gronski and his National Guard team had been in Ramadi since January 2005. Now a new leader stepped into the role of the commander of AO Topeka. Colonel MacFarland might have been new to Ramadi, but he was far from new to the insurgency in al-Anbar.

Sean MacFarland was born in Albany, New York, and raised just up the Mohawk River in Canajoharie. MacFarland graduated from West Point in 1981. He is a tanker, and most of his experience, both in his staff and command tours, had been with armored units. He holds a master's degree in aerospace engineering from Georgia Tech. MacFarland has an offhand, self-deprecating manner, and bears a striking physical resemblance to Mister Rogers of the TV program, something the SEALs in Ramadi picked up on immediately. None of this would seem to fit the mold of the commander assigned the difficult task of reclaiming the capital of al-Anbar province. But MacFarland had experience in this kind of operation; he had just come from Tall 'Afar. This new brigade commander was a counterinsurgency veteran, having worked with the highly regarded Colonel H. R. McMaster in northern Iraq. So along with an easygoing and approachable demeanor, he brought a great deal of experience to Ramadi. He also brought with him a number of seasoned veterans, what one Army officer called the Tall 'Afar mafia. MacFarland knew what had to be done, and he had a good idea of how he was going to go about it.

There were two battle plans on the table. For simplicity, I'll call them the Fallujah model and the Tall 'Afar model. The Fallujah model called for a full-on assault—a single operation. The line of this assault was to begin from the eastern part of the city in the vicinity of Camp Corregidor and sweep east to west with the Euphrates River, the battle-line border to the north, and the Habbaniyah Canal as the final objective of the sweep. As one Army officer put it, "We would just line up shoulder-to-shoulder and push the bastards west into the water." The Tall 'Afar model was a little more subtle. It was a modified inkblot strategy that called for a rolling assault—taking the city one neighborhood at a time. There was also a political dimension to this issue. No one, it seems, wanted a solution that would (1) overtly trash a major Iraqi city and (2) draw the media attention that attended the battle for Fallujah in late 2004. The 2004 assault destroyed a great deal of Fallujah, which, because of its intensity and scope, created a large number of refugees. A great many of the residents of Fallujah were caught between the insurgent forces and the advancing skirmish lines of marines. Those who could fled the city.

"To some extent," explained the new brigade commander, "the final plan for Ramadi was one born of necessity. Ramadi is significantly larger than either of the other two Anbari cities. We simply lacked the overwhelming force to achieve a Fallujah-style offensive operation." To underscore the colonel's point, the forces under his command were about the size of those at Fallujah, but Ramadi was more than twice the size of Fallujah. No one knew the actual numbers, but the enemy entrenched in Ramadi appeared to be far more numerous. "I had a few companies, which I could use as a 'swing force' to weight my main effort, which was to focus a battalion task force on the taking of one neighborhood at a time. So I formed the basic framework for my plan within a few days of arriving in Ramadi, along toward the end of May. In many ways, Tall 'Afar was a model for what I wanted to accomplish in Ramadi. In Tall 'Afar, we achieved penetration of all parts of the city with the Iraqi security forces, and we were making progress in forming a police department. We built a couple of new combat outposts where we thought enemy resistance was strongest, and that seemed to have a good effect.

"The significant advantage we had in Tall 'Afar was a strong mayor. He was my 'go-to guy,' and we worked closely with him on developing reconstruction projects. The 3rd Iraqi army division there was progressing well at all levels and they added a measure of stability. When we arrived in Ramadi, things were different. There was no police force, no mayor, and no city council. On the Iraqi side, I had a newly formed Iraqi division and very limited coalition presence in the core of the city. More important, I had no Iraqi civilian authority, no go-to guy, who could help us interface with the community at large—the citizens of Ramadi. So for a number of reasons, we were forced to take Ramadi a bit at a time over a period of time."

When this plan for the Battle for Ramadi was put in play, the action became more like a series of vicious skirmishes than a single, protracted battle. The plan called for establishing a series of combat outposts, or COPs—small fortified, permanently manned bases close to existing strongpoints, strategically placed, and gradually moving into the heart of the city. These COPs were to be sited in territory that in the spring of 2006 was fully under the control of AQI. The strategy was to place these outposts in such a fashion that they would be mutually supportive and incrementally deny control of the surrounding area to the insurgents. Each new COP was to reclaim a neighborhood or section of the city. This was the same "take, hold, build" strategy that had proved successful in reclaiming Al Qa'im and Tall 'Afar from insurgent control. But Ramadi was much bigger than either of those cities. The insurgents they would have to defeat were seasoned fighters, many of them veterans of the fighting in Fallujah, Al Qa'im, and Tall 'Afar. MacFarland's strategy was a proven one, but it had its drawbacks. While it allowed the Americans and the Iraqis to concentrate their forces and efforts on a single neighborhood, it also allowed the insurgents, whose tactics and mobility were every bit as good as our own, to resist in mass at each of these new outposts. The AQI elements in Ramadi were not going to give up without a fight. It was a task that promised to be a bloody confrontation, for the American soldiers and marines, for the new Iraqi army, and for the Navy SEALs.

"I had good people, many of them veterans of Tall 'Afar," Colonel MacFarland said, "and they knew what had to be done. My S2 [brigade intelligence officer] helped me determine the locations for the initial five COPs. After that, I selected the locations based on discussions with my task force [battalion] commanders, my S2 and, eventually, with input from the Iraqi brigade commanders and the tribal leaders."

This might be a good time to step back and take stock of the conditions in Ramadi and al-Anbar in June 2006. On the eve of the Battle for Ramadi and what may be, on reflection, one of the most significant and gallant chapters in the battle history of the Navy SEALs, let's again review the forces driving the dynamic in Ramadi.

All across Iraq we were paying dearly for the inattention to the power vacuum in Iraq created with the ouster of Saddam Hussein, the dismemberment of the Baath Party, and the disbanding of Saddam's largely Sunni army. Nowhere was this more apparent than in al-Anbar province. With the capital city virtually lawless, criminals joined the jihadists and the former Iraqi army soldiers in an insurgency that attacked American and Iraqi army patrols venturing out from their bases. The presence of foreign fighters was small, but highly influential. These were the true believers, and most of the suicide bombers came from these non-Iraqi insurgents. To add gasoline to this already combustible mixture, they had *plenty* of weapons and armament. Saddam Hussein had created multiple caches of weapons and ammunition along the Euphrates River Valley with large stockpiles at the Iraqi air force base at Habbaniyah and the Republican Guard compound near Fallujah. As Saddam's army fell into disarray, these arsenals were quickly looted.

As we mishandled the situation in Iraq and al-Anbar, al-Qaeda took full advantage of our mistakes and moved in. In many ways, they played on the Anbaris' natural resentment of outsiders and co-opted the insurgency. Yet, in the critical spring of 2006, there were already signs that the AQI-backed insurgent movement was having difficulties in al-Anbar. The Americans and the government in Baghdad might be resented, but AQI was becoming impossible in their dealings with the tribes.

The sheikhs are the key tribal leaders, and their leadership position within the tribes is social, cultural, and economic. Tribal commercial activity, which was everything from legal enterprise to cross-border smuggling, was threatened by al-Qaeda. Because tribal culture, like that of organized crime, is one of competing interests and turf management, there's a history of bickering and petty jealousy among the tribal sheikhs. This was a tailor-made situation for AQI to move in, isolate, and try to control these Anbari tribal sheikhs. When one of the sheikhs objected to the activity of AQI in their area, the sheik and his extended family became targets. When someone takes power tools to your brothers and your children, you're inclined to do what they tell you to do. Or at least you allow them to move about in your tribal area undisturbed. When the tribal leaders began to understand what was taking place, they tried to do something about it. But the life expectancy of a tribal sheikh who resisted AQI was not long. In its attempt to crush the tribal leadership, AQI was in effect going after the only functioning civil authority in al-Anbar. To the extent it succeeded, AQI would have a free hand to exploit the province. This bold and brutal approach did much to bring the tribal leadership to heel, but there was growing resentment for AQI within the tribes. It also opened the door to future tribal-American-Baghdad-government cooperation.

In June 2006, there were some twenty-one tribes in the greater Ramadi area. Only six of those were friendly to the Americans; the rest were hostile or, at best, sitting on the fence. The people of Ramadi were caught in the middle. The tribes and the people knew there was a fight coming, and they were waiting to see who was going to be the winner. On the eve of this battle, a significant event took place in Baqubah, a city twenty-five miles north of Baghdad and some sixty-five miles east of Ramadi. On 8 June Abu Musab al-Zarqawi was killed in an air strike. Just prior to his death, al-Zarqawi had proclaimed al-Qaeda in Iraq as the new caliphate with Ramadi as its capital. The death of this charismatic insurgent leader would have little bearing on the initial stages of the battle, but it would later serve as a last-ditch, rallying standard for AQI in al-Anbar.

Once the decision was made to take back Ramadi and the incremental, inkblot strategy was approved by the American high command and the government in Baghdad, there left only the execution of the battle plan. It was time for Colonel Sean MacFarland, the Sheriff of Ramadi, to step onto the street. When I told Sean of the title of the book, and my literary characterization of his role as the Sheriff of Ramadi, he smiled sheepishly and shook his head. "Don't forget," he said, "that I had a lot of help. And that some true American heroes died to make Ramadi safe for the Anbari people." I like to think of MacFarland as the Sheriff and his Army and Marine battalion commanders as his deputies. The Ramadi SEAL task unit commander acted as an important and valued "special deputy."

As for the Navy SEALs and the Ramadi task unit, their role in the brigade battle plan and their participation in the Battle of Ramadi evolved as the battle unfolded. In the overall scheme of things, they were a small element, and their operational portfolio did not require that they go out into the streets and fight in the way the Army and Marine, infantry and armor, were going to be asked to fight. They had options. And while the SEAL task unit was not MacFarland's to command, Jack Williams saw this as an opportunity to do what he had come to Ramadi to do—to make a difference.

"I had my marching orders from Commander Garrison," Jack Williams said. "We were to continue to train the Iraqi army scouts and make them better soldiers. We were also to conduct tribal engagement and to make ourselves useful to the brigade commander. But I had a great deal of latitude in the disposition of my task unit and in executing those orders. When Colonel MacFarland arrived, he was tasked with the job of taking Ramadi. I think he saw his job as twofold. First, he had to execute his battle plan, which became one of pushing out into the city and establishing outposts—to reclaim Ramadi step-by-step. Secondly, he had to engage the local tribes and encourage them to work with us against al-Qaeda. When I learned the Army and the Marines were going into the streets to take back Ramadi, I told Colonel MacFarland the same thing I told Colonel Gronski: 'Sir, what can we do to help?' When the rubber met the road, he basically wanted one thing from me; he wanted me to kill insurgents. So he incorporated the SEALs in his battle plan in that role. We became one of his supporting elements, just like his armor and his on-call air assets. We can and did do a lot more for him, but that's primarily how he used us to take back the city of Ramadi. We joined the battle by helping to establish the combat outposts."

There were variations on the theme of establishing a combat outpost. In many ways it was a complex venture with a lot of moving parts. In other ways it was a very straightforward, kinetic, and confrontational operation. Yet no two were alike save for the fact that they were bloody encounters. From the Army and Marine point of view it was a difficult but proven counterinsurgency tactic. For the insurgents it was an in-your-face surge or push that moved the line of scrimmage farther into their territory. For the SEALs it was an offensive operation that allowed them to use their direct-action skills to best advantage.

In early June 2006 the SEALs in Ramadi were preparing to engage the enemy in a way they had not done in their forty-five-year history. They would still operate with the *jundis* that they and the previous task unit had trained, and the intelligence and targeting cells would continue to crank out information on specific insurgent targets. But the focus of

SEAL operations would be to support the 1st Brigade Combat Team, 1st Armored Division of the U.S. Army in the battle to retake Ramadi. When the Sheriff stepped into the streets with his soldiers and marines, the Navy SEALs would back his play.

The order of battle on the eve of this struggle pitted four American Army battalions, one Marine battalion, and two Iraqi army brigades against an unknown and fluid number of entrenched insurgents. For the Americans there were the 1-35 and 1-37 armored battalions at Camp Ramadi, the 1-6 mechanized infantry battalion at Camp Blue Diamond, the 3/8 Marine infantry battalion at Hurricane Point, and 1-506 infantry battalion at Camp Corregidor. The Iraqi 7th Brigade was at Camp Ramadi with the Iraqi 1st Brigade just across Route Michigan from Camp Corregidor. All told, there were some 5,500 Americans and 2,300 Iraqis going into the Battle of Ramadi. Among them was a Navy SEAL task unit with thirty-some combat-ready SEALs.

The battle began on 17 June with two combat outposts being sited simultaneously in the southwest and southeast sides of the city. A third COP was established on 18 June in the southeast sector near Camp Corregidor. The outposts were named COP Iron, COP Spear, and COP Eagles Nest, respectively. These initial COPs were designed to block insurgent infiltration activity from the south. It took several days of fighting and building to seize and harden each of these three outposts and turn back the inevitable insurgent counterattacks. Over the course of the next seven months, thirteen COPs and several Iraqi police stations were established, then defended on a daily basis. SEALs were involved from the beginning in nearly all of these operations. Each of these outpost operations was an incursion into insurgent-controlled territory. Each one was different, but each was always combative—a story unto itself. I've chosen one of these operations as a surrogate for the SEAL's role in this battle as it related to these outposts in the Battle of Ramadi. It was the establishment of COP Falcon in southwest Ramadi on 25 June. This important COP was located at the intersection of Baseline and Sunset roads, in the heart of Indian country.

"There are a lot of moving parts to putting in a COP," Captain Mike Bajema told me. "It's a multilayered process that requires the organization of diverse forces and the staging of a lot of materials." Mike Bajema was the Bravo Company commander with the 1-37 battalion of the American 1st Armored Division at Camp Ramadi, and a veteran of close to *three years* of continuous duty in Iraq. Bajema grew up in Seattle and graduated from Washington State. He's an armor officer, a tanker, and professional soldier to the core.

"The site of a prospective COP is chosen by the higher-ups with some thought to its role in the overall battle plan, the logistics, terrain, and even the psychological impact it might have on the enemy and the people in the surrounding area. Lives are at risk, so each one is sited very carefully. Once a site is identified, the next step is for the company commander who will be in command of the COP to make a reconnaissance of the area, and, if possible, to put eyes on the buildings that will form the COP—kind of a combat suitability study. In the case of COP Falcon, I was the company commander, and I led the reconnaissance of the area, three days before we went in. It was an armored reconnaissance, and when we got close to the area, we began to get hit with IEDs. In those days, when you drove around Ramadi in a tank or a Bradley [Fighting Vehicle], expect IEDs. I did get close enough to see that the buildings we wanted to use would be inadequate, and we would have to have more structures than we'd initially planned on for this COP. This was a residential area, and our original plan was to occupy four residences. We ended up with eleven at COP Falcon. The taking and occupation of residents' houses are done with a lot of care and approvals that go up to the brigade level and beyond. We're not exactly the ideal tenants you want in your home, but the Iraqis we had to relocate for COP Falcon were well and fairly compensated.

"Once we've confirmed the location, a lot of planning and organization has to be done in short period of time. The quicker we can move, the better chance we have of achieving surprise. The taking of a COP is a battalion-plus operation with help from the engineers and the SEALs. The engineers take satellite imagery and any photoreconnaissance imagery, and design the outpost perimeter. This means they have to determine what exterior walls exist that they can make use of, and what concrete walls are needed to create a completely walled, defensible compound. The Army engineers, the Navy Seabees, and the battalion support platoon, along with my headquarters element, have to figure out how much is needed in the way of concrete barriers, food, water, concertina wire, generators, plywood, two-by-fours, ammunition, sandbags, et cetera, et cetera. In other words, what will it will take to build the COP and what will it take initially to sustain the COP? The materials, type and quantities, have to be calculated, staged, and some estimate made of how many flatbed trucks and how many trips it will take to move the materials from Camp Ramadi to the new COP location. For COP Falcon alone, the initial push called for 10,000 sandbags. In addition to erecting the walls, we had to build out eight fixed rooftop-fighting positions. We had to plan for new wiring, lighting, power distribution, and communications. There had to be a forklift at the COP to unload pallets and move concrete barriers into place. There also had to be a very brave combat forklift driver. The build-out was a seventy-eight-hour mission with the first forty-eight hours the most critical. I had to plan for rest breaks for all the engineers, builders, and drivers. The actual mission began with getting the security package in place, and that started with the Navy SEALs."

"We had gone in a few nights earlier to do our own recon of this COP site," Lars Beamon said of the COP Falcon operation. "It was one of several maritime operations we conducted in Ramadi." COP Falcon was the first joint combat operation conducted by Captain Bajema and Lieutenant Beamon. There would be more, as the SEALs would soon sortie often from COP Falcon into southwest Ramadi. Their relationship from the beginning was prototypical of the Army-SEAL bonding. Here's Mike Bajema on Lars Beamon: "We're brothers from different mothers." Lars Beamon said of Bajema, "I never met a more capable and dedicated warrior than Mike Bajema."

"We inserted by Marine SURC [Small Unit Riverine Craft] off the Habbaniyah Canal and patrolled in on foot," Beamon said of the SEAL recon. "The Marines have some great boats—quiet, well-armed, and with convenient bow-entry doors. The marines who man them know their business and are very professional on the water. We were very comfortable having them insert and extract us on missions. Once ashore we conducted a careful reconnaissance. We made a point to move about an extended area so we wouldn't tip off the exact location of the new COP. Yet we were able to get some good IR pictures of the COP buildings. This was a pretty dangerous area, down on the edge of the Al Mualemeen District. When we got to the neighborhood where the COP was to be sited, we found two guys in the street planting an IED. We shot them both. Then we completed our recon and got back to the boats."

The day before the operation was to kick off, a long train of trucks, tanks, supplies, and staged materials were carefully assembled at Camp Ramadi. Then there were extensive briefings for all units involved. There were final operational orders to be given, communications plans distributed and radio checks performed, premission inspections held, and a massive amount of details that needed attention. Captain Mike Bajema was everywhere. Everyone involved were professionals and pretty much knew their jobs, but Bajema checked everything. This would be be his COP and his company's home for the next six months or more.

After dark on the evening of 24 June, an expanded SEAL element was again inserted by Marine SURCs. Those living in the houses that would compose the COP were still unaware that their world was about to change. The SEALs, their EOD techs, a Marine ANGLICO (Air Naval Gunfire Liaison Company) air controller, interpreters, and their contingent of scouts quietly made their way to the objective. They were all traveling heavy, as they would be out several days, and, in anticipation of heavy fighting, they carried a great deal of ammunition.

"We didn't have to wait long to make contact," Beamon said, "as we killed an armed insurgent on the way in. It let the Army know we were on the job; when they rolled up, there was a muj facedown in the street at the entrance to their new COP. We went into the main house, a tall three-story residence. The scouts and the terps explained to the residents what was coming, and they took it stoically. These are people used to war. We set up shooting positions in the upper stories, and called Mike to tell him we were in place. Our job now was to provide a sniper overwatch along the routes that the lead Army elements were going to use to get to the COP location."

Since this area was known to be liberally sprinkled with IEDs, the Dagger clearance teams came in first, ahead of the armor. These brave soldiers and their heavily armed vehicles are charged with route clearance—in this case from Camp Ramadi to COP Falcon. These are the IED-removal specialists. They have a variety of equipment from specially configured Bradley Fighting Vehicles to large trucks called Buffalos that look a lot like garbage trucks. These vehicles have wire roller brushes, mechanical arms, and other physical-removal apparatus. They also emit a broad spectrum of radio frequency energy to disrupt radio-controlled or cell-phone-initiated IEDs. There is nothing subtle about a Dagger Team. They have racks of spotlights and they make a lot of noise—audibly and electronically. And, again, they are manned by some of the bravest soldiers in the battlespace. The SEALs watched as they approached, specifically looking for insurgents with RPGs who could threaten the Dagger Team vehicles.

Next comes the armor, the regular M3 Bradleys and the M1A2 Abrams tanks. They follow the Dagger Teams in and fan out around the COP to provide a cordon of security around the site. Close behind them is a company of infantry soldiers for additional security. There needs to be an area sufficiently cleared around the Falcon site in order to protect the builders of the COP. This could be a radius of a city block or more. With armor and infantry in place, Captain Bajema, his Bravo Company Bulldogs (the nickname for the soldiers of Bravo Company of the 1-37 infantry), and their supporting elements come in and occupy the buildings. For COP Falcon, Bajema has two mechanized infantry platoons, a mortar platoon used as a light infantry platoon, a tank platoon, an engineering platoon, and a headquarters platoon. As Mike Bajema and his people move in, Lars Beamon and his snipers move out. Sometimes the SEALs will leave an overwatch element at the COP, but not this time. They patrol out from the new COP, past the infantry and armor, to set up sniper overwatch positions along the routes they've determined the insurgents are most likely to use to mount a counterattack.

"We liked to get out and into our shooting positions well before daylight," one of the platoon snipers told me. "Usually we've identified the buildings where we wanted to set up, but sometimes we'd make a last-minute decision to change from one to another. It becomes an issue with the security of the position and the fields of fire. It seems as if it's always a compromise between good shooting positions and good security—offense and defense. It's never a perfect world, and in Ramadi we nearly always had to trade off one for the other. No two overwatches are the same. We like a building that has high shooting positions and fields of fire along two avenues—more if we can find the right location. This is not rocket science, and the bad guys know what makes a good shooting perch as well as we do. As much as we want the good shooting positions, we're always looking for a building that doesn't have too many blind spots—avenues of approach where the enemy can sneak up and get close."

I spoke with a number of SEALs about these operations and their accounts varied along a familiar theme. This might be a good time to outline the mechanics of a sniper overwatch as they evolved in the Battle of Ramadi. On occasion, a suitable abandoned structure was found, but for the most part they were residences that were occupied, and the occupants had to be dealt with. This was done in various ways, by a polite knock on the door up to a full-on explosive breaching and building takedown, but usually the former. The residents were told what was happening and given assurance that they'd be paid for their inconvenience. Once the SEAL element went inside, no one was allowed to leave until the mission was finished. Sometimes these residents were cordial and amenable, and made tea for their surprise guests; other times they were withdrawn and hostile. But the work had to go on. In most cases, the scouts held the residents on the lower floor and tended to security while the SEAL shooters took to the upper floors or rooftops. Depending on the building and its configuration, it takes a while to get set up. And it also depends on how many guns were sent in for the overwatch. When there were no suitable shooting stations from windows or rooftops, the latter proving dangerous as the battle wore on, a hole had to be made in the walls for the sniper-rifle barrels. This was sometimes done with a loophole charge—a quarter-pound block of C-4 explosive to punch a shooting hole in the adobe-style walls. Most Iraqi homes and buildings were of a cinder-block, stucco-covered type of construction. This made for solid defensive shooting positions but was often hard to punch holes in for sniper work. Here, again, the residents were compensated for this damage. That said, it's hard to picture some American GIs in a French farmhouse paying for any damage they might have caused while they fought the Germans, but that's how it was done in Ramadi. The Iraqi scouts held security in the lower floors and watched the residents while the SEAL snipers looked over their precision weapons and waited for insurgents. Once secured and sited, the residence became an overwatch position, sometimes called an OP.

"Once the SEALs got in place on the outer perimeter," Mike Bajema said of the Falcon operation, "we were as prepared as we could be to defend the battlespace around the COP. Now the Army engineers, the Navy Seabees, and the support elements rolled into Falcon and started a forty-eight-hour nonstop build-out of the site. Trucks began to ferry equipment and building materials in from Camp Ramadi, often taking sniper fire as they came and went. They dropped more than two hundred twelve-foot concrete-wall T-barriers, set up two thousand meters of concertina, and strung God knows how many feet of electrical wire. It was a minor construction miracle."

"Those of us on the operational end of things often don't understand, or get the chance to appreciate, the work of the engineers," Lieutenant Commander Jack Williams said of the COP construction crews, "but they were totally awesome." Williams came into COP Falcon with armor elements to see his SEALs in their initial overwatch position at the COP site. He remained there after they moved out into the outlying overwatch positions to ensure that amid all the commotion, their locations and area clearances were known to other friendly units. "It takes some courage to do what we do, but in my opinion it takes a whole different kind of courage to keep your mind on your job—unloading trucks, setting up barriers, installing generators—while insurgents are out there trying to kill you. They worked like dogs, eighteen hours a day or more—exposed, wearing helmets and body armor in 115° heat. Those Army engineers and Seabees were true heroes. When they were building those combat outposts, all of us worked to keep them safe. We SEALs stood in their shadow; they were nothing short of magnificent."

Inside the perimeter of the new COP, engineers and soldiers alike worked at a fever pitch, laying concertina wire, moving supplies, and carrying sandbags amid the drone of generators. Outside the outpost grounds, between the new concrete-barrier walls and the tanks and Bradleys on the outer security perimeter, soldiers patrolled the streets, carefully searching the upper stories of buildings for insurgent activity. Skirmishes happened often. Overhead, F/A-18 fighters and drone aircraft circled the new COP while keeping human and electronic eyes on the surrounding area. At night, there were AC-130 gunships overhead as well. And well outside the foot patrols and the armor, Lars Beamon and his snipers kept watch on the streets of Ramadi, specifically along the routes the insurgents might take to get to those building COP Falcon. This was a relatively new game for the SEALs and the insurgents, and a learning experience for both.

SEALs train for this and know how to conduct sniper overwatches, but usually in the context of covering a single special mission, such as a raid or an assault, or to protect a conventional force patrolling in the street. They also train for these overwatch operations with the idea that they would be shooting from positions unknown to or hidden from the enemy. And for the most part, their training is for short-duration missions. Now they were going out and sitting in shooting positions from two to four days at a time. Sometimes the objective of the overwatch was area denial, as with COP Falcon, and sometimes it was to provide top cover for soldiers and marines patrolling in the streets in support of an extended combat operation, like a cordon-and-search operation. The insurgents quickly became adept at locating these overwatch positions. And if the SEALs managed to set up in an overwatch undetected, that advantage went away with the first shot taken. With this first shot, the overwatch often became nothing more than an elevated, covered position from which to engage the insurgents in a sustained gun battle.

The insurgents knew the city and the neighborhoods far better than the Americans. If they didn't intuitively know the location of the best and most likely positions the overwatch might use, they quickly learned. They also learned how to move in the dead spaces where they were screened from their enemy's fields of fire, both from the COPs and from the sniper OPs. For the insurgents moving on the street, these were life-and-death lessons in trigonometry; those who didn't master this skill, or were careless or less nimble, were quickly killed. They learned from bitter experience just how accomplished these sailors with sniper rifles could be. The SEALs took a grim harvest of insurgents in Ramadi, especially early on during the building of the initial COPs. In many cases, each of these insurgent deaths was a mistake on their part—and a lesson learned. They soon began to understand the methods and tactics of these skilled urban shooters and to develop countermeasures.

"Shooting these guys was very easy at the beginning," a SEAL sniper told me. "They were careless. One day there were these two muj heading for a new COP on a motor scooter. One had an AK-47 and the other an RPG launcher. One of our snipers got them both with a single round— one shot, two kills. But it gradually got harder. It was a Darwinian thing. We shot most of the stupid ones, and that left the smarter ones to evolve and survive. But we evolved as well. And even for some of the hard-core fighters out there, all they had to do was make one wrong move at the wrong time or take one too many chances. When they crossed an open area, we might not get the first one, but we'd get the second—and the third if they were dumb enough to try it. We're SEALs, and we were very good when we got to Ramadi. For the insurgents in Ramadi or who came to Ramadi, they became good or died in the process."

SEAL contributions to the battle extended well past precision shooting. In their role in Ramadi as "another warrior in the battlespace" they came to be looked on by the conventional forces as a brother warrior rather than a special warrior. Yet few warriors arrive in the battlespace better prepared or with more extensive training. Most first-tour SEALs will have trained for *two-and-a-half years* before they go in harm's way. Given that they have a maritime skill set that can command a third of that time, it's still far more comprehensive than the basic and advanced infantry training afforded new soldiers and marines. These sailors train and drill in ground assault and fire-and-movement—repetitively, and in different kinds of terrain. They practice these disciplines at all levels of training with live fire. Jack Williams likes to tell the story of one of his new assistant platoon OICs on his first combat tour. He was in one of the COPs when a call for help came in. One of the Army military transition teams and some of their Iraqis were pinned down by snipers and unable to move. This young officer quickly collected a squad of SEALs and *jundis* in two Humvees and hurried to their location. When he got to the MiTT and the Army major in charge, they were still taking fire from the insurgent snipers. He immediately sent a SEAL-scout element to flank them. With suppressing fire from the flank, he split his remaining element into two groups and began to leapfrog toward the enemy position. They were able to kill one of the insurgents and drive the others off.

"You guys were terrific," the major said in thanking his rescuers. "You must have a lot of experience in urban combat."

"Not really," the SEAL, a junior-grade lieutenant, replied. "This was my first firefight."

While the Ramadi SEALs were learning about the conventional forces and making themselves useful, the Army and, to a lesser extent, the Marines were learning about SEALs. This was the first time in their history that SEALs had operated in direct and continuous support of conventional forces in combat. When Jack Williams went to Colonel John Gronski, and later to Colonel Sean MacFarland, and made his SEALs available for brigade-support duty, this put Navy SEAL–U.S. Army relations on a totally new footing—at least in Ramadi. The respect went both ways. The SEALs had nothing but admiration for the soldiers and marines. Lars Beamon said it this way: "In writing this book, Mister Couch, I want you to never lose sight of one thing. The bravest and noblest men in uniform are those Army specialists and Marine lance corporals. They're our most courageous and patriotic fighting men, and they're out there day in and day out. For many of them, it's becoming year in and year out. We SEALs are honored to call them brother warriors."

Over at Camp Corregidor, Lieutenant Sean Smith and the Delta Platoon SEALs were bonding with the 1-506. At Corregidor they lived, ate, and worked in close proximity with the Army. At the daily battalion staff meetings, Sean or a platoon representative was present. The SEAL camouflage uniforms and battle dress differed from those worn by the Army. Smith found Army uniforms so that his SEALs would look like their Army counterparts. More important, during the Battle of Ramadi, they went out into the streets and bled with them. "We asked the 1-506 if we could wear their battalion insignia on our battle dress," Smith said. The insignia of this storied battalion is the famous ace-of-spades patch. "We were honored that they allowed us to do this. We earned the right to call ourselves soldiers."

But what did the Army think of these SEALs and the SEAL task unit in Ramadi? Many had experience with Army Special Forces and a few had worked with the classified special missions units. The majority of the soldiers and marines at Ramadi had never worked with SEALs, so I made it a point to ask them what they thought of these sailors in their battlespace. I started with Mike Bajema.

"My first impression of the SEALs was in meeting Jack Williams and his senior chief petty officer in the brigade operations center at Camp Ramadi. It was just a few days after we arrived. We shook hands and he nearly broke all the bones in my right hand. Simply put, Jack appeared as this massive, intense, fighting machine—very intimidating. But one thing that came across right away with Jack and the other SEALs I met that day was their honesty. They didn't care about a man's branch of service or rank or physical size. I found that the SEALs tended to judge a man on his character, his courage under fire, and his determination to kill the enemy. I was never treated as anything less than an equal and always given the respect of being a different type of warrior on the battlefield. My preconception of the SEALs was solely based on my experience working with the Army Special Forces teams. Those experiences were not positive, as the Army SOF community, in my experience, is quick to assert their sense of importance in most situations. First meetings are always a 'tab check' of who has the most Army [shoulder] tabs and school identifiers—airborne, Ranger, Special Forces, sapper, et cetera. This never happened with the SEALs. They only cared how a man performs or reacts when in contact with the enemy—in a tank, as dismounted infantry, as a medic, or as an operations center communicator. They just wanted a man to do his job like his buddies lives depended on it—and in Ramadi they often did.

"The Army SOF community I worked with previously was very reluctant to share their information with conventional forces. It seems like the information they had is too valuable or too secret to get passed on to others in the battlespace. The SEALs always followed the rules of disclosure, but they worked really hard on passing information down to the conventional guys on the ground. In return I passed all informants

I came across to the SEALs to develop as sources, as I was restricted as to how I could task these informants in the gathering of intelligence. The SEALs had the specially trained folks that could task and even pay sources for information.

"After that first day, after we seized COP Falcon, the SEALs and Bulldogs were joined at the hip. It was a team atmosphere. There was no rivalry—just how each group could support the other in killing AQI fighters. When those SEALs first came back into COP Falcon, some of them had been out there seventy-two hours on sniper overwatch. They were nearly heat casualties—hungry and dead tired. Still, they would join a line of Bulldog soldiers to carry endless supplies of sandbags to the rooftop fighting positions before eating and resting. That's what really makes them special—they don't act special. We worked with the SEALs of Charlie Platoon of SEAL Team Three in Ramadi for those first three terrible months, and they were always there for us. And we'd go anywhere in Ramadi to help them out if they got in trouble. They were our brothers."

"Did you ever have any reservations about working with the SEALs?" I asked.

"My only reservation was on how the chain of command would work if the SEALs were operating in my battlespace. As the local battlefield commander and 'landowner,' it was my responsibility to command the activity in my area. The SEALs had a separate chain of command. Before we started to work together, I was concerned that the SEALs would be rogue operators. I thought that they might refuse to work within our parameters or just to leave me in the dark—go off on their own and do their own thing. After the first day on the battlefield, this concern was quickly erased. They always briefed me ahead of time, and they would send their after-action reports through their chain of command and keep my operations center in the loop. We did the same by including their TOC in our reporting. Basically, we traded all requests for clearance and all situation reports to fully sync our operations and theirs. This created one force out of two separate groups, and no one was confused by the other's actions. And we could support each other if the need arose.

"I think what made us a big fan of the SEALs," Bajema continued, "was the respect they showed us. Here we were a company of dogface Army soldiers, and here they were, these BTFs—big tough frogmen. I think they secretly liked it when we called them that. Right from the start, they treated us as equals, and they'd been in the battlespace longer than we had. They had tremendous intelligence assets and resources, and they went out of their way to share information with us.

"They had this one officer fresh out of the Naval Academy—looked like he was a teenager, but he was really sharp. His name was Hedberg—Ensign Hedberg. Jack Williams always introduced him as the smartest ensign in the United States Navy. Lars Beamon called him the King of Imagery. He was a genius at downloading Web-based imagery and could tap into any government or military database and find things. Whenever we were planning an operation, he or one of the SEALs would turn up with an armload of reconnaissance photos and satellite imagery—everything from MapQuest-type stuff to NSA data. The kid was incredible. It wasn't long before he became the go-to guy for the other Army and Marine battalions for imagery. So it wasn't just the SEALs; all the people in their support package were very helpful and willing to share information."

Lieutenant Lars Beamon had equally good things to say about Mike Bajema and his Bulldog soldiers. "We felt a little more comfortable when we were operating near COP Falcon. If we needed a QRF [quick-reaction force] or a CASEVAC [casualty evacuation], we knew Mike and his guys would come for us. And they did. The Army patrols out of COP Falcon often operated under a SEAL sniper blanket. And a great many SEAL operations were conducted from COP Falcon. As the Battle of Ramadi ground on, this relationship evolved on a personal and professional basis. A great deal of the SEAL success in Iraq has been credited to our ops-intel fusion. In Ramadi much of it was due to the SEAL-Army fusion."

I asked Colonel MacFarland about the interface of the SEAL task unit and his requirements at the brigade level.

"I didn't know what to expect—I had never worked with SEALs before. My most recent experience in Tall 'Afar with Army Special Forces had not been very good. It seemed to me that they were intent on pursuing an independent agenda. I was hoping that it would be different in Ramadi. As it turned out the SEALs were exactly what I had hoped for—and, in some ways, even more. They were very interested in working as a part of a team, as well as being incredibly good at what they do. I won't say that their competence surprised me, but I wasn't sure just how adept sailors with guns would be in a counterinsurgency fight. It quickly became evident to me that they were tremendously effective and versatile warriors who were highly motivated and thoroughly professional."

I asked him about any reservations he may have had.

"Again, I was new to working with SEALs," the colonel said, "but I can honestly say that with the exception of Delta operators, who are the crème de la crème of our Army SOF components, I had never worked with warriors of such high caliber. I think that opinion was shared at all echelons, from colonel to private. My soldiers and junior leaders came to respect the big tough frogmen and would do anything for them. The losses that the SEALs suffered in Ramadi cemented that relationship in my mind. Anyone who shed blood, sweat, and tears in Ramadi with us will always be a part of our band of brothers. The names of those SEALs lost in action were inscribed on our [division] memorial plaque in Germany when we got home. We like to think that this respect was mutual."

Since Jack Williams and his task unit specifically asked to be involved in the brigade battle plans to retake Ramadi, I asked Colonel MacFarland just what he asked of "his SEALs."

"I gave them a wide range of missions, all of which they accepted without complaint and executed superbly. They helped us establish our COPs by sending in small kill teams to help seize the buildings we wanted, then they moved out to positions outside the perimeter in order to disrupt any enemy counterattack. At COP Falcon alone, they killed some two dozen enemy fighters in those first twenty-four hours as they attempted to disrupt our COP construction. We also employed SEALs as part of our counterfirefight—inserting them near historic enemy mortar points of origin. The enemy feared snipers above all else, and for good reason. Our sniper teams were incredibly lethal. Of all our sniper teams, the SEAL teams were the best. But all of our snipers benefited from their presence because they were also great instructors. Operationally, I tried to put them in the seams of the battlespace—places where they could go because of the small size of their patrol elements and the places where we couldn't go.

"Another function that they performed for me was training the Iraqi security forces. They worked with the Iraqi army scout platoons. They also helped us to provide rudimentary training to tribesmen who 'flipped' to our side and established neighborhood watch positions to defend against AQI. They also helped us to train new Iraqi army and Iraqi police recruits at Camp Ramadi after they returned from their basic training, raising the competence level of the soldiers and policemen in Ramadi to well above their peers elsewhere.

"Finally, the SEALs conducted targeted raids on individuals on which they had developed target folders. They shared their intel with us at intel-fusion and targeting meetings, and were happy to pass over targets best suited to conventional forces."

In light of Captain Bajema's and Colonel MacFarland's comments and praise for the Ramadi task unit, I'm going take a moment here for a brief editorial comment regarding the mission set of Navy SEALs as compared with Army Special Forces. Having spent a great deal of time with both SEALs and Special Forces, I think I understand the issues of both regarding their integration with conventional forces. First of all, high praise goes to SEAL leaders like Jack Williams who took the initiative to engage and work with the Army and the Marines. That kind of outreach and user-friendly approach is not that common with Special Forces units. Special Forces are primarily trainers, and while they have a broad range of talents, they seem to be most effective working with tribesmen and indigenous forces in remote areas. They do better when they're operating independently, away from conventional forces, and can be a tremendous force multiplier when employed in this manner. Given their training and cross-cultural skills, they have the ability to live and work with the locals, and this kind of venue is usually found in more rural areas where theirs is the only presence on the battlefield. Not everyone can meld in and live with indigenous populations. Special Forces can and do.

SEALs, on the other hand, are direct-action animals. While they can be very capable trainers, their training and their historical preference are to engage the enemy in combat. Sean MacFarland gave them the opportunity to do just that, and they were all over it.

The comments of Colonel MacFarland and Captain Bajema also reflect the long-standing competition between conventional Army and Army SOF. The Special Forces, as a career Army branch, draw away a good number of promising and proven officers, and capable sergeants, from the conventional units. This has led to a natural rivalry and, inevitably, some resentment. The SEALs have no such issues with the blue-water Navy—the fleet. Since 9/11 the SEALs have done most of their work on deployment in Army and Marine battlespace. As a result they've become quite good at finding their niche in that battlespace, and developing good relations with those conventional commanders.

Over at Camp Corregidor, Lieutenant Colonel Ron Clark, commanding officer of the 1st Battalion of the 506th, had nothing but praise for the SEAL task unit's Delta Platoon. "I was very impressed with their humility and their willingness to conform to our tactics and operating procedures in the fight for Ramadi. They were adaptable and very professional. They were proficient shooters as well as proficient trainers. Our SEALs were a definite force multiplier in the training and mentoring of the Iraqi scouts, the most experienced and capable Iraqi soldiers.

"The SEALs also worked well with our battalion snipers to become a potent force in our battlespace. On one operation, we had mounted a large cordon-and-search effort to clear insurgents from just west of the Mala'ab District—one of the most dangerous parts of the city. It involved sizable elements from my battalion and the Iraqi 1st Battalion. The SEALs, along with our battalion snipers, set in a series of mutually supporting positions. This guaranteed the success of the mission right from the start. These sniper teams killed eight insurgents and prevented others from moving into the area from other parts of the city. One of the SEAL snipers killed an enemy fighter in the act of placing an IED. The operation went off with outstanding results and with no friendly casualties. I firmly believe that operations like this and others paved the way for the Awakening and the peace and stability the citizens of Ramadi enjoy today. We're very proud of our association with the SEALs and their contributions to the history of the 1-506 infantry."

A driving force in the emerging Army-SEAL fusion in Ramadi was the need for precision shooters in the battlespace and the ability of the SEALs to shoot. It requires talent and a great deal of time and training to create a combat sniper. And it's not just a matter of pure precision shooting. There are the issues of patrolling through hostile territory to get into position, and adjusting to the difficult and imperfect conditions found in a combat environment. This is not match shooting, it's combat sniper work—precision, long-range killing. Competition shooters often make poor snipers, and a good sniper is sometimes an average marksman in long-range match competition. A military sniper must be able to shoot, but he also has to be a functioning member of the patrol and the combat team. Early on, the SEALs relied on the Marines to train their snipers because the Marine scout-snipers are among the premier military shooters in the world. For many years now the SEALs have trained their snipers in-house and have come a long way in this regard. Sniping is an individual talent, and talent will win out. Yet in my opinion, as a group, the SEAL snipers are the best combat snipers in the world. In short, the SEAL teams have the talent and the weapons, and their shooters are given a lot of time on the gun.

That said, there are varying degrees of competency within the best of the best. Whenever I asked who *the* best of the SEAL snipers was, there was always discussion of where and under what conditions—urban shooting or open space, single shot or multiple targets. But one name always came up: Cam Kellogg. Petty Officer First Class Camden Kellogg was the lead sniper in Charlie Platoon and in Ramadi. He's also a shooting legend in the SEAL teams. This was his third combat tour and second tour as a platoon sniper. On his first tour he was among the first SEALs in Iraq, serving as an M60 gunner on a SEAL desert patrol vehicle during the preinvasion operations to take and hold the Iraqi oil-tanker terminals and petroleum pumping infrastructure. On his previous rotation, in 2004, he was one of the SEAL snipers in the Battle of Fallujah. He was wounded there and is still being treated for that injury, but that didn't keep him from taking part in the Battle of Ramadi. It was in Ramadi that his shooting took him into the ranks of the military sniper elite.

Cam Kellogg grew up on a working ranch in Texas. He was used to hard work, dealing as he did with cattle, and shooting on the open range. A solid work ethic is a key ingredient for a sniper. It's a difficult and hard-won skill. Eyesight, nerve, judgment, and patience all have their place in the making of a sniper, but to be *really* good, you have to work at it. SEAL sniper training is a popular and sought-after school for the platoon SEALs, yet few who enter this training realize just how hard they must work. It's a mentally and physically demanding calling. Kellogg spent a year on the professional rodeo circuit as a saddle bronc rider before joining the Navy at twenty-four for SEAL training. He graduated with BUD/S Class 233. Kellogg is a large man, perhaps six-two and 230 pounds. Big shooters have an advantage with a higher human mass to weapon mass ratio. And like many snipers I spoke with, Cam Kellogg has a soft manner, almost shy in explaining his duties. Early in this tour in Ramadi he worked with the Marines at Hurricane Point and trained Iraqi army scouts at Camp Blue Diamond. But when the battle started, he became a pure sniper in a very target-rich environment.

"We did a lot of shooting," he said of those initial months of the battle. "And there were a lot of bad guys to shoot at. I have to credit my teammates with a lot of my success. They spotted for me and provided the security, so I could focus my time and attention on the gun." When I asked which gun, he answered immediately. "Three hundred WinMag [.300 Winchester Magnum]. The best sniper rifle in the world—a Remington 700 rifle set up for the .300 WinMag cartridge. It's a great round with a lot of punch—very heavy and a very flat trajectory. Its only downside is the noise and the flash. Even with a suppressor it has a loud bark, and it's hard to mask the muzzle flash. It lets everyone know exactly where you are."

In addition to the favored .300 WinMag, the SEALs also use two other sniper weapons. One is the SR-25, a semiautomatic rifle designed by Eugene Stoner and manufactured by the Knight's Armament Company. The Navy calls it the Mk 11 Mod 0 Sniper Weapons System. This rifle uses the NATO 7.62 match-grade ammunition, combining this superb round with an accurate, semiautomatic capability. It's a true sniper weapon that enjoys a great deal of utility in a standard firefight. The other is the Mk 12 Mod X Special Purpose Rifle, a "sniperized" version of the M4 rifle. Without going into the details, it's a highly accurate version of the standard SOF rifle with a sound suppresser and scope. The Mk 12 also has the option of frangible .556 ammunition that has applications for reducing collateral damage in long-range shooting situations. All of these weapons have their place in mission-specific environments. A few of the snipers I spoke with favored the SR-25 in Ramadi because they seldom made a shot longer than four hundred yards, well within the capability of the weapon, but with the ability to quickly engage multiple targets. But most preferred the absolute precision and stopping power of the .300 WinMag. It's a punishing weapon, for shooters as well as those on the business end. It has a brutal recoil, and SEAL snipers, perhaps more than other military snipers, put a lot of rounds through their weapons. The SEALs also have a .50-caliber sniper rifle in the inventory, but it had limited use in Ramadi. Currently, the SEALs are looking at the next generation of special-purpose sniper weapons in the .338- and .408-caliber range.

"You can always tell one of our snipers," a SEAL platoon chief told me. "They walk around with one shoulder lower than the other. That's why it sometimes helps to be a bigger guy; you can take the recoil from all those training rounds without developing an unconscious flinch-type reaction in anticipation of the kick."

I asked Cam Kellogg about the number of kills he'd made, and he told me the exact figures. For this text I'll just say that it was *well* over a hundred in Ramadi, and this was in addition to the nearly twenty he accounted for in Fallujah. "These were the confirmed kills," he said in his quiet, precise way, "the ones who were shot dead on the street. We don't count the ones who managed to crawl off and probably bled out. But I didn't have too many of those." I asked about his longest shot. "A little over fourteen hundred yards," he replied. In Ramadi, the insurgents came to know and fear Cam Kellogg. They called him *al-Shaitan Ramadi*—the Devil of Ramadi. There was a reward out for Kellogg and his fellow snipers. AQI would pay $20,000 for any insurgent who could kill a sniper and bring in his weapon. It has been estimated that more than eleven hundred insurgents were killed during the Battle of Ramadi. A third of those have been credited to the SEAL snipers.

The insurgents also had snipers. Most of them used the Dragunov sniper rifle, a dated, semiautomatic 7.62-millimeter weapon of Soviet design. Neither the weapon nor the insurgents who had it were in the same league with the SEAL shooters and their guns, but they were still a threat for the Americans patrolling the streets of Ramadi.

Ninety-six Americans died in the nine months during the Battle of Ramadi. All but two of those were soldiers and marines. I have to wonder how many more would have been killed in the battle without the grim harvest of snipers like Cam Kellogg.

A discussion about snipers is incomplete without speaking about the rules of engagement. The ROEs are the restrictions and guidelines that govern military activity and combat engagements. These apply to the snipers as well. These rules can vary from region to region and situation to situation. And, in many instances, I'm restricted from talking about them in detail because the rules that permit or restrict the shots our snipers can take are of use to our enemies. In Ramadi the ROEs allowed for an enemy combatant to be taken under fire if he was armed and moving with tactical intent, or clearly presented a threat to soldiers or civilians. There are finer points to these ROEs, but their purpose is to allow for the killing of bad guys while safeguarding innocents. An insurgency is a battle for the people, and killing an innocent civilian may do far more harm than the good that comes from killing an insurgent who deserves a bullet. This becomes a complex issue with the insurgents hiding among the people. In the early days of the battle when the first COPs were being established, there were more than enough targets in the form of armed insurgents moving tactically in the streets.

Rules of engagement come from the theater commander and are passed down through the chain of command. For the SEALs in al-Anbar, that chain of command is the commander of the Joint Special Operations Task Force at Balad Air Base to the squadron/SOTF–West commander in Fallujah to the task unit commanders. It's the task unit commanders who ensure operations conform to the ROEs. Since the Ramadi SEALs were operating in his battlespace, Colonel Sean MacFarland took an interest in this as well. In Iraq it was SOF policy regarding snipers that for every enemy combatant killed in action (KIA) or wounded in action (WIA) there had to be a statement from the shooter and a statement from a witness, usually the sniper's shooting partner or spotter. In addition to these statements, an operations summary that outlined the tactical and operational conditions that accompanied the shoot was required. Given the heavy toll of human life taken by the SEAL snipers in Iraq and Ramadi, these measures were put in place to protect the shooters should there be a question of impropriety. If these parameters were burdensome or a source of complaint, I never heard it voiced, and I spoke with a lot of SEAL snipers. I read a lot about soldiers and marines who do have issues with rules of engagement. If the Navy SEALs had any issues, they said nothing to me.

The ROEs and statements aside, it really all comes down to the decision of the man on the gun. He must decide whether a shooting is justified—whether the man in the reticle of his scope qualifies for and deserves a bullet. In my opinion it goes much deeper, to the heart of the shooter—his instincts and his judgment, even his compassion. Few warriors have the opportunity and burden, on an ongoing basis, to end a human life. Snipers do. I spoke with more than a few snipers who took a great deal of life in Ramadi. I found them to a man to be serious and professional about their duties, and proud of the fact that they had not exceeded their moral or statutory boundaries.

By the first week in July 2006, Ramadi was very hot. The temperature often reached 120°, even as the battle raged for control of the streets. Five new COPs had been established as the Americans and the Iraqi army edged into the city, the last of these being COP Hawk, established on 5 July. The insurgents now knew the strategy of the Americans and were determined to stop them. Another player was beginning to show itself on the battlefield of Ramadi—the Iraqi police. The Americans and the new Iraqi army continued their push into the city, reclaiming neighborhoods and doing what they could to keep them insurgent-free and safe. The tribal sheikhs began to see that the Americans were serious—that they were successfully executing their battle plan and beginning to bring parts of Ramadi under control. So the tribal leaders began to encourage their young tribesmen to join the fledgling police force in Ramadi. On 17 July the Jazeera police station was established. This was the *first* police station in Ramadi since the insurgency began, but others would follow. The location of this station was suggested by the sheiks and the new police force.

The COP strategy, as Commander Cally Garrison put it, was to "isolate, seize, clear, hold, and build." That month in Ramadi, "hold" was the operative term. Once the new COPs were put in place, they had to be held—held and defended. These were also centers of influence, and that influence and the safety net around the outpost had to be expanded and made secure. To do this the area around each COP had to be purged of insurgent elements and the streets had to be patrolled—to keep them clear of insurgents and to let the people know that those streets now belonged to the Americans and the Iraqi army. The plan called for the police to be the most visible force in the streets, but that would come later. Most of July was taken with patrolling the streets around the COPs and beating back insurgent counterattacks. In addition to keeping patrols on the streets, there were cordon-and-search operations to flush out the last of the insurgent presence in the cleared areas and all-out assaults on enemy strongholds. It was on one of these operations that the first SEAL was killed in action in Iraq.

During the early morning hours of 2 August, the SEALs of Charlie Platoon, which was garrisoned in Camp Ramadi, were supporting Iraqi army soldiers in a clearance operation in south-central Ramadi, a very dangerous area. As these elements moved along the street, they were protected by bounding overwatches—SEALs and a few Iraqi scouts moving from position to position in order to protect those engaged in the clearance work. This job usually amounted to knocking on a door and asking whether they could search the premises. Permission to do so was granted in most cases, with the Iraqis conducting the search. They were looking for insurgents and evidence of insurgent presence. Shortly after the operation commenced, a SEAL in one of the overwatch teams was struck in the face by a single round. Ryan Job (pronounced "Jobe"), a first-tour SEAL from Seattle, Washington, was down. The round hit the top of the receiver of his Mk48, a compact 7.62-millimeter squad medium machine gun. The bullet then fragmented and skipped into his face, metal shards shattering his right cheekbone and entering his right eye.

The Charlie Platoon SEALs reacted as they had in their drills. The platoon corpsman raced to Job's side to render aide, working to keep his airway clear as his face began to swell. Several SEALs took up positions, often intentionally exposing themselves to enemy gunners, and laid down a base of covering fire. Other platoon SEALs carried Job from the exposed rooftop. One of those providing cover for the extraction of the fallen SEAL was Petty Officer Marc Lee. The platoon took no further casualties in this action, but Ryan Job would ultimately loose the sight in both of his eyes.

The element commander, Lieutenant Lars Beamon, called for a casualty evacuation. A Bradley Fighting Vehicle came from COP Falcon for Job, who was taken to the hospital at Camp Ramadi. The rest of the patrol returned to COP Falcon to rearm, as most of their ammunition was expended in the exchange. Everyone in the platoon was shaken with this serious wounding of Ryan Job. Out on the streets, the insurgents pressed their attack, and several Army patrols were in heavy contact. ISR (intelligence, surveillance, and reconnaissance) from orbiting F/A-18s reported several bands of armed insurgents moving in the area where Job was hit. With the other Army patrols still fighting and the enemy clearly mounting counterattacks, Beamon made a difficult decision. He ordered his SEALs to gear up and get ready to return to the fight. They were tired and battle weary, but then that's why SEALs train to such a rigorous standard. The F/A-18s orbiting over the city kept them advised of the insurgent locations. The Bradley Fighting Vehicles carried the SEALs back to the fighting in south-central Ramadi. This time they were without their Iraqi scouts. Their operating procedures called for them not to go into the battlespace without Iraqis in their patrol element, but the scouts did not want to go back out onto the street. This was the first time many of them had seen a SEAL go down. With Army patrols in close contact, the SEALs returned to the fight without their scouts. Their mission now was to help support those Bulldog soldiers from COP Falcon still engaged in the street battle.

The SEALs, supported by Bradley Fighting Vehicles *and* M1A2 Abrams tanks, attacked an insurgent stronghold not far from where

Ryan Job was wounded. After a thorough raking of the building by the heavy weapons of the armor, the SEALs began to clear the building. They cleared the ground floor and began to move to second floor. As they started up, several SEALs were taken under fire from a building across the street. The enemy fire poured in through a window near the stairwell. Marc Lee stepped into the window with his Mk48 to provide suppressing fire for his teammates and was struck down. An enemy round took him in the head, killing him instantly. Once again, the SEALs had to fight, maneuver, and care for a fallen brother. Once again, platoon SEALs took exposed positions to provide covering fire while others took Marc from the building to a waiting Bradley, but there was nothing that could be done for him. When the SEALs had withdrawn and other friendly units in the area had been accounted for, air strikes were called in to extinguish the insurgents who had fired on them. But Marc Lee from Hood River, Oregon, was dead. He was the first SEAL to be killed in action in Ramadi—in all of Iraq.

The death of Marc Lee, just hours after the wounding and blinding of Ryan Job, shook the entire task unit. Indeed, Captain Mike Bajema and his Bulldogs felt the loss of a brother as well; Charlie Platoon had conducted many of their operations from COP Falcon. These casualties came thirteen months after the eleven SEALs were killed in Afghanistan. There had been no deaths among the Navy SEALs in that intervening period.

The decision to take to the streets in support of the Army and the Marines in the Battle of Ramadi had largely been Jack Williams's. As a SEAL task unit commander he did not *have* to support Sean MacFarland and his brigade battle plan in this way. He might well have directed his SEALs to continue in their roles as trainers and continue to provide the Army and Marine battalions with intelligence and targeting information only—not become shooters. Or he could have restricted his operations to those traditionally considered "special," keeping his SEAL operators poised for high-value targets, such as key foreign fighters and known al-Qaeda operatives. And my guess is that he would have been supported in this by his SOF chain of command. But you'd have to know Jack Williams to understand that he was not going to step back from this important battle. Nor did the SEALs I spoke with wish to remain on the sidelines. On the eve of the Battle of Ramadi, when he said to Colonel Sean MacFarland, "Sir, what can we do to help?" he meant just that. And his decision to take to the streets in this battle was well supported by his platoon OICs, his senior enlisted leaders, and the task unit SEAL operators.

"The loss of wounded Ryan Job and the death of Marc Lee was hard on everyone," Williams said. "It was hard on me. But those soldiers and marines went out there every day, and we'd all have felt terrible sitting back cleaning our guns or reviewing target folders while they were fighting for their lives on the street. It wasn't an option for us. We were in Ramadi, and we wanted our guns in the fight; we wanted to make a difference. Lars did his duty—what was expected of him as a combat leader. Anything short of that would have been dereliction of duty."

I asked Lars Beamon about his decision to go back out.

"I think about it a lot—every day, in fact. I'd give anything to have Marc back. I'd give anything for Ryan to see again. It was my decision, and I'll live with it. I'm not sure I could live with myself if we'd stayed in the COP while our Army brothers were out there in close contact. That's just not who we are."

A short time later, the Ramadi SEAL compound known as Shark Base was renamed Camp Marc Lee.

Two more COPs were established in August and two more Iraqi police stations were opened in September. Each operation was a little less of a struggle, but they were never really easy. The Army and the Marines knew what they had to do, and they did it. The insurgents knew what was coming and knew they had to oppose these incursions into their turf. For them, this meant moving onto the streets and risking death at the hands of a sniper. They didn't know when or where the next COP would be sited, but they were learning to react more quickly when the Americans and the Iraqis moved into a neighborhood and began construction. They were also learning how to deal with the sniper overwatches. Yet with each operation, the Americans and their Iraqi allies became a little more proficient at the seizure and building of these outposts. Nevertheless, most of these COPs were on the periphery of the city. The insurgents still held a firm grip on the center of Ramadi. The structures around the Government Center, in the words of Sean MacFarland, were "little more than shells of buildings to hide snipers and IED triggermen." The seeds of change were being sown by the building of the COPs, but the insurgents still controlled more of the city than they had lost. Of concern to the SEALs, who continued their deadly overwatch operations, were the insurgent countermeasures to their sniper overwatches. In their efforts to disrupt the construction of these COPs, they had begun to target the SEAL snipers that had so devastated their numbers. Between these major COP-construction operations, the task unit SEAL elements continued with cordon-and-search operations and patrolling with their Iraqi scouts to help the Army and the Marines with a visible presence in the city. They also set in overwatches to protect the Army and Marine patrols. As each neighborhood or area of the city came under the influence of the expanding system of outposts, the newly repatriated sector had to be patrolled. Insurgents filtering back into these cleared areas had to be dealt with. This extension of influence at the expense of the insurgents sent a strong message to the people of Ramadi and their tribal leaders. In many ways, it paved the way for the tribal movement that became know as the Awakening. This important development had its beginnings in August 2006.

Al-Qaeda and its allies had been at odds with the tribes in and around Ramadi for some time. In an effort to gain influence and control, AQI first tried to marry senior al-Qaeda members into the tribes, a strategy that had proved successful in Afghanistan and in the border reaches of Pakistan. When the tribes resisted this, AQI intensified its campaign of murder and intimidation. Along with these M&I tactics came the imposition of sharia law, a strict interpretation of Islamic laws based on the Koran, something most unwelcome in Anbari tribal society. Smoking, for example, was punishable by the removal of the fingers holding the cigarette. While the tribes viewed the growing AQI influence with alarm, there seemed to be little they could do about it. Whenever a tribal sheikh opposed an AQI overture, he was killed or members of his family were killed—and often tortured in the process. With tribal leaders being killed at an alarming rate, many fled to Syria or Jordan. In the wake of the death of Abu Musab al-Zarqawi in June 2006, his followers seemed to press even harder in their efforts to control the Anbari tribes.

As the American and Iraqi security forces began to extend their control into Ramadi proper, the tribal sheikhs started to encourage their young men to join the local police. The tribal leaders were induced to support local police recruitment by Sean MacFarland and his senior leadership; they told the sheikhs that the new policemen could serve at home and protect their own neighborhoods. MacFarland offered further support in the way of police station construction and police

How to Win the War in Al Anbar   by CPT Trav

This is an American Soldier. We'll call him Joe. Joe wants to win in Al Anbar. But sometimes it seems like other people don't share that idea.

How can Joe win in Al Anbar? By fighting the insurgents?

This is Joe with all his gear on. It weighs 80 pounds. He can't fight insurgents very well in all this gear. Survive attacks? Yes. Fight well? No. (Have you ever tried to climb a six foot wall in the middle of the night with 80 pound of gear so you can sneak up on insurgents? Joe has. It's hard, and it makes him sad when the insurgents have already run away because they heard him and his squad coming three blocks away..)

The PowerPoint presentation "How to Win the War in Al Anbar," created by Capt. Travis Patriquin, USA, is presented here verbatim; it is taken from http://www.blackfive.net/main/files/how_to_win_in_anbar.pdf.

This is Mohammed. He's in the Iraqi Army. He is from Baghdad, and he has a lot of the same problems that Joe has in Anbar.. Except ALL the people here hate him!

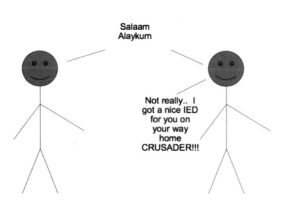

On the right is an insurgent. He is bad. On the left is an Iraqi Man, who is not an insurgent, but is scared of them. He doesn't necessarily like Joe, but he doesn't want to hurt him, and he does want to protect his family, but he's afraid of the insurgents. What to do??

There's Joe and Mohammed! They don't know if these are good Iraqis or bad Iraqis..
What to do?

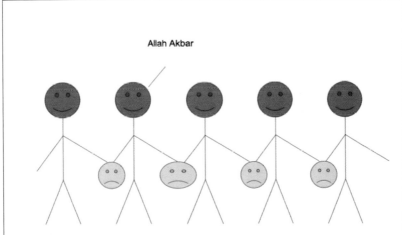

This is a group of insurgents. They like chaos and power. They get it by sawing heads off of and intimidating good Iraqis

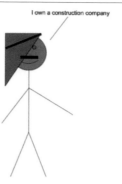

This is a Sheik. They've been leading the people of this area for approximately 14,000 years. In spite of many, many conquering Armies trying to remove him, this man and his family have been involved in the politics here since recorded time began.

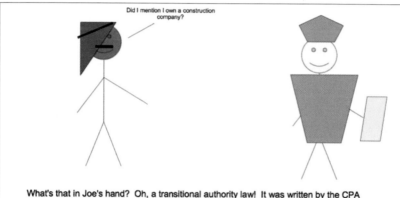

What's that in Joe's hand? Oh, a transitional authority law! It was written by the CPA (25 year olds from Texas, and Paul Bremer) and it says NO SHEIKS! ONLY ELECTED GOVERNMENT!!! "That's OK", says the Sheik. "Can I have some contract work?"

These guys, however, can win elections if they want. More importantly, they can make good Iraqis not vote! And control ministries and other government offices! Smart Insurgents! Humdillillah, they say, that the Americans can't tell us from the innocent Iraqis!

Poor Joe can't tell the terrorist from the good Iraqis. Neither can Mohammed.

This is the Sheik with his militia. Militias are bad.. "But they just protect my family and tribe.." Says the Sheik. "Let's have Chai.." (In order to protect their families, many young men have resisted joining the Iraqi Army, because they might be sent elsewhere in Iraq while the security suffers in their home areas. Iraqis hate even the thought of their family suffering while they're gone. Come to think of it, Joe feels exactly the same way..)

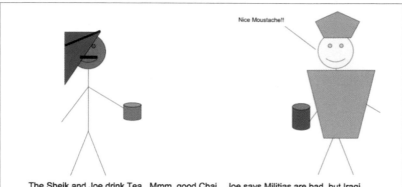

The Sheik and Joe drink Tea. Mmm good Chai.. Joe says Militias are bad, but Iraqi Police are good. Would the Sheik Let his men join the Iraqi Police? Yes, yes he will. (Iraqi Police stay in their local areas, and can effectively defeat murder and intimidation campaigns by their presence, unlike the Iraqi Army, which might send him somewhere far away..)

Remember the militia? Now half go to Police school while half protect their families.

Then they come back, and they're police! Then the other half goes to school.

Now can you tell the difference between the insurgent, the normal Iraqis, and the Iraqi Police man? Kind of? Don't worry, because the Iraqi Policeman can tell the difference. And the insurgent knows that. See, that's why he's sad.

That terrorist is sad.. He just got caught. Joe is happy. The normal Iraqi is happy. The Iraqi Policeman is happy. The Sheik is happy.

The Sheik brings more Sheiks, more sheiks bring more men. Joe realizes that if he'd done this three years ago, maybe his wife would be happier, and he'd have been home more. Mohammed gets to meet the Sheiks. They realize he's not such a bad guy, which is good for Iraq. Joe grows a moustache, because he realizes that Iraqis like people with moustaches and have a hard time trusting people without one.

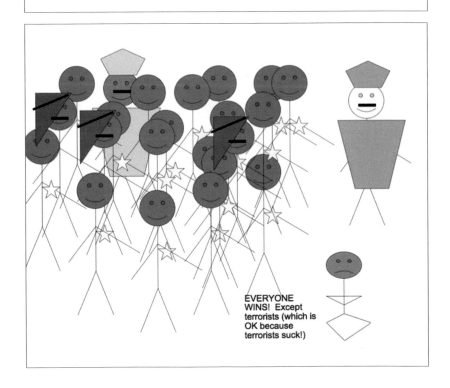

training. During the first half of 2006, there had been very few police volunteers—fewer than three hundred total. That changed in August, when close to a thousand signed up for police training in Ramadi. Most of them were from the Albu Ali Jassim tribe. A local, robust police force would deal a severe blow to the insurgency, and al-Qaeda knew it. AQI had to strike back against the tribal leaders. This led to the kidnapping and assassination of the tribal leader Sheikh Khalid (often reported in the press by his tribal-leader title, Sheikh Abu Ali Jassim) on 21 August. Al-Qaeda further angered his followers by hiding the sheikh's body in a field rather than returning it to the family for prompt burial, as is the custom. If there was a turning point in the tribal sheikhs' and the Anbari people's opposition to the AQI-led insurgency, this was it. This brutal murder and desecration of the remains pushed many sheikhs off the fence and in favor of cooperation with the Americans and the fledgling Iraqi security forces.

Colonel Sean MacFarland and his brigade staff recognized this as an opening and renewed their efforts to reach out to the tribes. This fell in line with the incremental strategy to regain control of Ramadi. The combat outposts and the security patrols in the vicinity of these outposts had begun to purge these areas of insurgent elements—and to make them safe for the people. As the neighborhoods near the COPs became safer, the tribal police began to appear on the streets—often not in uniform, but still a local, coalition-friendly armed presence on the streets. With the tribal police on the streets, the Army, Marine, and the new Iraqi army patrols could move on to support offensive operations—and more COPs.

After the death of Sheikh Khalid, a group of remaining sheikhs met on 9 September and signed a declaration of solidarity pledging to fight al-Qaeda and to support the Americans and government security forces. Colonel Sean MacFarland was present. The declaration agreed upon at this meeting led to the movement known as the Awakening, and the formation of Sahawat Al Anbar—the Awakening Council. This formal stand against al-Qaeda was to have a profound, rippling effect across al-Anbar and all of Iraq. The Awakening Council also became the forum for a colorful and charismatic Anbari leader, Sheikh Abdul Sattar Baziya of the Albu Risha tribe. As the emerging leader of his tribe, he was best known as Sheikh Abdul Sattar Abu Risha. Sattar was a brash, defiant, chain-smoking sheikh who made no secret of his opposition to AQI, nor of his embracing the Americans. He and Sean MacFarland quickly became friends and confidants. His aggressive nature and willingness to take a stand against insurgents in Ramadi became the trademark of the Awakening. This handsome, belligerent leader *looked* like an Arab tribal leader—he had *wasta,* that magnetic, manly quality so important in Anbari tribal culture. That he had a shady background, as well as former insurgent ties, were forgotten when he became leader of the tribal revolt in Ramadi. As the fall of 2006 wore on, the animated Sheikh Sattar and the laid-back Colonel MacFarland were often photographed together. This odd couple was to change the face of the insurgency in al-Anbar and beyond. In Ramadi the embattled Sheriff was now gaining the backing of the townspeople.

Yet tribal politics in al-Anbar is never clear or predictable. Sattar and the Albu Risha tribe had a long history of criminal activity going back to the days of Saddam's regime, including the smuggling of oil out of Iraq during the UN embargo. And Sattar himself was a minor tribal leader until his stance against AQI and his open alliance with the Americans elevated him to something close to "sheikh of sheikhs" status. An opportunist? Unquestionably. A courageous leader—that, too. In some respects, his newfound favor was reminiscent of Lucky Luciano and the Mafia's role in cooperating with the Allies against fascist Italy during World War II and against Communist influence immediately following the war. Sean MacFarland, being an experienced and capable counterinsurgency practitioner, saw in Sattar and his fellow sheikhs a means to bring the people to the side of the coalition. He seized the opportunity. "The real prize is the population," MacFarland said during the battle, "and that's where we were making the most dramatic gains through tribal engagement. Without that, the enemy could regenerate and replace his losses indefinitely."

The Awakening and the reluctant journey of the tribal leaders from insurgent-friendly/insurgent-supportive to neutral, to wait-and-see, and finally to coalition-supportive was an important yet poorly understood evolution. It was a bottom-up movement, one that was eventually supported by the government in Baghdad, but it was never a government-sponsored enterprise. The Awakening bloomed of its own initiative. Its decisiveness in the Battle of Ramadi may never be calculated, for the battle lines were blurred. The rank-and-file insurgents in Ramadi were Anbaris—they lived there. They were the insurgent foot soldiers. They were also members of their tribe. So when an insurgent, at the direction of his tribal sheikh, laid down arms as an insurgent and took up arms as a policeman, it was a double victory. There was one less of them and one more of us. And when an insurgent became a policeman, he brought all that knowledge of insurgent activities with him. Strange and suspicious by Western standards—certainly. In keeping with tribal culture going back to ancient times—absolutely. And totally acceptable within *their* frame of reference. So throughout the battle, insurgents were being killed and insurgents were changing sides. Just how loyal were these insurgents-turned-cops in Ramadi? The answer: as loyal as their sheikhs. But their loyalty was and is to the tribe, not to the central government in Baghdad. This bottom-up, sheikh-led revolt was a grassroots movement and a key element in the winning of Ramadi and all of al-Anbar. Yet this movement and the Awakening might have been stillborn had there not been a resourceful and adaptive Colonel Sean MacFarland to midwife this important development.

With the bulk of the forces under MacFarland, including the SEAL task unit, now engaged in the difficult and methodical process of pushing into the city, key members of the 1st Brigade Combat Team staff busied themselves in supporting the Awakening. Of those working with the tribes, perhaps none were more effective or influential than an Army captain named Travis Patriquin.

Patriquin enlisted in the Army out of high school and served as an intelligence specialist with Army Special Forces in Latin America. He had a flair for languages and spoke Spanish and Portuguese. After becoming an officer he deployed to Afghanistan, again in support of Special Forces. He was trained in Arabic, and in Afghanistan he became conversant in Dari and Urdu. He joined Sean MacFarland and the 1st BCT in Tall 'Afar in January 2006. MacFarland made him his brigade S5 (plans) officer in Ramadi. By this time he had become fluent in Arabic, and an expert on Sunni tribal customs.

"Travis was unique in his ability to engage the tribal sheikhs," one of his fellow officers said of him. "He was part American Indian—a big guy with a full mustache. Whenever he met with the tribal leaders, speaking easily with them in their language, their eyes would light up. They knew they were with a friend. I still can see him huddled in a corner with Sheikh Sattar, smoking cigarettes and plotting their next move against al-Qaeda. The tribesmen instantly liked and trusted him. We never saw Travis much in the evenings. He was always out dining in the home of some Iraqi. Iraqis are very social in the taking of their meals, and Travis was a much-sought-after dinner guest."

Tribal politics and the relationship of the tribes to the Americans, the Iraqi army, and the government in Baghdad during the Battle of Ramadi were complex and often mystifying. Warriors like Travis Patriquin were essential to establishing the cultural bridge between the Anbari people and their leaders and the American and Iraqi security forces. Patriquin was also able to articulate what we had to do to win in al-Anbar. His famous "Stick Figure Briefing" appears in this chapter. This presentation did much to help American military and political leaders understand what was taking place in Ramadi and al-Anbar, as well as what we needed to do to win out west in the Sunni tribal lands. He understood this early on, but he would never live to see it become a reality. Travis Patriquin was killed in Ramadi by an IED in December 2006.

The roadside explosion that took the life of Captain Patriquin was costly for the Army, for the Marines, and for the United States. Major Megan McClung, USMC, was killed in the same blast. Major McClung was serving as a public affairs officer in Ramadi. She was the first female Marine officer and first female Naval Academy graduate (Class of 1995) to be killed in this war.

In late September, Squadron Three and the task unit at Ramadi were looking at their last few weeks in Ramadi before their scheduled rotation back home. Those at Camp Lee were beginning to notice some changes. Days went by without taking fire on the base. Over at Camp Corregidor, the SEALs were still taking fire daily, but the intervening periods of quiet were becoming longer. They still couldn't go to the toilet or to chow without a helmet and a flak jacket, but there was a feeling that things were getting better. The COP strategy was beginning to pay dividends; the neighborhoods around the COPS were gradually being purged of insurgents and insurgent violence. Tribal policemen were seen more frequently on the streets near the COPs. In these areas there were the beginnings of normal life and normal commercial activity. There were still districts within the city fully under insurgent control, but their influence was shrinking. On their final operation the Corregidor SEALs of Delta Platoon from Squadron Three were scheduled for a thirty-six-hour overwatch operation. The SEAL squad assigned to this operation was already packed and ready to leave for Camp Lee on the first leg of its journey home. The platoon's other squad was back at Camp Corregidor, staging its equipment for redeployment. A contingent of scouts from the 1st Iraqi Brigade at Corregidor were with the SEALs. The mission was to set in two mutually supportive overwatch positions to protect a platoon of soldiers stringing razor wire along the rail line that ran across the southern outskirts of the city. By this stage of the game, it was a familiar drill, but they were taking nothing for granted this close to the end of the tour.

This was not the first time the men had operated in this sector of the Mala'ab District, and the SEALs knew it to be dangerous turf. The insurgents were still active, both offensively and in planting IEDs. Only two weeks earlier two soldiers with a Dagger clearance team had been killed in action nearby. It was from this sector that insurgents gathered to launch attacks on COP Eagles Nest. The previous SEAL operation in this area had led to a forty-five-minute firefight and six enemy KIAs, with the SEAL element maneuvering in a running gun battle for half a mile to get back to the COP.

During the present operation, the SEAL elements patrolled out from COP Eagles Nest on foot and seized two buildings that were about a block from each other. (The name "Eagles Nest" was chosen in honor of Easy Company of the 1-506 in World War II; in 1945 they occupied Hitler's mountain retreat, which was called the Eagle's Nest.) Lieutenant Sean Smith was in command of the easternmost overwatch, while Lieutenant (junior grade) John Seville commanded the other. Seville was the Delta Platoon assistant officer in charge, or AOIC. There were twelve to fourteen men in each element. A third of them were SEALs. The teams settled into their positions about 3:00 AM on 29 September. Both had excellent fields of fire to protect the soldiers who would be working along the rail line after sunup. The scouts dealt with the building residents and held security on the lower floors while the SEALs set in shooting positions on the roof of the third floor. The latter were exposed on the roof but protected by a short stucco-and-concrete wall that bordered the open flat roofs. In order to make their shooting positions more secure, the SEALs cut holes in the wall with loophole charges. Their positions were tactically solid, and both overwatches were in communication with the TOCs at Camp Corregidor and COP Eagles Nest.

"As soon as it became light, we knew it was going to be a day of fighting," John Seville told me. Seville was a former enlisted marine who took his degree and commission at Texas A&M. Instead of returning to the Corps, he opted for a commission in the Navy and for SEAL training, graduating with BUD/S Class 247. This was his second combat rotation in Iraq as a SEAL. He had spent time in Ramadi in the summer of 2005. Seville had begun this tour with his SEAL squad working out of Shark Base, before it was renamed Camp Marc Lee. With the persistent insurgent presence in south and eastern Ramadi, he had been detailed to Corregidor to help Sean Smith and the 1-506.

"The muj were out moving early, scouting our position," Seville said of the mission. "We shot two of them, and the other overwatch to our east shot one. Then civilians began blocking off the streets with rocks and trash to warn people away. By midmorning, vehicles began pulling into view. Someone inside would send a few rounds at us, and then they'd drive off. These were long-range, drive-by shootings. At noon, we got hit by an RPG that dusted up everyone inside our building."

From his command position in the other overwatch some 150 meters to the east, Sean Smith could see the RPG strike and knew Seville's overwatch was under siege. So was his position, for that matter. He also trusted John Seville as capable combat leader; he and his SEALs, all seasoned veterans, could hold their own in a fight.

While their position on the roof at Seville's overwatch was reasonably secure from direct fire, the SEALs were vulnerable to indirect fire, handheld rockets, and RPGs. Into the early afternoon, both positions were under steady insurgent fire. It seemed that on this day the insurgents in the Mala'ab were focusing on the SEALs rather than the soldiers stringing wire along the railroad. Employing small periscopes, the kind used by the gallery at professional golf tournaments, the SEALs watched as individual insurgents tried to maneuver close to the overwatch buildings. They were able to drive most, but not all, of them off. At Seville's overwatch one of them managed to get in close, under the guns of the SEALs on the roof. It was from there that he managed to hurl a grenade up to the roof. It was a well-placed toss.

Petty Officer Mike Monsoor was on one knee behind the covering wall. The grenade hit Monsoor in the chest and dropped in front of him. He leaped to his feet, then dropped to the ground to smother it with his body. John Seville was a few steps to Monsoor's right and another SEAL was less than five feet to his left. Both Seville and the other SEAL were in prone shooting positions; they had no room or time to maneuver away from the grenade—to avoid the blast.

Mike Monsoor was the only one of the three who could have dived away from the grenade that had landed in their midst. In the split second it took for Monsoor to assess his position relative to the vulnerable position of his brother SEALs, he made a fateful decision. He dropped on the grenade and absorbed the blast with his body armor and his body.

"He never took his eye off that grenade," John Seville said of Monsoor's last courageous act. "His only movement was down toward it. He undoubtedly saved my life and probably saved Danny's [the SEAL to Monsoor's left] as well. We owe him."

Mike Monsoor was twenty-five and on his first combat rotation as a SEAL. He was handsome, just over six feet, easygoing, and a devout Catholic. He had failed in his first try at SEAL training, only to return more determined than ever. The second time, he succeeded. At SEAL Team Three, his quiet presence and cheerful willingness to carry the heavier Mk48 made him a well-liked and respected member of his platoon and his team. This was not his first courageous act on the battlefield. On 9 May, not quite a month after the task unit had arrived in Ramadi, Monsoor and his element were engaged in a firefight with insurgents. Moving through the streets, one of his teammates was taken down by enemy fire. Shot through the legs, he was exposed and immobile in the street. Mike raced to his side, shooting on the move. Enemy rounds kicked up the dirt around him. He helped to drag the fallen SEAL to safety, while continuing to lay down suppressing fire with his Mk48. For his courage under fire, he was awarded the Silver Star.

After the grenade exploded, there was a great deal of confusion. Seville and Danny, on either side of Monsoor and the smothered grenade, both absorbed shrapnel, mostly in their legs. Neither was able to walk. Three of the scouts on the roof, shaken at the sight of three SEALs down, ran from the rooftop into the safety of the building. The fourth scout went fetal, unable to move from fear and shock. The wounded men needed help, but the blast had also knocked out the SEAL radios. John Seville crawled to the immobilized scout and took his radio, calling to the other overwatch position to say he had men down. Bobby, the fourth SEAL on the roof, was only slightly wounded. He managed to drag Mike away from the building wall edge to assess his wounds, but there was little to be done; Monsoor was still alive, but his breathing was labored. Calling the other scouts back onto the roof, Seville managed, with some difficulty, to get them to take up positions and return fire.

At the other overwatch, Sean Smith and his SEALs were already on the move. Knowing that Seville and his team were hit and needed help, they broke from their position. The second they stepped into the street, they were in a running gunfight as they battled their way to Seville's location. The fire was so intense that Smith's Iraqi scouts refused to leave the protection of their overwatch building. Smith and his four SEALs didn't have that luxury. There were brother SEALs in trouble, and they had to get to them.

"It seemed like it took them forever to get to us," Seville said of the wait, "but time was distorted for me. It was probably well inside of ten minutes. That was pretty quick, considering they were moving under fire. I was experiencing a lot of pain and a lot of frustration. And I remember how badly Mikey was hurt. I knew we had two priorities until the CASEVAC arrived—win the fight and keep Mikey alive. Bobby, a professional warrior to the core, had taken Mike's Mk48 back to the wall and was firing down on the enemy. Then Sean was there, kneeling beside me and taking charge. One of my lasting memories of that day, before they dragged me off, was Bobby still fighting, a look of anger and determination on his face."

Lieutenant Sean Smith called for a casualty evacuation and two Bradley Fighting Vehicles were dispatched from COP Eagles Nest. The three wounded SEALs were rushed back to the COP and on to the hospital at Camp Ramadi, but it was too late for Mike Monsoor.

"I met Mikey at communications school during our predeployment training," Seville said, recalling his friend. "He was from Garden Grove—your typical Southern California boy. He drove a Corvette and always had a laid-back, I'm-cool, no-sweat attitude. But that was just on the surface. He took important things seriously. When we were working, he was always there, 110 percent and all business, yet in a nice way. When Mike was around, things seemed to go better—easier. He was very good at SSE [sensitive site exploitation—the searching of buildings and rooms], and he was always careful when we were searching a building or structure. One time I'd given a room a quick search and found nothing. Then Mike pulled back a dresser and found an AK-47. He handed it to me with that Mikey smile of his. He didn't say anything, but I knew he was thinking, 'Hey, come on, Lieutenant, you can do better than that.' Mike came from a very loving family, and when you met his folks, you could understand how he came to be such a likable guy and such a great team player. Y'know, he never made a big deal about it, but somehow he always managed to go to Mass on Sunday. He was our best, and now he's gone. We all miss him."

At the headquarters of the U.S. Army's 1st Armored Division in Stuttgart, Germany, there's a dedicated field of honor with a planting of evenly spaced trees. By each tree is a small monument with a plaque to honor a fallen member of the 1st AD. Among these soldiers' memorials are those for two sailors—two SEAL petty officers: Marc Lee and Mike Monsoor.

On 9 April 2008 President George W. Bush presented Mike Monsoor's parents the Medal of Honor. Mike is the fifth Navy SEAL to receive the Medal of Honor and the second since 9/11. He alone among these SEAL heroes chose to give his life in a willful and deliberate act to save his teammates. Mike had options. He *could* have turned away from that grenade and saved himself. His teammates *might not* have died from the blast. Mike Monsoor chose instead to protect his teammates. *Greater love hath no man than this, that a man lay down his life for his friends.* John 15:13. This was Mike Monsoor.

Armed patrol. Humvees, trucks, and armor rumble through the streets of Ramadi toward the entrance of COP Falcon during the height of the battle. *Courtesy of Captain Mike Bajema*

The Battle Turns

The men of Naval Special Warfare Squadron Five and its associated components began to relieve their brothers from Squadron Three in October 2006. This change-out of SEALs across al-Anbar would be the first squadron rotation with the incoming squadron commander based in Fallujah *and* in command of all special operations forces in al-Anbar province. As with his predecessor, the first SOTF–West commander, he reported to the Joint Special Operations Task Force commander at Balad Air Base. His responsibilities included the NSW task units in Fallujah, Habbaniyah, and Ramadi as well as the Army Special Forces advanced operating base located at the Marine base at Al Asad. The special missions units, while very much SOF elements, operated under the direction of the JSOTF at Balad. For the most part, these special and highly classified units continued to operate as unilateral tactical strike elements, often called in to deal with high-value targets. The previous June, they played a key role in the death of Abu Musab al-Zarqawi. The SEAL and Special Forces elements under SOTF–West scattered across al-Anbar were certainly keeping an eye peeled for high-value targets, but their duties usually involved the day-in, day-out counterinsurgency operations—working with the fledgling Iraqi security forces and supporting their Army and Marine battlespace commanders. These special missions units kept the senior al-Qaeda and insurgent leaders looking over their shoulders, as these exceptional warriors can appear anywhere at any time. Nevertheless, it's the opinion of this author that the important work of SOF in al-Anbar was and is being done by the SEAL task units, the SEAL platoons, and the Special Forces detachments. These are the warriors closest to the Anbari people, and they're the ones most adept at developing the wealth of targeting information that can only come from local sources. They're the ones who will ultimately help to bring the local security forces to a level of self-sufficiency such that we can go home.

I called on the Squadron Five commander shortly after his return from Iraq and al-Anbar. He had just reverted to his predeployment status as commanding officer, SEAL Team Five, and would soon leave his team en route to his next command. When a squadron/team returns from deployment rotation, many of the key senior leaders will move on to new duty stations. Junior leaders will step up to positions of greater responsibility. The platoon officers in charge and the platoon chief petty officers will usually remain with the team but not with the platoon. New task unit commanders and task unit chiefs are often selected from the outgoing platoon OICs and platoon chiefs. But the team commanding officer will always move on after the tour to make way for a new CO and future squadron commander. Commander Rick Leonard met me at the back gate on the Pacific Ocean side of the Team Five compound. I was surprised to see that he was walking a brown and white dog that looked like a spaniel.

"It's a Fallujah terrier," he explained after we exchanged greetings. He led me and the dog up to his office in the Team Five spaces. "This was Clark Schwedler's dog. We had a hell of a time getting him back here from Iraq, but his parents said they wanted the dog, so we were able to bring him to the States. Like many of us here at Team Five, he's in transition. We hope to get him on a flight back to the East Coast in a few days."

Petty Officer Clark Schwedler had been killed in action near Fallujah in early April 2007, only a few days before Squadron Five was to redeploy. Schwedler was one of the Squadron Five SEALs from the East Coast. He was assigned to the task unit in Fallujah from the Virginia-based SEAL Team Four.

Rick Leonard gave me an overview of his task group and what the SEALs had accomplished out west in al-Anbar. "Things turned around while we were out there, not that they still don't have a long way to go. Ramadi and all of al-Anbar are much different than they were when we arrived. Most of the credit goes to those soldiers and marines who shed their blood to help the Anbaris reclaim their towns and cities. And I can't say enough about what the guys from Squadron Three did over there. I'd like to think that we picked up from where they left off last October and continued the progress they and the previous squadron started. When we arrived, things were still pretty unsettled—it could have gone either way. However, the tribes were already beginning to fight back. Much of al-Anbar was still being contested, but all eyes were on Ramadi. There were indications that we were making progress in Ramadi, but there were also street battles every day. Credit the Army and the Marines and men like Colonel Sean MacFarland in Ramadi for turning things around. The feeling was that if we could make it work in Ramadi, we could make it work in the rest of al-Anbar.

"From my perspective in Fallujah, reading the message traffic and situation reports, things still appeared uncertain last October. Some intelligence estimates being leaked to the press had us losing in Ramadi and in all of al-Anbar—that AQI had the upper hand. That was still the case into November. Yet when I spent time with our operational units, I got the feeling that we were doing a lot more than holding our own out west, especially in Ramadi. We were winning the ground and were winning over the people through our efforts to engage the tribal leaders. The Awakening was beginning to result in more Iraqi police taking to the streets. But Ramadi was far from won. All our task units in al-Anbar were engaged, but none more heavily than the TU in Ramadi."

As with most SEALs and SEAL commanders I interviewed, Leonard cautioned me about giving undue or disproportionate credit to the SEALs. Without question, he was very proud of the combat record of his squadron, but I sensed it was an issue of proportion and a measure of quiet professionalism. I had yet to speak with a SEAL veteran, from squadron commander down to junior platoon enlisted operators, who didn't openly praise the Army and the Marines. I was to hear it many more times as I began my work with Squadron Five.

"We followed in the footsteps of Squadron Three in that we made ourselves useful to the commanders who owned our battlespace," Commander Leonard said. "The operative phrase was 'What can we do to help?' I had my mission direction from my JSOTF boss, but we were all aware of the load the Army and Marines carried. We saw ourselves as enablers for the conventional-force presence. My task units were given a great deal of latitude in the conduct of their operations, but their direction from me was to serve as a value-added component to our conventional forces and to do what they could to make the Iraqis a more effective security force in their battlespace. Our mandate, as with the previous squadrons, was that we would conduct no unilateral operations. At all times, SEALs were to conduct their operations with Iraqi soldiers. In Ramadi, Tim Ryan stepped in right where Jack Williams left off.

"Ramadi was especially tough, and our task unit there was in the thick of it. They were still in the fight to establish combat outposts and purging the city of insurgents. Putting in the outposts got easier toward the end of their tour, but in October and November of last year, the insurgents still had the run of the town. The COPs that were in place were taking fire daily, as were the guys out on patrol. It was still a very dangerous city. It wasn't until early 2007, as we were preparing to redeploy, that things got turned around.

"The biggest thing for us in all of al-Anbar was the transition from working with the Iraqi army to working with the Iraqi police. Things didn't really settle down in al-Anbar until we got the local police on the streets, and nowhere was that change more important and more dramatic than in Ramadi.

"As you spend time with Tim and his task unit, they'll tell you about our decision to shift away from overwatch engagements. That was a sea change for us, but it allowed us to move on and be more engaged with the tribes and the Iraqi police. And another thing," he said at the end of our interview, "I know your focus is on Ramadi, and they were in the center of things, but my other task units did some great things as well. Talk about some of them if you can."

"Aye, aye, sir," I replied.

The task unit that arrived in Ramadi in October with Squadron Five could not have stepped into a more challenging situation. Unlike the task unit from Squadron Three before them and the TU from Squadron Seven that was to follow, they had little time for area familiarization or training or any kind of gradual operational transition. The Battle of Ramadi had been ongoing for close to four months. It was still raging. At the end of October there were ten COPs fighting to hold their ground and the neighborhoods around them, and there were four functioning Iraqi police stations. Each of these new emplacements had to be continually defended. The insurgents still controlled the Government Center in Ramadi and the core of the city. The level of violence had not slackened. Yet the U.S. commanders in Ramadi sensed that the battle was starting to go their way. This optimism was buoyed by the recent pledges of support from the Ramadi tribal leaders. Led by Sheikh Sattar, the Awakening now counted eleven sheikhs and their tribes as allied with the Americans and the Iraqi army against al-Qaeda. Volunteers for the Iraqi police had been barely a trickle throughout the summer of 2006. Now, with the full backing of the more influential sheikhs, this trickle had become a flood. The last quarter of 2006 saw close to two thousand new Anbaris volunteer for police duty— nearly a thousand of those in December alone. Many of these new police volunteers were former insurgent fighters who had "flipped" to our side as their tribes joined the Awakening. Things were clearly changing in Ramadi and, indeed, all of al-Anbar. But the insurgent tentacles still had central Ramadi in their grip, and they were not going to give up easily.

The fall of 2006 also seemed to be a time of "sorting out" for local tribal leaders as well as for al-Qaeda and its constituents. The tribal leadership appeared to want to reengage in the national political process, demanding greater recognition and participation in the government along with a more equitable sharing of the oil revenues. Oddly enough, they also petitioned the al-Maliki government in Baghdad for a withdrawal of U.S. forces—even as they were moving toward a closer working relationship with those same forces. It may seem like the sheikhs were talking out of both sides of their mouth, but that's not inconsistent with Anbari tribal politics. It was a reminder to the American-led counterinsurgency effort in al-Anbar that this new sense of cooperation on the part of the tribes was fueled by the threat posed by AQI. Al-Qaeda and its allies in the region continued on in what, in retrospect, was a disastrous course. In the wake of the death of Abu Musab al-Zarqawi the previous June, AQI leaders renewed their efforts to establish the Islamic State of Iraq and set up governing councils across al-Anbar to impose their will on the population. They even designated certain al-Qaeda operatives as emirs to lead a campaign against those who opposed their vision for Iraq—a vision that continued to be at odds with tribal culture. AQI continued to insist on establishing strict sharia law in this new Islamic State of Iraq, something the more secular and tribal Sunnis of al-Anbar opposed. This kept AQI on an adversarial track with the sheikhs, causing an increasing number of these tribal leaders to reject the insurgency and join the Awakening. In essence the al-Qaeda-sponsored Islamic State of Iraq had the effect of driving more of the tribal leaders into a partnership with American and Iraqi security forces. This new and emerging Anbari-American alliance was a marriage of convenience, as neither the tribes nor the Americans seemed able to manage the insurgent presence on their own.

A key element in the Battle of Ramadi was the emergence of the Iraqi police. The Army and the Marines could take the streets, but holding them on an ongoing basis was a police function. The presence of soldiers and marines on street corners in Ramadi was at best a temporary solution. Even the Iraqi army, with its Shiite bias, was unwelcome in Ramadi on any kind of permanent basis. When Sean MacFarland and Sheikh Sattar hatched a plan to recruit, train, and pay men from the local tribes to serve as policemen, the streets of Ramadi began to change for the better. There was now a force in waiting that could come in behind the soldiers and marines as they cleared the neighborhoods of insurgents. A key element of this plan was for the new police force to be recruited locally and trained locally—at least initially—and to serve in their local communities. Still, there was a great deal of fighting to be done.

The task unit from Squadron Five relieved the task unit from Squadron Three in mid-October. The actual turnover took only a few days. By this stage of the conflict, most of the SEALs and all of the senior task unit leadership were combat veterans, so these changeovers were seamless. And as is the current practice, a small cadre of Team Five SEALs from the task unit had visited Ramadi several weeks earlier for a site survey and a ration of "ground truth." They had gone into Ramadi on operations with the SEALs from Three for a firsthand look at a war they would soon inherit. Armed with this information, they had returned to Coronado to guide their task unit's final preparations. For Lieutenant Commander Tim Ryan, this deployment marked a return to Ramadi. It had been a little over a year since he had operated here as a platoon OIC with Squadron Seven in Habbaniyah. As Jake Williams took him around to meet the senior Army and Marine commanders, he was greeted by a more robust infrastructure at Camp Ramadi and Camp Lee. And a full-on battle for the city.

"When we came up here from Habbaniyah in the summer and fall of 2005, the insurgents were not so entrenched or organized. The streets were dangerous and you could get shot at, but they had yet to be able to claim control of whole neighborhoods. Now they had a much greater presence, at least in those parts of the city where there were no outposts. A great many insurgents had been killed in the fighting, and others had left the city or had joined the police. But the real hard-core fighters had pulled back into the districts and areas they still controlled. There were the foreign fighters still filtering across the Syrian border. Taking back these neighborhoods from these veteran insurgents was still a torturous business. The task unit from Three did a great job, and we had to step in and pick up where they left off.

"The bad guys still operating in Ramadi seemed to have taken their urban-warfare skills to the next level," Ryan said, "but then so had we. I had a lot of veteran SEALs in my task unit who were no strangers to urban combat. There were a few new men in the platoons, but the nature of our predeployment training had brought them up to speed. On balance, the task unit was an experienced and mature force. As for the enemy, there was probably a distillation process at work. The dumb ones had been killed off, and those not committed to the insurgency had faded away. The ones that stayed with it were pretty good. They could move tactically in five- to eight-man elements, they knew the terrain, and they could conduct fire-and-maneuver tactics as well as we could. And they were organized; they could still mass a great number of fighters at any one location. As we continued to reclaim parts of the city, the ones that survived got better.

"The talent in my task unit extended beyond the SEAL operators. The outgoing task unit has some terrific people in their intelligence and targeting components. I had good people as well, and they made sure there was a smooth transition in those intelligence-related areas. Those coming and going sought each other out. The master-at-arms, the medical people, the mechanics, the Seabees—all connected with their counterparts and helped with the transition. By this stage of the war, there were a lot of veterans, both on the operational side and the support side. They were all professionals, and made sure their relief had a handle on the work before they stepped back."

Tim Ryan is a more compact and blonder version of Jake Williams. He grew up in southern New Jersey and was recruited by the Naval Academy to play football. He played linebacker for four years and graduated with the Class of 1997. Before coming to Team Five, Ryan had served with SEAL Team Eight and SDV Team One. Before 9/11 he had served in Kosovo and participated in maritime interdiction operations in the Persian Gulf. As a platoon OIC in Habbaniyah, he was one of the few SEALs in his task unit with experience in both training and operating with the Iraqi army scouts. Like most of his veteran SEALs, Ryan had seen combat in al-Anbar. But the rotation of this task unit from Squadron Five into Ramadi was different, even unprecedented. Never in the history of the Navy SEALs had SEAL platoons been so heavily engaged in an ongoing urban battle—an all-out war for a city. So never before had a new task unit stepped into a pitched battle like the one under way in Ramadi.

"Our mission in Ramadi was not a lot different from the task unit we relieved," Ryan said. "We wanted to do what we could to support the conventional forces. We were also to help with tribal engagement and to work closely with the Iraqi security forces. In short, my job was to use the assets of my task unit to support the brigade battle plan. We especially wanted to use our intelligence assets and targeting cell to best advantage, both for our own operations and for the benefit of the Army and the Marines. We inherited the army *jundis* who were trained by the previous task units. But they were getting a little battle weary, and there was always the issue of new soldiers joining the scouts. We had no choice but to go into battle with these scouts. So we had a lot on our plate in Ramadi and not much time to make ourselves battle ready. Past going into the streets of Ramadi and trading bullets with the insurgents, our biggest challenge became working with the Iraqi police. This was something we had neither planned nor trained for. Fortunately, it didn't come about until the last half of our tour. There were very few volunteers for the Iraqi police when we got there, but that began to change, and we were pressed into service as police trainers."

I asked Tim Ryan what they had done differently than previous task units to prepare for coming to Ramadi.

"I was satisfied with our training and predeployment work-up. The [Naval Special Warfare] Group One training detachment conducts West Coast predeployment training. They do a great job, and their curriculum is constantly being refined. We were the first squadron since 9/11 to have a full eighteen-month work-up—at least most of the squadron did. [Tim Ryan had moved from Team Seven to Team Five, allowing him only a year away from Iraq and al-Anbar—a year to train with his task unit before going back on deployment.] Tactically, it was probably little different from Squadron Three's professional development training and unit level training. During the squadron integration phase of our training, we had some trainers from the Joint Special Operations University [JSOU] in Florida come to Coronado and give us some counterinsurgency and culture-awareness training. It all helps, especially for the new guys and for some of the vets who may have only worked with the ISOF and are now entering a pure counterinsurgency environment. And a few of my people had previously only deployed to Afghanistan. Going into Ramadi, we knew our job was to support the conventional forces and to work with the Iraqis. Anything we could do to learn about the people helped. The

JSOU trainers also helped us with some advanced planning techniques and command-and-control issues.

"One thing available to us that I don't think the previous squadrons had was the Group One cultural-training unit. We knew that if and when we got past the kinetic operations, we'd be dealing a lot with the Iraqi people. There's a Defense Language Institute extension that makes language and cross-cultural training available to deploying SEAL squadrons. It was up to us at the team and squadron level to schedule what time we could for this training, so we worked it in. We thought it would help us better understand the people in al-Anbar."

This cultural/language-training unit amounted to a small section assigned to the Group One training detachment. Two civilian employees staff this training unit, one of them a native-Arabic speaker. Rasha was of Egyptian descent, and when I met with her, she was wearing traditional Arab dress.

"We try to tailor our training to the requirements of the deploying SEALs," Rasha told me, "depending on what they think they'll need, given where they are going and what they will be doing there. We have to fit our training around their schedule—they are very busy. Some squadron components want a week of continuous training and will make that time available to us. Other deploying units may want two hours a day, once a week, over an extended period of time. Most of this is cultural information for everyday use—customs such as the use of the right hand in greeting or eating, or the custom of entering a Muslim home with the right foot, never the left. We try to acquaint them with the Arab concept of honor and shame, and what constitutes an insult. We talk about small things, such as the Arab sense of time and the importance of eye contact, even when communicating through an interpreter. We give them handbooks of useful phrases in Arabic, both for day-to-day dealings and in military context."

"How is this training received?" I ask her.

"For the most part very well," she said. "There are always a few who only come to class because they are ordered to. They typically tend to be the younger men. Most of the SEALs want this information and use it. Often they will stop by the office when they return and tell us about how something they learned in class helped them in Iraq. Sometimes they tell us about a lesson learned that we can add to our training to make it better." A big smile creased her dark features. "And sometime they bring me presents. I just received this." She took down a folded flag from a shelf and held it up for me to see; it was green with Arabic script on it. "Green is the symbolic color in Islam. It's often used on banners and was the color of the first Islamic flag."

I spoke with Tim Ryan as he was leaving Team Five for duty as the executive officer at one of the SDV teams. He's married and has three children. "This next tour will probably be a good one for me," he said, referring to the largely administrative duties that fall to a team exec. "The CO usually does the traveling, so I'll get stuck at home with the paperwork. No complaints here; I'm looking forward to some family time. I'm overseas a great deal, and I need be around home for a while."

The task unit from Squadron Five in Ramadi began its tour in support of the 1st Brigade Combat Team of the 1st Armored Division and its assigned battalions. That October there was a combined force of five battalions—four Army and one Marine. By the end of Squadron Five's tour, an additional Marine infantry battalion had been added to the mix. Tim Ryan deployed his task unit in Ramadi in much the same way as Jake Williams, but with some modifications. Ryan elected to break his two platoons into three assault elements, one at Camp Corregidor and the other two at Camp Marc Lee. With a few extra SEAL operators at his disposal, he was able to put three elements in the field with roughly twelve SEALs per element. The bulk of the task unit personnel settled into Camp Lee in support of Ramadi-wide operations.

The Ramadi task unit transition had about a hundred people coming in and a hundred rotating out. The two task unit commanders had been in contact by e-mail and phone, as had the senior TU leadership with their opposite numbers throughout the TU organization. For the new arrivals there were the mechanics of introductions to the conventional players and in-briefings on the current battlefield. At Camp Lee there were base familiarization, tactical-operations-center procedures, and intelligence updates. There was also the careful handover of the interpreters and scouts. Underlying all this was the nonoperational side of the changeover. For the outgoing group there's the emotion and anticipation that comes with going home—family, friends, time off, lots of sleep, and the delicious feeling of being out of danger. And the memory of teammates killed and wounded to bring into perspective, once out of the combat zone. For the new task unit, this is the culmination of up to a year and half of predeployment work-up. Within the platoons, there is the anticipation of close combat. For the new men, a chance for validation after two and a half years of continuous training. For the veterans, many of whom are returning in positions of increased leadership, it's a return to the fight. Many of the SEALs I spoke with said they returned to Iraq with a mixture of anticipation and anxiety—eagerness and apprehension. There's the expectation of the adrenaline high that comes with going into danger, combined with the individual pride in having mastered a hard-won combat skill set. For the platoon SEALs, it's about the job—they're warriors who see themselves as quiet professionals. For the platoon leadership, there's all that plus the heavy responsibility that goes with planning combat operations and leading men in harm's way. I spoke at length with several of those junior combat leaders from Squadron Five, shortly after they returned from Ramadi.

At first glance, Lieutenant Ned Stallard is an unlikely looking SEAL. He has a bleached, youthful California look; he's five-seven, a solid 160, and not a terribly imposing figure. Yet there is a maturity and measured intensity about him. He's a very careful listener. He'll wince when he reads this, but it's easier to picture him in a Boy Scout uniform than a set of body armor leading a squad of SEALs into battle. He deployed as an assistant platoon OIC and became one of the assault element leaders for the Camp Lee–based SEALs. This was his second combat rotation. He graduated from the Naval Academy in 2000 and with SEAL Class 234 in 2001.

"I grew up in Utah and was recruited to play soccer at the Academy. When I got to Annapolis in the summer of 1996, I didn't really know what a naval officer was or even did. It's been quite an adventure and learning experience, coming from Salt Lake City to the SEAL teams. Fortunately, I've been blessed with great SEAL operators and great enlisted SEAL leaders. They looked out for me during my first tour and again on this last one—especially the last one."

Stallard had been back from deployment only a week and will be leaving Team Five for duty at Group One with one of the operational support components. He's been married only a short while—no children but one dog, a husky. Ned Stallard is the first SEAL I've met who drives a Toyota Prius.

Petty Officer Don Wettack is a different sort; where Ned Stallard is reserved and measured, Wettack is outgoing and animated—a stocky man with rounded features, soft brown eyes, and an easy smile. He talks with his hands. He's not much taller than his lieutenant, but he has a good forty pounds on him, and he is a much coarser article. Wettack was the leading petty officer of Stallard's element in Ramadi and his senior enlisted SEAL. He graduated with Class 231. This was his second tour in Iraq and third combat rotation. There's a restless energy about him compared with his lieutenant's near stoicism. This, too, is Wettack's last rotation with Team Five, at least for a while. When we spoke, he was scheduled to attend the Defense Language Institute in Monterey. He's a Spanish speaker and wants to learn French. While the two are a study in contrasts, there's no question that they are brother warriors—same mold, different ingredients.

"After we changed out with the guys from Squadron Three, we immediately began drills with our Iraqi army scouts," Ned Stallard began. "This was a crash course—to get us familiar with the battlespace and familiar with our scouts. They needed to learn about us as well. They were in various stages of training. Some had been in the army and with the scout platoons for some time and many were relatively new. From the beginning, our biggest issue with the scouts at Camp Ramadi was the large numbers and the turnover. Of the close to two-hundred-some soldiers in the scout platoons, only about half of them were at Camp Ramadi at any one time. They had other duties besides working with us. They served as scouting elements for the Iraqi army and they were often detailed as bodyguards for senior Iraqi army officers. So on any given day we didn't know what we had to work with. Aside from turnover, there was the war; we were in the middle of an urban offensive, so any training or familiarization had to be done quickly.

"We began with individual and squad movement, and patrolling, and quickly moved on to some range work, room entry, close-quarter battle. Most of the *jundis* had at least some of this training from the previous task units. We had four groups of scouts at Camp Ramadi, the three Iraqi battalion scout elements and our brigade's special missions platoon. But they were continually rotating out of garrison on leave, usually to Baghdad. Ramadi was true combat duty for them, and many simply just didn't return; they didn't want to go back out there. To be fair about it, some of them were serious about their duty and their training, while others were basically civilians in uniform. With SEALs, soldiers, or marines, we've all had the same baseline training, so you can grab a guy from one service and put him in the squad file, and for the most part, he'll do fine with the basics—patrolling or fire and movement. We had no such assurances with the scouts at Camp Ramadi."

"Most of our scouts were Shia from Baghdad," Don Wettack said, "so while they could speak to the locals and help us conduct residential searches, they really didn't know the locals or the neighborhoods. They were outsiders—foreigners like us. When we went out on operations, we would request a half dozen scouts to go with us. What would show up could be anywhere from four to ten. Some of them we came to know on sight, but there would always be new faces. The preoperation rehearsals became important, just so we could see who was there and make sure they were all good to go."

"The bottom line," Ned Stallard said, "was that we came to have a low degree of trust in many of our scouts. Some of them stayed away longer than they should have when they were on leave from their units. We knew, from our interpreters, that a few of them were spending extended off-duty time in the service of Muqtada al-Sadr and his Mahdi Army in Baghdad. They were part-time Shia militiamen." Stallard voiced these reservations regarding the Iraqi scouts very carefully. "Our situation regarding the scouts in Ramadi was a little different from that of the previous task units. We simply didn't have the time on the range with them or in a noncombat environment. The previous TUs had the luxury of an extended training period and time for break-in patrols in relatively safe areas before things got hard. We had to jump into the middle of a war with them. Our plate was pretty full; every week there was either a new COP or a new police station going in. When we were out there, we were always in contact. Don't get me wrong, many of the scouts were brave and patriotic, and did their job. In some situations they were an asset, and sometimes they weren't. We often simply didn't have the time to work with them and get things right. We were getting shot at all the time."

Over at Camp Corregidor, Lieutenant Craig Thomas quietly took over from Lieutenant Sean Smith as OIC of the Corregidor SEAL element. Smith took him around and introduced him to the conventional commanders, including Lieutenant Colonel Chuck Ferry, commanding officer of the 1-9 infantry battalion in the 2nd Infantry Division, which had relieved 1-506. Ferry was an experienced commander and one of few battalion commanders to have experience with both SOF and SEALs. He was an enlisted Special Forces soldier and had spent time as an officer with the 75th Ranger Regiment, including the heavy fighting in Mogadishu.

"I had worked with SEALs before and, by chance, had worked with Craig Thomas on a training exercise at the National Training Center the previous summer. They quickly became an essential part of our battalion task force at Camp Corregidor. They jokingly called themselves Army SEALs, but they were true team players. They did a lot for us—raids, sniper work, source operations, and training our Iraqi scout and police elements. When they were not on missions, I asked them to teach sensitive site exploitation, breaching, and other special skills to my soldiers. For me as a conventional commander, it was a great relationship. Bottom line, this was a great group of SEALs and a good example of conventional-SOF integration under difficult combat conditions."

The Sean Smith–Craig Thomas relief left Ferry wondering about the Navy's template for SEAL platoon OICs. At six-five and close to 230, Thomas was only slightly taller than Smith. Both were towheaded blonds. Like Sean Smith, Thomas was a Naval Academy graduate. He graduated with BUD/S Class 228. He had come to Team Five from a staff tour in Germany, but he was no stranger to combat in Iraq. He was with the deployed SEAL squadron based in Kuwait during the opening days of the Iraq War and was one of the first SEALs on the ground. Thomas had led a SEAL element in the capture of a key pipeline valve station as the SEALs moved to secure the Iraqi oil-exporting infrastructure. The details of that action, and Craig Thomas's role in seizing that important facility, are detailed in chapter 5, "Night of the Navy SEALs," of *Down Range: Navy SEALs in the War on Terrorism*. Since his last trip to Iraq, but before leaving for Germany, Thomas became engaged and married. On the eve of this deployment, his wife was five months pregnant with their first son.

There was a second officer with Thomas at Corregidor. They were the Mutt and Jeff of the SEAL element leadership there. Lieutenant Chuck Wall is dark-haired, with the compact, muscular build of a wrestler, and close to a foot shorter than his OIC. Yet when they're together, they come across as brothers and equals. Wall is a former fleet enlisted sailor from Texas. He qualified for the Navy's Seaman to Admiral program and took his degree at the University of Oklahoma.

"I always wanted to be a SEAL and a career naval officer. The Navy gave me the chance to do both. I got through Oklahoma in three years by taking classes year-round. Instead of going back to the fleet, I began SEAL training with Class 235. Then I got hurt in training, and that set me back a while. I thought I was going to be in BUD/S longer than I was in college. When I finally graduated with Class 238, I was lucky enough to deploy right out of training with the Squadron Five detachment in the Philippines. This was my third rotation with Five." He will be with Five for the next tour as well. Chuck Wall will be a platoon OIC for the next Squadron Five rotation.

The Squadron Five SEAL element at Corregidor quickly settled into the Full Metal Jacket building, which was left to them by their departing brothers from Squadron Three. They did this quickly and immediately began looking for work and targets. The SEAL element's petty officers were immediately out linking up with available sources of local military intelligence and battlefield knowledge. These ranged from the Army intelligence specialists to the civil affairs cadres to the military transition teams—the MiTTs. Like their brother SEALs at Camp Lee, they had to become familiar with their Iraqi army scouts quickly.

"We inherited a great bunch of scouts," recalled Petty Officer Byron Abdul. "We were lucky in that regard. It's hard to compare our scouts with the *jundis* at Camp Lee. Theirs was a different situation. With a few exceptions, our Iraqi scouts were good to go. The guys from Three said they'd bleed for us, and they were right. They were good, and we worked to make them even better. By the time we left, the lead group of scouts from our Iraqi brigade's 1st Battalion were able to run their own operations. We had the 2nd and 3rd battalion scouts also doing pretty well."

The Corregidor SEALs' liaison with 1st Division Iraqi scout contingent couldn't have been a better fit. Petty Officer Byron Abdul was on his second combat rotation and had seen action in both Iraq and Afghanistan. His father is Iraqi, and he has the strong dark features of his heritage. Abdul has limited conversational Arabic, but he can make himself understood, both on the street and in working with the brigade scouts.

"They were selected pretty carefully to start with, and they'd also had six months of work with the previous platoon here. We put them through a quick two-week training course to see what they could do, and there wasn't a lot we needed to teach them. They knew each other and, after a few operations, we came to know them as well. The two weeks of training was primarily to make sure our tactics and procedures matched up with theirs. We trained at Camp Corregidor and very quickly took our training sessions on patrol in the Mala'ab District."

"The difference between the scouts at Camp Ramadi and Camp Corregidor was turnover," Tim Ryan explained, "and they came from different divisions of the Iraqi army, and their respective brigades each had its own character and level of experience. The Corregidor scouts were smaller in number, and they were allowed to function as a unit. It takes time to build unit cohesion and a sense of unit integrity. So it was easier for the Corregidor SEALs to get close to their scouts. And," Ryan said with a smile, "Byron Abdul was a natural as liaison petty officer with the scouts. A lot of it has to do with personality, and Byron was as capable as he was affable and outgoing."

"These guys genuinely liked Americans," Abdul said of the Corregidor scouts. "There were a few we had questions about, but for the most part they were all right. In their barracks, they had little American flags on their lockers and pictures of Mike Monsoor. Our casualties were their casualties. When we left, we traded gifts with them. They were our brother warriors."

I pressed him on the reasons for the success of the *jundis* at Camp Corregidor. "It just takes time—time and leadership. There were some seasoned enlisted leaders in the Corregidor scouts, men who took pride in their units. And we were physically closer to them. It was a little easier for us to look after them and make sure they were getting paid and they were getting good chow. You take care of them and they'll take care of you. We proved that on the battlefield."

The Corregidor SEAL element began its combat operations where their predecessors left off, with a combination of direct-action raids and overwatch operations in support of Marine and Army patrols. These overwatch operations in support of the Battle of Ramadi came to a head on 19 November during a joint operation with the SEALs from Camp Lee.

Every few weeks, the SEALs from Corregidor made their way over to Camp Lee to reconnect with the full task unit and the ongoing operations in western Ramadi conducted by the Camp Lee SEALs. They did this in mid-November and returned to Camp Corregidor with a mission in hand for the morning of 19 November. The Army and the Marines were going to be patrolling in force in several sectors of the city, and they had requested whatever help they could get from the SEAL task unit. Given the number of soldiers and marines that were going to be on the street, both Camp Lee SEAL elements and the Camp Corregidor element planned overwatch operations to support them. The Camp Lee SEALs were set in two separate sniper overwatches in the Al Iskan

District in support of Army and Marine patrols working out of Camp Ramadi. These overwatches would be close to each other and mutually supportive. The mission of the soldiers and marines that day was cordon-and-search operations in the Al Iskan and Al Andols districts. The Corregidor SEALs were to set up three overwatch positions in the southern Mala'ab District to serve as a blocking element in support of the overwatch positions of the Camp Lee SEALs; they were to guard their eastern flank. Both the Army and the Marines would be on the street with elements of the Iraqi army. As they had done many times before, the overwatch teams were to patrol in that night, set up their positions, and be ready in their shooting perches at first light.

"This was still early in our deployment," Craig Thomas said of their overwatch operations, "but we knew the drill and we knew the dangers. We were also prepared to accept more risk in these overwatches as we were working in support of our other SEAL elements. On this operation, we were going to be in the southwest part of the Mala'ab District, a particularly dangerous area. All the SEAL elements out that night were operating in support of the Army and Marines. Their mission was to push their patrols into some of the more contested neighborhoods, and the SEAL mission was to do what we could to keep them safe while they did. The insurgents knew what we were doing in these overwatches, but we had to balance our risk with the added security we could bring to the patrols in the streets. We knew this would probably be a contested operation, so we made sure we had some of our best *jundis* from the Corregidor brigade with us."

Just before midnight they drove in Humvees from Camp Corregidor to COP Eagles Nest, the outpost that would support the operation. There they conducted their final briefings and set up the procedures for QRF and CASEVAC help—a standby quick-reaction force and a casualty evacuation capability—should they be needed. Shortly after midnight, the SEALs and their support elements patrolled en masse to their preplanned overwatch positions. The Corregidor SEAL element had close to a dozen scouts along with EOD techs and Marine ANGLICO personnel. There were close to fifty in the patrol. Their mission that night was to set up three overwatch positions and wait for daylight. As they approached the target area, they split into their assigned three groups and made for their separate overwatch sites. Craig Thomas was in charge of one, with Chuck Wall to be a block away leading another. Their element chief petty officer was in the third overwatch a short distance from Wall's position. They had selected the three overwatch positions so they served as a blocking-force line to protect the planned operations to the east *and* to be mutually supportive of each other. But when they arrived at the preplanned sites, they found they found them unsuitable to for both objectives. New sites were quickly selected and seized. These new locations were sited in such a way that they protected the Marines, but couldn't directly support each other. All three overwatch teams were in their sites by 3:00 AM and began to set up their positions.

"It didn't feel right from the beginning," a SEAL in Craig Thomas' group said. "When we set up in an overwatch position, we usually have to take over the home of some luckless Iraqi family. Most often, they make the best of it, and some even welcome us and make us tea. Arabs take guests and these courtesies seriously, even uninvited guests in wartime. And they know we'll pay for anything that gets broken. But in my overwatch, the family was very sullen—quiet and fearful, like they knew something was up. Still, we had a job to do. The Army and Marine patrols were scheduled to be on the ground midmorning. We went to the upper floors and began to set up positions and fields of fire. Since Mike Monsoor's death, we tried not to go on the roofs, preferring to remain inside and better protected from grenades. To get one of the sniper rifles where we needed it, we had to knock a hole in an exterior wall so we could cover one of the cross streets. We did it, but we made a lot of noise in the process."

"We began to get more apprehensive after it got light," recalled Craig Thomas. "There was none of the normal movement on the streets—no women or kids. But the F/A-18s overhead now had visual surveillance and reported, through the ANGLICO controllers, movement throughout the area and armed men closing on the overwatch positions. Something was definitely up, but it was still quiet. So we spend an uneasy morning watching the streets. There were kids out moving and we knew they were probing our position. Midmorning we shot two armed muj on the street, a few blocks from our position. Then the midday call to prayer came, but it ended in an unusual way. Our senior enlisted *jundi* came running in to warn me that something was all wrong. And then the grenade came in.

"I don't know how that guy did it," Thomas said as he recalled the beginning of the fight, "but he must have been Spider-Man. He also must have had a huge set of cojones. He had to have jumped from a neighboring roof and onto our building, then crabbed his way down to the shooting port we opened in the wall to toss in the grenade."

The insurgents were learning that gun battles with SEALs were not a good idea. If the insurgents could shoot at them, the SEALs could shoot back, and they were much better shots—advantage SEALs. Increasingly, the insurgents' tactics were designed to locate the SEAL overwatch positions and move fighters in as close as possible, moving in the blind spots to get under the SEAL sniper rifles. Their objective was to get within grenade-tossing range, or, in this case, get to an adjacent building and lob a grenade through a window or a shooting port.

"I was on the lower floor and on my way up when I heard Eddie yell, 'Grenade!' and then there was an explosion," Thomas recalled. "When I got there, Petty Officer Ed Marcum was down and he was badly hurt. By now we're under small-arms fire from several directions, as were the other overwatch positions. The grenade seemed to be the initiator for a coordinated attack on our three overwatch positions. But now all our focus was on caring for Ed. He needed more medical attention than we were able to provide. There was nothing to do but to call the QRF and prepare to extract under fire. As we prepared to leave the overwatch site, things got quiet—unnaturally so."

Lieutenant Thomas raised COP Eagles Nest to alert the QRF and the CASEVAC that they needed both. By this stage of the battle, the SEAL-Army relationship was well cemented. The outpost soldiers were more than willing to come for their SEAL brothers when things got out of hand, or, as in this case, when they had wounded.

"We waited inside the door until we heard them coming for us," one of Thomas's SEALs said. "It was quiet on the street, but we're never more vulnerable than when we're entering or leaving vehicles in the street. Armored vehicles make a lot of noise and draw a lot of attention. The plan was to get our four *jundis*, Ed, and the SEAL who was carrying him into the first Bradley, and the rest of us would follow in trailing vehicles. As we left the entrance to the overwatch, there was this huge explosion. I thought we got hit by an RPG; it was all very confusing—lots of smoke and noise. As it happened, one of the scouts had tripped an IED that I *know* wasn't there when we went into the building. The blast wounded three of the four *jundis*. Ed took another round of shrapnel, as did Jim Heller, the SEAL who was carrying Ed. Both SEALs were down, bleeding, and on fire. Their legs were broken and laid at odd angles—unnatural angles. We had no choice but to get Ed, Jim, and two of the wounded *jundis* back inside to safety. And now we were under fire from several directions. The muj had sprung a pretty good ambush, and they weren't about to call it quits, nor did they have any intention of letting us leave."

Once back into the relative protection of the overwatch, Craig Thomas called the other overwatches and told them he couldn't extract without help. "Ed and Jim were in a bad way. Their body armor had protected their torsos, but their legs and arms had taken a lot of shrapnel. Ed was incredible. He was our corpsman and he was badly hurt, but that didn't keep him from telling us what to do. We got a nonstop tutorial as we attended to Jim. He insisted we treat Jim first, then we started back to work on him. All the while, Ed never stopped talking treatment. Two of our scouts were not hurt too badly, but one died in short order. He had been closest to the IED, and it nearly cut him in half.

"After the IED went off," Thomas continued, "I was dazed and barely functioning. I wasn't hurt, but it knocked me down and I got my bell rung. It took me a while to get straight. Meanwhile my platoon communicator stepped up and took charge. He saw to the wounded, set up security, and managed our position. He was everywhere. I remember him running through fire to drag wounded men back inside—he had Ed, and I wrestled with Jim. Then he was on the radio coordinating the QRF and the CASEVAC. He calmly and courageously did what had to be done. I couldn't have been prouder of him. He consolidated our position and made us safe. Throughout all of this, we were taking a great deal of fire. I'm not sure we'd have got out of there if the other overwatch teams hadn't got back to us."

"I knew Craig had wounded, and they'd been hit again as they tried to extract from their overwatch position," said Chuck Wall of the action. "I knew if another couple men went down, then we'd have been in *real* trouble. There was nothing for us to do but to collapse back on Craig's position to help. When we stepped out onto the street we came under fire. There were bad guys everywhere. It became a fire-and-movement drill with rounds chipping at the buildings as we moved. My chief and his overwatch team moved in along one street and I came in on another. We could only move by leapfrogging under covering fire; it was a full-on fire-and-movement drill. It took us about five minutes to get to where Craig's element was pinned down."

Craig Thomas just shook his head as he remembered the battle. "I was scared, frustrated, and really pissed off. Then I saw Chuck and the others working their way toward us. They took up positions along the street to support us. That allowed us to focus on Ed and Jim. Both were still bleeding and Ed was in a lot of pain. We had applied tourniquets and pressure bandages, and did what we could to get them ready to move. We had our pill packs, and used them once we had the major bleeding controlled." The SEALs all carry preloaded pill cases that have a mix of antibiotics and painkillers. IVs are seldom used, unless the wounded man can't be moved for a while, as they thin the blood and impede clotting. "However, in a situation like that, the best medicine is fire superiority."

"Craig looked like a man possessed when I got to him," Chuck Wall recalled with a grin. "His face was flush and smeared with sweat, dirt, and smoke. He'd been yelling so much that he could hardly talk. Once we got some more guns in place along the street, it took some pressure off the wounded men and the SEALs who were tending to them. Yet we were all on the street level and most of the fire was coming from the second and third floors of the buildings along the street. After a while we were all pretty much pinned down—Craig and his people in their building and the rest of us in doorways along the street. We all knew the really ticklish part was going to be covering the guys inside as they dashed from the relative security of the building to the Bradleys. 'Dash' is maybe not the right word. Neither Larry nor Ed could walk. So when the Bradleys finally got to us, I told them to work out on the upper floors of the buildings on both sides of the street. As they moved down the street toward us, they tore into the upper floors of the buildings with their 25-millimeter chain guns. We took refuge in the doorways and hunkered down. It was kind of frightening with them shooting just over our heads; like the end of the world. There was debris flying everywhere. A couple of the SEALs in Craig's overwatch building had to shield the Iraqi residents with their own bodies.

"The Bradleys gave us the covering fire we needed to get our butts out of there," said Wall. "A Bradley is only supposed to carry six armed men, but we stretched that a bit. We were packed in there like sardines, shooting over the top of the ramp as it came up and trying not to jostle the men who were hurt. One guy was banging away while another guy was tending a tourniquet. What a day; it was wild! I'm just thankful we got the wounded and everyone out safely. It's too bad we lost the one scout; he was a brave one—one of the go-to Iraqis that you could count on."

"It seemed like it took forever for the Bradleys to cycle through and get us all out of there," Craig Thomas added, "and it seemed as if we were in a full-on firefight the whole time. I had to hand it to those Army guys who made the return trips. They were driving into a lot of fire, down streets that could have been mined with IEDs, but they kept coming for us until they got us all out. Those Bradley crews hung it out there for us that day, and none of us will forget their courage and professionalism. And I know my element wouldn't have made it without Chuck and the chief coming back to help us. As we were carrying the wounded men to the vehicles, they were out in the street, shooting and intentionally exposing themselves to draw fire while we loaded up. Besides Eddie and Jim, about half the guys there that morning had shrapnel wounds. It was a messy affair, and I was lucky. I had my SEAL brothers and my Army brothers on the street with me that day. Otherwise, I might not be here. All of those men were heroes, every one of them."

Not more than a half mile away in the Al Iskan District, the overwatch manned by Lieutenant Ned Stallard and Petty Officer Don Wettack was taking heavy fire, but had sustained no casualties that would put a man out of the fight. Less than a block away, the other position, manned by Camp Lee SEALs, was similarly engaged. The insurgents in their area as well had largely ignored the soldiers patrolling on the street and were focusing on them.

"We expected to be in contact, but nothing like this," recalled Don Wettack. "We'd not seen the muj move on us in force like this before. We'd heard that our SEALs over in the Mala'ab were in a fight as well, but we had our hands full for most of the day."

The previous afternoon, their work-up and their mission briefing cycle at Camp Lee had paralleled that of the Corregidor SEALs. Along with their Iraqi scouts, they had arrived at COP Iron after midnight and went into their final preparations for the foot patrol to their overwatch. "We arrived at the COP about 0100 or so," recalled Lieutenant Ned Stallard, "and got straight to the business of getting a local update. The COP commander knew of our mission, but it's always good to go over it with him face-to-face. Those Army troops manning the COPs were terrific and very supportive. When they were pushing out and building the first COPs, including COP Iron, the SEALs from Three sat on overwatches for them, and they never forgot it. 'I don't care where you are in the battlespace,' one of them told me, 'we'll come and get you anywhere, anytime.' Those guys out there living in those COPs were some of the bravest soldiers I've ever met."

"We patrolled out from the COP on foot about 0200," said Don Wettack, "with our point man and an EOD tech out front. There were seventeen of us, including five scouts. The second Camp Lee element was about the same size. We had a long walk in, about fifteen hundred meters. This time, we didn't have to concern ourselves with taking our building. There was a squad of Army troopers already there, and they had secured the building—a three-story residence. They held security on the lower floor while we went upstairs and set up our firing positions. We made our setup in a corner building where we had good fields of fire to the west, east, and especially to the south where the Army patrols were to be working. The other element was in another corner building a block away with a half-torn-down structure between us. This two-position setup gave us some measure of security. As in all setups, we looked for good fields of fire to reach out and cover the Army patrols we're there to protect and to reduce the dead spaces where the muj could try to sneak up and get close to us. It all takes time, even with the Army squad holding the overwatch sites for us. You never get exactly what you want, but you do the best you can. By this time, both we and the enemy knew the deal. That's why we were starting to call these Alamo operations. We were just setting up fighting positions. Since the Army guys were already there, we had to assume the muj knew something was up. The residents of both sites were very cold to us; they probably knew they were going to be in the middle of a fight.

"Once you're in place there's not a lot to do but wait for daylight. We went in heavy on this one," Wettack continued, "and in retrospect, it's a good thing we did. In addition to the sniper weapons we had the Carl Gustav launcher and about ten rounds. Our scouts are good for packing two rounds each. The Army guys couldn't believe we carried that much firepower."

"After we were in position," said Ned Stallard, "we immediately began to get reports of activity—lots of people gathering in groups and moving within a few blocks of our position. Fortunately, the ISR [intelligence, surveillance, and reconnaissance] coverage couldn't have been better. That night we had a Navy pilot with us to serve as our JTAC. Many of us are trained as joint tactical air controllers, but there's nothing like a pilot on the ground speaking with a pilot in the air. In this case it was Navy pilot to Marine Corps pilot, but they're both naval aviators. Our aviator was attached to the task unit, and usually he's back in the TOC. This time he was with us—and was now probably wishing he were back in the TOC. Our pilot had a rover—a laptop-like computer so we could see on the ground what the Marine pilot was seeing in the cockpit. We had an eye in the sky and a good interpretation of what was taking place on the ground. We watched the IR presentation that night and the video into the daylight hours. As soon it got light, the only activity we saw on the streets was the kind we don't like to see—unarmed civilians walking innocently by in plain sight and men peeking around corners. This activity around us told us they knew exactly where we were. And there were groups of armed men that we couldn't see from our shooting perches, but that were plainly visible on the video feed from the ISR. They know the terrain, and they're trying to close in on our positions in the dead spaces. This is not how we like to begin our day in an overwatch. It didn't look as if it were any better for our SEAL brothers over in the Mala'ab District.

"Then our JTAC pilot tells me we have a group of twenty to thirty armed males on the move through a series of abandoned buildings, moving in our direction. We can see them on the overhead imagery, but we can't see them line of sight; their movements in the street are screened from us. Yet we know there's a bunch of armed men, and they were working their way toward us. But we could see the buildings."

"We were lucky," said Wettack, picking up the story. "We knew which buildings they were hiding in, and we had the Gustav. You can't always use it as the backblast is almost as lethal as the business end of the rocket." The Carl Gustav is an 84-millimeter shoulder-launched rocket that carries a seven-pound warhead and is very accurate. It's an unwieldy weapon on patrol, but against armor or in defense of an urban static position, it can come in handy.

"There was a half-story on the top of our building that gave me a good field of fire and a safe area to the rear for the backblast. The backblast can be devastating. By now, we were taking small-arms fire, so you had to be careful in exposing yourself with the launcher. It takes coordination with the other shooters and the guy with the Gustav so he has covering fire. We fired into the one building and a bunch of muj ran from that building to the next. So we put a rocket into that building, and in the next one they ran to after that. We couldn't see them from where we were on the roof, but our pilot was watching the show on his laptop. He said that each time they moved to the next building, there were fewer of them. With the Gustav rockets, you can set in a tenth-of-a-second delay on the warhead, so you get an internal explosion. I don't know how many of them we killed, but the overpressure of that bursting charge had to be taking out their eardrums and really screwing them up."

As the day wore on it became a game of cat-and-mouse, with insurgent fighters trying to get close to the overwatch sites. The two positions, to some extent, were able to protect each other. From their mutually supportive positions, the SEALs kept the insurgents at bay with their precision shooting of their sniper weapons and the indirect fire of their M203 grenade launchers.

"The 203s were very effective when the muj got in close," one of the SEALs told me. "Late that morning, a half dozen or so of them managed to get behind a wall that was only fifty meters or so north of our position. We couldn't get at them with rifles, and if you were to wait for them to pop over the top of the wall to make a shot, you were leaving yourself exposed for an extended period. Not good. We were pretty good with the 203s, and soon we were hitting the top of the wall with 40-millimeter HE [high explosive] grenades. It was enough to send shrapnel and chunks of concrete into the muj crouched behind the wall. That was enough for them; they pulled back, and they had to carry a few of their number out as they were too shredded to walk by themselves."

By early afternoon, the Army commanders were calling their patrols in from the Al Iskan and Al Andols districts. There was little left to do for the Camp Lee SEALs, who were running low on ammunition and getting very weary. "These things can drag on," Stallard related, "and it's a given that you're going to be on your feet for thirty-six hours. We were tired and worried about the overwatch teams from Corregidor; we now knew they had wounded. As we were getting ready to leave, another group of enemy fighters gathered in a nearby building. They were shooting at us, and we knew it would be a little dicey getting out of there—we'd be under fire in the open once we got into the street. We were out of rockets, so we requested permission for an air strike. That's something we very seldom did at that stage of the game because of collateral damage. But we got the clearance and one of the F/A-18s put in a laser-guided Maverick missile." A Maverick packs a 125-pound warhead. "We were all hunkered down, thinking it would be raining concrete from the missile strike, but it was no more of a bang than the Gustav rounds. The missile warhead must have had a delay, as it detonated well inside the building. However, we took no more fire from the building.

"We sent the Army squad out ahead of us, covering them but waiting to see if any of the muj took the bait. Sure enough, a few insurgents began sneaking up the street, thinking we had all left the two buildings.

We took them under fire, and I know we killed at least one of them. That seemed to take the heart out of the rest of the street fighters. They were probably getting as tired as we were. There didn't seem to be any movement along our return route, and that was confirmed by ISR overhead. Still, you have to be careful. So we set up a bounding, leapfrog rotation as we moved back toward COP Iron. By this time we were really low on ammunition, so the Army captain at the COP sent out his Bradleys to pick us up. It wasn't until we got back to the COP that we learned the details of Craig's element—that their two wounded were seriously hurt and that they had lost one of their scouts.

"The overwatch operations were becoming something of a catch-22 for us," Ned Stallard said carefully. I could tell he had mixed feelings about it. "This kind of operation meets many of our tests. First of all, we have the shooters and we have the guns. From a unilateral, offensive standpoint, it's something we do very well, and our long-range shooting capabilities are something the Army and Marines need. If the Army and the Marines are going out there to patrol with their Iraqi counterparts, well, we want to do all that we can to make it safer for them. The scouts that accompany us are learning something every time we go out— they gain confidence, if nothing else. Nevertheless, it was getting very dangerous for us. There was very little we were doing out there that the insurgents didn't know about or couldn't anticipate. They know our size and our capabilities. They know that if they can put us in a bad way and keep us there, then they can attack the QRF and CASEVACs when they come for us. So they were ignoring the patrols and targeting us in these static firing positions. In some ways we were creating a bad situation for the Army QRFs who had to bail us out.

"We usually get a chance to kill a lot of bad guys on these operations, but just who are these bad guys? Are they hard-core AQI fighters, or are they some out-of-work teenagers who just had the muj shove a gun in their hands that morning and push them out into the street? I suspect a lot of the insurgents we shot were new recruits or new draftees—the ones who were easy to kill. And it can't be a good experience for the residents to have us come into their homes and make it Fort Apache, even though they get compensated. I wasn't the only one who was beginning to sense that there was a better use of our time and talent than setting up fixed fighting positions in the nastier parts of the city. One thing was sure; the muj kept getting better at anticipating our moves and targeting the overwatches."

Reflecting on the events of 19 November, Lieutenant Commander Tim Ryan had this to say: "What happened that day certainly caused us to take a closer look at the cost-benefit of the overwatch operations. By cost-benefit, I'm not just speaking of the danger to our people out there in the overwatches. A part of our job was to support the soldiers and marines who had to patrol the neighborhoods with their Iraqi counterparts. If we could support them, then it was a good mission for us. That was especially true during the installation of a new COP. When we got into December, the COPs became a little easier, so our guns were not needed as much. The insurgents were obviously targeting us as much as the patrols on the street or the COPs. The overwatches were simply leading to pitched battles from a static position. Every time we put in an overwatch, we trashed a neighborhood. That's not what we want. The overwatches were becoming a series of escalations that caused collateral damage and cost us good relations with the local population. Anytime the insurgents can get us fighting amid the citizens, then *we* become responsible for the damage and any noncombatant deaths.

"Now, don't get me wrong, there were still more than a few guys out there who deserved a bullet, and the overwatch operations gave us opportunity to do this. We simply can't allow insurgents to move about the streets in force with guns. However, this was an insurgency—a battle for the people—and we had to evaluate our operations in light of that. Does this operation or that combat mission help us in winning the support and trust of the people? In that context we had to step back and *really* be sure who we're killing, no matter what the provocation.

"When the last task unit was supporting the placement of the first COPs, the overwatches were important—essential, really. They saved the lives of a lot of soldiers and marines. Even then, killing insurgents at long range, something we do very well, can be a two-edged sword. Killing a guy because he has a gun or is out digging a hole for an IED by the side of the road, while he may deserve a bullet, can do more harm than good. His whole extended family might take up the cause. So we moved away from the overwatch operations. There were better things for us to do than just shoot insurgents—and maybe get ourselves shot. Insurgents are a renewable resource; only the Iraqis themselves can correct that.

"I also had to look at the overwatch operations considering the tribal engagement that was starting to pay big dividends. That November we were just starting to see the surge in volunteers for the Iraqi police in Ramadi. Insurgencies are much more vulnerable to a police force than to a national military force. It's simple: the police are locals—it's their turf, their neighborhood. So we shifted our focus on getting *them* on the streets and getting *us* off the streets."

I asked him about how this change in tactics affected his SEALs. His answer was measured.

"In some ways it was difficult for them to accept. The overwatches were difficult and dangerous work, but it's what we trained for. It's warriors' work, and our guys are primarily warriors. And our soldiers and marines, and their *jundis,* really appreciated it when we were out there. It was a mission we inherited from Jake Williams's task unit and, up to a point, it was a good mission for us. Without sounding too bloodthirsty or macho, killing guys who are out there trying to kill our conventional brothers can be satisfying. Like I said, it was warriors' work. For the snipers, it was a validation of their long-range shooting skills; they're proud of their abilities. In the end I think they understood why we stood back from the overwatch operations. Even some dirtbag insurgent has a family who will take up the cause if we kill him, and our talents were better employed elsewhere."

In talking with Tim Ryan, I recalled my conversations with Commander Rick Leonard and the decision to abandon the full-on sniper operations.

"We're Americans, and we're a conspicuous presence here in Mesopotamia in general and certainly out in al-Anbar," Leonard had said. "There's always going to be somebody taking issue with our presence, no matter how justified our actions. I remember one of our snipers saying that he had his scope on four kids out digging a hole by the side of the road. He was a good four hundred meters away from them. So he waited until the kids were finished and left. A short time later, this muj steps out of the shadows with a 155-millimeter shell, all wired up for burial as an IED. The sniper takes him out, and we send some EOD techs out to police up the explosives and the initiator. So what's their next step? What are we going to do when four little kids come out with the 155-milimeter shell in a litter, trailing a firing lead, and roll it into the hole? Now it's a functional, command-detonated IED. So what do we do—shoot the kids? We had to get out of the game of shooting insurgent foot soldiers. With the local police beginning to patrol streets and in the neighborhoods, things changed. *They* know the foot soldiers from the senior insurgent leaders from the foreign fighters. They put us in a position to go after the people who counted rather than to just shoot some guy on the street because he has a gun or was given fifty bucks to plant a bomb.

"Had we stopped the overwatches when we arrived or a month earlier," Leonard had continued, "it'd have been too soon. To stay with them longer than we did in Ramadi would have been too long. What those brave SEALs from Squadron Three did was to put fear into the hearts of the muj and made the fight for those first COPs a little easier—a little less costly for the American and Iraqi forces. Thanks to their work, we had the opportunity to shift our focus and move on—to spend more time with the Iraqi police."

"I think Tim and the commanders up the line were right to move away from this," said Craig Thomas. "When we first arrived, most of the guys were anxious to get out there and mix it up. It's not that hard to do. You can go out on any given day in Ramadi and get into a firefight. After we got shot at a few times, we were maybe not so anxious. And the platoon veterans knew we had to work smarter. I know that after November 19 *I* wasn't as keen on it as when we first got here. Fortunately, we had some opportunities to engage with the tribes and work with the tribal police. I think in our hearts we all knew the police were the answer, although it's not the work we train for. Working with the scouts, it was combat FID. We knew that training the police was going to be more like the standard foreign internal defense. We were going to be basic trainers."

"It was time," echoed Ned Stallard. "And maybe a little easier for us at Camp Ramadi. We were not as close to our scouts here as the SEALs were over at Corregidor, so maybe we were more ready to engage with the Iraqi police. Once we started to get the police on the street, the intelligence really began to flow."

The SEALs at Camp Corregidor were settled and reasonably comfortable in their relationship with their Iraqi army scouts. The prospect of training and going into the streets with the new and inexperienced police volunteers was not all that appealing for them.

"We had gotten to know the scouts," said Byron Abdul, "and we'd been on the street with them. There was a range of personalities and abilities with our *jundis,* but the few really good ones were just like having another SEAL alongside you in a firefight. Then, all at once, we were being asked to work with these local Iraqis off the street—guys who all of the sudden had decided they want to become policemen or were told by their tribal sheikhs to become policemen. It was a big change for us. About the time we were wondering how all this was going to work, we were thrust in the middle of it. You might say that the Sufia District made police trainers out of us, almost overnight."

The large Sufia district immediately north of Camp Corregidor was still Indian country in December 2006. The district is dominated by the Albu Soda tribe and, to a lesser extent, the Albu Ghanam tribe in the southeastern portion of the district. Both of the tribes were on the fence and had yet to join with Sheikh Sattar and the Awakening. The Albu Soda had links to other tribes in Ramadi, particularly in the Al Mala'ab District, where pockets of the Albu Soda lived. Most of the tribes were linked in one way or another. To the extent that the U.S. and Iraqi security forces were purging parts of the city of insurgents, it was in the western districts, specifically in the Ta'meem District and those close to the Marines at Hurricane Point. Insurgent elements still moved freely in most of the districts in the south and the east. They also moved in and out of Sufia at will. When the SEALs or their conventional allies ventured into Sufia, they usually did so at night, when they held the tactical advantage with their night-vision optics. A daylight patrol invited sniper attacks and command-detonated IEDs.

One of the problems with the Sufia District was its proximity to Corregidor—well within mortar range. The insurgents would slip into the district and launch mortar rounds into the camp. These mortar attacks invariably invited a response in the form of Army counterbattery fire. The Army has portable radar installations that can quickly and accurately pinpoint where the rounds are coming from, and can return fire with its own mortars or artillery in a matter of seconds. But the insurgents fire their mortars from the bed of a pickup truck in a residential area, or even near a school. When the counterbattery fire arrives, the insurgents and their truck are long gone. It was a convenient exchange of fire on both sides as the Sufia population centers were some three to four thousand meters from Camp Corregidor. Then the Albu Soda tribal leaders stepped in to try to stop this exchange of mortar rounds.

"I don't think they had a real problem with the insurgents coming in and mortaring us," one of the Corregidor SEALs told me, "but they didn't much like the counterbattery."

Sheikh Jassim al-Suwaydawi knew he had to get the insurgents to stop mortaring Camp Corregidor if he wanted to stop the Americans from returning fire. At Jassim's direction, district tribesmen set up checkpoints to restrict the al-Qaeda elements and nonresident insurgents from entering the district. As with all the Anbari tribes, they know who has business in the area and who does not; who lives there and who is an outsider. Initially, they were able to turn back the foreign insurgent elements and things quieted down. However, AQI took exception to this and warned the sheikh to let them through the checkpoints or suffer the consequence. When the sheikh refused to back down, AQI decided to reassert its access and control in the Sufia District.

One afternoon in late December, a large contingent of AQI fighters overpowered a checkpoint and swept into the district. They began to look for tribal members who had manned the checkpoints, and even those who didn't. And they began to do what al-Qaeda does best—kill indiscriminately. As they moved toward the home of Sheikh Jassim, the slaughter continued. A coalition informant inside the Sufia District had been provided a cell phone and reported what was taking place—perhaps the first 911 call in the Sufia District. This alerted the Army at Camp Corregidor. One of the Predator drones that are usually over Ramadi came over to take a look. The video feed back to the TOC at Camp Corregidor captured the killing of Albu Soda tribesmen by al-Qaeda. The home of the sheikh was under siege. That was enough for Lieutenant Colonel Chuck Ferry at Corregidor. He launched Bravo Company of his 1-9 infantry battalion to go to the aid of the tribesmen. The relief column rumbled into the district, and the insurgents melted back into the town when the Americans arrived in force. After they set up security, the rescuers began to tend to the local tribesmen. The insurgents had killed more than thirty of them and wounded many more. Al-Qaeda had sought to make an example of those who opposed them, but they didn't figure on the Americans moving so quickly, or the stubborn streak that seemed to be growing within the tribes.

Sheikh Jassim was evacuated to Corregidor for his personal safety, but not before he told his tribal elders that the Americans were to be welcomed and treated with respect. Bravo Company set up a security perimeter and continued to render medical treatment to wounded tribesmen. They remained in place for the afternoon and a very tense night. Back at Camp Corregidor, Lieutenant Colonel Ferry and his new tribal-leader friend came to an agreement on how to make the district safe. Tribal engagement with the Albu Soda tribe was going into high gear.

"I think we were all taken by surprise," one of the task unit intelligence specialists told me. "Surprised that AQI would take on a whole tribe like that and that the tribe would so readily accept our help. I also think the tribal leaders were surprised that we would come in force as well as all that we were prepared to do for them. Yet that's how al-Qaeda was reacting in the face of the Awakening. If they felt their influence was slipping in an area, they became incrementally more vicious. It played right into our hands. I think the Albu Soda had been led to believe that we were there to occupy their land and take advantage of them. When they understood we wanted only to help, things changed in a hurry. Probably in some ways, I suppose they had little choice."

"We were quick to exploit this opening," Lieutenant Colonel Ferry said. "After our QRF secured the area, we did all we could for their wounded. We saved many lives that afternoon and evening. We knew the insurgents were still hiding in the area, so we took the sheikh out to keep him safe. I have to say that it was with a certain amount of misgiving that I left Bravo Company out there that first night, but it was the right thing to do. Our presence in force and Sheikh Jassim's assurance that we were there at his invitation seemed to quiet things down. I didn't get much sleep that night, not with a full company outside the wire. Nevertheless, we now had a combat outpost in Sufia and we didn't have to fight for it; all we had to do was hold and build. It was a little primitive at first, as we were working out of an abandoned house. But the company stayed on, and now we had a presence. In a single day the Albu Soda had become our allies against al-Qaeda."

Sheikh Jassim returned to his compound four days later with additional Army personnel and a squad of SEALs for security. They set in a forty-eight-hour overwatch near his home to keep him safe from residual insurgent activity. The squad then returned to Camp Corregidor to refit, and was back in Sufia a few days later to begin to train the sheikh's tribesmen as policemen. The day following the return of the SEAL trainers, 176 Albu Soda tribesmen mustered outside the SEALs' quarters, ready for police training.

"I didn't believe him," Craig Thomas said of the police-volunteer muster. "The night before Sheikh Jassim said, 'We will have 170 new policemen for you to train tomorrow.' I thought, 'Yeah, right,' but the next day, there they were."

"It happened very quickly for us," said Chuck Wall, "and that was probably a good thing. One day we were sifting through intelligence data and looking for targets to hit, and the next we were committed to a full-on training regime in Sufia. Craig and I split our SEALs into two squads and went to work. Our new quarters were a gutted house out in the district, but living at Corregidor had conditioned us to do without creature comforts. There were security issues as well. Half of us remained at Corregidor while the other half stayed in Sufia and trained the new police volunteers. Then we swapped out—a week or so in Sufia and a week back at Corregidor."

"This was a real change of pace for us," said Byron Abdul, "especially in the beginning. As I've said, we enjoyed a good relationship with our *jundis,* and, with a few exceptions, we trusted them. They had fought alongside the SEALs from Three and they had fought with us. But the police were different. They were like a group of illegals for hire, like you might see on a street corner in LA. They were dressed in old clothes and T-shirts, and looking like what they were, unemployed Anbaris. They were ready to start training, even eager, but we knew nothing about them or what they could do."

The Corregidor SEALs set up a three-week training course in Sufia and taught the basics—individual and squad movement, security procedures, patrolling, prisoner handling, and basic small-arms handling and safety. There was also training in the basics of room- and building-clearing procedures, but all drills were very simple. While the training was under way, they were able to do a full biometric screening of all police volunteers. The SEALs were the only unit at Camp Corregidor with this capability. The screening included fingerprinting and photos. Without getting too deeply into the subject, the U.S. military has an extensive and user-friendly database in Iraq that tracks known al-Qaeda operatives and sympathizers, as well as those with a history of insurgent activity. This allowed the SEAL trainers to carefully screen the volunteers and pull aside those few who appeared in the system. The system is not 100 percent foolproof, but it is an effective screening tool, both in deselecting questionable individuals from joining the police and in discouraging those with ties to AQI from trying to join in an attempt to infiltrate the new police force. The biometric screening also had intelligence-gathering benefits. Those who surfaced in the system with known insurgent ties became some of the best sources of useful tactical information.

"The training and the screening process led to a new operational dynamic for us," said Thomas. "While we were in Sufia conducting training, the new recruits and Sheikh Jassim were feeding us all kinds of intelligence. When a squad rotated back to Camp Corregidor, they uploaded and analyzed this intel and conducted time-sensitive operations in eastern Ramadi. In one case, it led to a raid on the compound of the number one high-value AQI leader in the area. Because of these developing relationships with the Albu Soda, we often had informants to lead us on these operations."

"Regarding working with the new policemen," said Byron Abdul, "we had to understand that we were no longer working with soldiers, and that we were working with policemen—police trainees. They needed what we could teach them in the way of tactical skills, because they were definitely going to be trading bullets with insurgents, but their real contribution to the effort was their local knowledge. Local knowledge trumps all. They knew the neighborhoods and the people. Their presence on the street, with or without us, was with the permission and at the direction of their sheikh. Ultimately, that changed everything. It put pressure on AQI. Shooting at us or at Iraqi soldiers was one thing, but shooting at the police was a direct attack on the tribes—the people."

The Corregidor SEALs had more than a few stories about training the Albu Soda tribe. "Some were quick studies," one of the SEALs recalled. "We could tell that many of them had military training, probably in the Iraqi army under Saddam. A few of them knew how to handle weapons, but none of them could really shoot well. More than a few were former insurgents. We were showing them how to look for explosives hidden in the undercarriages of cars. One of them says, 'That's not where the insurgents put the explosives. They're trained to put them here on this part of the frame.' 'OK,' one of our SEALs said, 'why don't you give this class?' and he did."

"Not all of it was good or set well with us," another platoon SEAL said. "Our interpreters told us that some of these police volunteers would openly talk about their battles with our marines—how they had ambushed them or hit them with an IED. Still, they were on our side now, and we needed them. I guess it takes a thief to catch a thief. When we went out with them, they knew who the insurgents were, and where the weapons and explosives were hidden. Still, we also knew that we had been trading bullets with some of these guys not too long ago, and that made us a little uneasy—in some cases, very uneasy. I can't help but wonder when and if they'll take the training we're giving them and go back to the other side. We can only hope that our vision of a free and independent al-Anbar is more of what the Anbaris want than al-Qaeda's vision for al-Anbar. And that we can get them strong enough to resist AQI after we're gone."

"It didn't take long for this new relationship with the Albu Soda tribe to start to pay off," Chuck Wall said. "Keeping half our SEALs with the police trainees and the other half at Camp Corregidor gave us a lot of flexibility. Things had quieted down in the district, but al-Qaeda had not given up on Sufia. As security was always an issue, none of us slept too well in our little training compound. Since the insurgents now had difficulty getting into the town, they began observing checkpoints to identify and target tribal members who were working with us. When they could ID someone as a police volunteer or someone in the sheikh's or a tribal elder's family, that tribal member became a candidate for reprisal—murder and intimidation. When that individual left the district, AQI would try to kill or capture them. We learned that they'd been successful with this tactic in other districts as well.

"Then one day when Craig and his squad were training the police in Sufia, I get a call from him on the Iridium—a secure satellite phone. One of his tribal police trainees told him there was a car sitting near a checkpoint that shouldn't be there. The driver was a known insurgent and he was watching the comings and goings at the checkpoint. It was about a thousand meters from the camp, close enough for me to climb up on the roof and spot the car with a set of binoculars. It was also close enough for one of our snipers to keep an eye on him and the surrounding area. After I got a sniper in place for some top cover, we mounted up in a couple of 113s [an M113 is a tracked armored personnel carrier] and drove over there. We had a squad of Army soldiers from the QRF in one vehicle and my SEALs in the other. You could see this muj's eyes getting bigger and bigger as we got closer," Wall said with relish. "He couldn't believe it. We made a quick assessment before we got out of our armored vehicles; some of these dudes will blow themselves up when you corner them. He finally put his hands up, and we motioned him out of the car. We had him cuffed and blindfolded within fifteen minutes after I got the call from Craig.

"Craig sent two of the police trainees over and they named him as a known AQI soldier," Chuck Wall said of the new capture. "He later popped up on our database. That started us to thinking that maybe working with the police wasn't going to be such a bad thing after all."

"It was definitely different when we began training with the new tribal recruits," Don Wettack said of the police training at Camp Ramadi. "The training cell did a good job of setting up the training, and as operations permitted, we all went out to the ranges and helped. As you know, we had issues with some of the scouts, and I suppose we had our issues with the police recruits as well. Very few of them had military training, but several of them had terrorist training. We could tell that right away. And as opposed to the scouts, they had no uniforms at first; most of them turned up in jogging outfits or loose trousers, collared shirts, and sandals.

"It's never a perfect world, and both the scouts and the police had their drawbacks. We knew that some of our scouts were going to Baghdad on leave and taking to the streets with the Mahdi Army. We also knew that some of the guys who were now volunteering for police training were the same guys were shooting at us only a few weeks ago. Yet we knew that having local fighters on our side was going to be a huge plus. So we sucked it up and cast our lot with the new police trainees."

"I'd have to say that most of them genuinely wanted to help make their city and their neighborhoods better," said Ned Stallard. "Some of them were out there because their sheikh had ordered them to volunteer, but most of them were there because they wanted the violence to stop. Once we started working with them on operations, they proved their worth immediately. The task unit targeting cell would work up a list of three or four insurgents we'd like to take into custody, and we would plan an operation around those targeted individuals. After we briefed the Americans and the interpreters, we'd go out to meet with the policemen assigned to us that day. We'd meet them at a COP or one of the new police stations. They would usually know the bad guys or know of them. Sometimes they'd say, 'He used to be here, but he moved. If he's the guy you want to arrest, then right now he's living over here in *this* house.' The police would either corroborate our intelligence, or have better or more current information. They were also good to work with on follow-ups. We'd grab a targeted individual, and, depending on the mission, we'd interrogate him on the spot with the Iraqi policemen doing the talking. Our interpreters would give us a running update on the Q&A. If the guy had information that could take us to a good target, then the police would get the guy to lead us there."

Don Wettack put it this way: "When the police got on the street in significant numbers, then things began to go our way. They were a good source of intelligence and a good source of quality control for the intelligence we developed in-house. There were things they couldn't do tactically in the way some of our Iraqi army scouts could, and when they were out with us, we handled most of the patrolling and operational tasks. But when it came to working with the locals, they were an asset. They got better as time went along and, after a while, they were out in their neighborhoods operating on their own. That's something that the scouts could never do; they were out-of-towners, just like us."

I asked Don and Ned Stallard about a good operation with the Iraqi police.

"Probably the smoothest operation that comes to mind," Ned began, "was the one where we were going out after a Vee-bid [his pronunciation of "VBIED": a vehicle-borne improvised explosive device] maker—someone who makes car bombs. Toward the end of our tour, the explosions were getting fewer but a whole lot bigger. The insurgents had taken to packing cars and trucks with lots of explosives, parking them along the side of the road, and then waiting for a U.S. or Iraqi army patrol to come by. So when we got some information on a guy who was supposed to be making these things, we moved on it.

"We were working out of COP Warrior with some policemen from the Jazeera police station, and met up with the Army unit that was going to support us. This Army unit was relatively new in Ramadi, but they understood the importance of stopping Vee-bids. Initially, they wanted to go in hard and fast with armored vehicles. Sometimes when they do that, and when there's a concern about IEDs, they use the 20-millimeter broom—that is, they shoot up the ground and any debris in front of them with their 20-millimeter cannons. It can occasionally be an effective tactic, but not very subtle. We suggested that they lay back and let us patrol in quietly ahead of them and try to catch the guy. Most of these insurgents, especially the guys making bombs, know they're wanted men—by us and now by the local police. If they hear you coming, it's out the back door and gone."

"The Army readily accepted our plan," Wettack said, picking up the story. "They set up as a standby QRF and gave us good support.

We went in quietly and without raising an alarm. The area was a cul-de-sac-like street with five houses in a circle. There was a dump truck parked by one of them, and that got our attention right away. Was this a big, command-detonated Vee-bid? Was this guy waiting for us to get close and then crank it off? Long story short, we quickly cleared all five houses, but only one was occupied. Thanks to our policemen, we quickly learned that our target wasn't there. While the Army rolled up in their Bradleys, our EOD techs cleared the occupied house and the dump truck.

"All the while, our policemen were chatting with the residents of the one house. One of them told the police he knew where the guy we were looking for was. We asked him to take us there, and at first he wanted nothing to do with that. Then the police, after a little discussion, helped him to see that it was in his best interest to take us there. It was less than a mile, so the Army element stood by with their Bradleys and we patrolled off to the new location. Once there, the informant pointed out the house and we got a quick setup on the place. The EOD tech checked the entrance area and door for booby traps. When you're after a bomb maker, you have to be extra careful. We took the door with an explosive breach and began to carefully clear the bottom floor."

As patrol leader, Ned Stallard was toward the middle of the patrol file, in a command-and-control position. "I was several people back in the stack," Stallard said, "and the SEALs up ahead were moving carefully and professionally. Then this guy comes charging down the stairs with an AK-47. It took Don and one of the other guys about a nanosecond to react; they both fired at the same time. He was dead before he hit the floor. What impressed me, in retrospect, was how easily the shooters handled this. After they dropped him, they kept moving, clearing the building and looking for more insurgents. We're well trained for this, but it was nice to see how professionally they handled it. It's a tribute to just how professional our SEALs can be. They put an armed muj down and continued with the mechanics of clearing the house without missing a beat.

"I think a mission like that one is a good example of what we could now do working with the police. We could carry the tactical load, so they could engage the locals and get us updated information. Once the people knew we were out there with their local police, they were much more willing to rat out bad guys. The neighborhoods in Ramadi are tight little communities, and the people are close to each other—like ethnic neighborhoods in a big American city used to be. Everyone knows what's going on—who belongs and who doesn't. They would tell the police and the police would tell us. Then we'd recalibrate our plan, and move on it. Credit the police and their local knowledge, but also credit our SEALs for their ability to adapt and move quietly and professionally over dangerous ground as a new target developed. The police were learning, but they still needed us to do the heavy lifting. Usually, if the door needed taking, we took it. Watching our SEALs work was good OJT [on-the-job training] for the policemen. Also, credit to the Army for a successful mission like this. Knowing that they were only a few clicks away with an armored QRF allowed us to move into an unknown neighborhood with a little more confidence."

"And the bomb maker?" I asked.

"We got him and his tools. He was our guy," Wettack replied. "You take a guy like that off the street and it does a lot for the cause. The people will talk about this in the coffee shops the next day. It'll be known that we came in the night with their policemen and took a violent dude out of their community. It's a win-win all around."

At Camp Corregidor the training of the local Iraqi police continued in the Sufia District. Here, too, the relationship with the Albu Soda tribe in Sufia began to pay off in the way of intelligence—operational intelligence that reached into other districts in eastern Ramadi. With the Americans and the tribal police now patrolling in the district, the local residents were more willing to pass along information. Sunni tribal relationships reach across tribal boundaries. These tribal entities are very social—they talk, especially the women. They can make a great deal of information available about "outsiders," whether they are foreign fighters, other Iraqis who have come to fight in Ramadi, or insurgents from other tribes. Or they can withhold information. Tribal interests come ahead of provincial or national interests. When AQI began to push its agenda ahead of the tribal interests in Ramadi and al-Anbar, it began to loose the people. In Sufia, when it outright attacked the tribal structure, it made a grave tactical error. The resentment for the American presence that had been so deeply seeded was, if not extinguished, put on hold. For now, most of the tribes across Ramadi were willing to work with the Americans—or, better said, work with the tribal police who were working with the Americans.

"Our training of the police in Sufia created many opportunities for us," Craig Thomas said of their police academy duty. "Training is something we can do, but we'd rather be out chasing bad guys. However, there's no question that our training of the police won us some friends and provided us with some specific and accurate intelligence that we'd not had earlier."

I asked him if he could give me an example.

"Well," he replied, "There was this one shooter we were looking for. He was sniping at Humvees that were going between Corregidor and COP Eagle in the Mala'ab District. It was more of a nuisance than a threat, but sooner or later he was going to get a round into a ring-turret gunner or graduate to something more lethal. Things were getting better in the Mala'ab, but this guy was becoming a real pain in the ass. We put the word out in Sufia that we'd like to get him. A few days later an informant, a member of the Albu Soda tribe who lived in the Mala'ab, got word to one of the policemen we had trained that he knew the guy we were looking for and knew where he lived. He came into a police station in Sufia, and we talked to him. After hearing him out, we thanked him and told him we'd get back to him. Following the interview, we checked him out with some of our other sources in Sufia. They vouched for him and corroborated some of his story, so we decided to act on his information."

"There are several things that have to line up before we go out like this," said Chuck Wall. "We do everything we can to check the informant out without burning him with the locals. Anyone who helps the Americans can be a candidate for a very ugly death. Then we have to plan how we're going to run the operation, keeping three things in mind: We have to protect ourselves, protect our informant, and accomplish the mission. With our informant, it means protecting his identity from our Iraqi army scouts and from other members of his tribe, even the police. People talk and people have divided loyalties. While we may think he's telling us the truth, we're never 100 percent sure. If we buy into his program and he's setting us up, we could get a lot of guys killed. If we decide to go on his information, the only variable we can work with is when we go. So we don't tell him when we're going to do this, or even if we're going to do it. If he's genuine, he'll go anytime we decide the time is right.

"In keeping with our normal procedures, we work up the mission and clear ourselves into the area. On this one we took along our Iraqi scouts rather than the police. After the warning order and patrol order at Corregidor, we went over and collected our scouts. Then we drove down to COP Eagle, and held final briefings with the outpost commander. We seldom go anywhere without some Iraqi presence, except when we're working with an informant. This informant lived only a few blocks from the COP, so four of us with our lead interpreter patrolled out to pick him up. He came to the door all sleepy-eyed, surprised to see us. Through the interpreter, we told him that we were ready to go now if he would lead us. 'We go! We go now!' he said; he was really excited—and so were we. With a willing, vetted informant to take you to the target, your chances for a success go up dramatically."

"Good informants are precious," Thomas continued. "We take care of them and treat them with respect, especially guys like this who put themselves at risk to help us. One of the ways we can best do this is to protect his identity. This time we dressed him up in cammies, and had him put on a helmet, flack vest, and pair of dark glasses. We left his house with him in the squad file and hopefully no one in the neighborhood the wiser—just another visit in the night by a small armed force. Back at the COP, we held him just outside while the rest of the patrol got ready to move out. We knew generally where this shooter lived and had planned our route accordingly, but our informant took us a different way. He knew where he was going and moved very quickly, leading us to an apartment complex less than a quarter mile from the COP. He took us right to the door and said the guy we wanted would be on that floor and in the last bedroom on the left."

Thomas suppressed a smile, then looked at Wall. Both of them were suddenly grinning broadly.

"What?" I asked.

"We went out on a lot of missions," Wall explained, shaking his head, "and the operations sometimes tend to run together. But this one was a little different, at least right at the end it was."

Thomas went on with the story. "There was nothing left to do but to kick the door and clear the house. The scouts went in first and took the front rooms, and we went to the back to get this dude. We were moving very quickly, and he really didn't have time to do anything—or to stop what he was doing.

"I don't know what he could have been thinking," Chuck Wall explained. "When we kicked the front door, he must have just thought that it was a mortar round or an IED down the street, or he was just having too much fun. When we bowled into the bedroom, he was still in the saddle."

"Ah, you mean he was . . . ?"

"Yep, we caught them in full stride. We pulled him off the bed before he knew what was happening, slapped on the cuffs and blindfold, wrapped him in a blanket, and hustled him out of there—zip, zap. She just lay there, clutching a sheet under her chin and her eyes as big as saucers. The scouts collected some IED materials and some weapons, and we were out of there. We were back in the COP in less than forty minutes. It was a struggle, trying to run a good patrol on the way back—trying to keeping from giggling. We talked about it for days, and every time the operation came up, we'd break out laughing. But we never got shot at on the way to COP Eagle again, at least not by him."

"So what happened to his partner?" I asked.

"Who knows? Maybe she's now being serviced by the informant. Maybe that was what it was all about. If so, good on him—he earned it."

Things continued to change for the better as more police appeared on the streets. With the people of Ramadi increasingly turning against them, the insurgents were being denied sanctuary in the city. Army and Marine patrols were fired on less frequently. The citizens of Ramadi began to point out IEDs to the police, who told their American advisers. Until recently, the key interface advisers were the military transition teams—the MiTTs. Now the go-to advisers were the PTTs—the police transition teams. With the police taking to the streets, the Battle for Ramadi was coming to a close.

"We could see things changing, and we were grateful for it," Byron Abdul said, "but my heart was still with the scouts. We continued to operate with them when the opportunity and targeting arose. Some of those *jundis* had been fighting alongside SEALs for close to a year. They proved their loyalty and their worth in battle. They helped us to turn the tide. But the day of the Iraqi policeman had arrived in Ramadi. They still needed us and the Iraqi army on occasion, usually when the muj came out in force, but the police were taking ownership of the streets."

"Looking back on the tour, we struggled a bit with Iraqi scouts," Ned Stallard said, "and working with the police is not without its issues, but on balance I think we're heading in the right direction. A lot of Anbaris here in Ramadi want to be policemen. If we can keep up with the demand for training and they do well on the streets, then there's a light at the end of this tunnel."

As the Ramadi task unit and the rest of Squadron Five prepared to leave al-Anbar, a tragic event took place just outside Fallujah. This tragedy was also marked by a single act of individual courage and warriorship the likes of which is unparalleled in the history of the Navy SEALs. A SEAL element from the task unit in Fallujah was looking for a high-value AQI leader who was thought to frequent a compound near that city. The SEAL element inserted by helicopter and made a quick assault on the main building. They had no idea whether this individual was there or not. As it happened, he was, and with his bodyguards.

Several hours before the SEAL assault, a section of H-60 Blackhawk helicopters had, by chance, overflown the compound. This may or may not have alerted those inside. When the SEAL element arrived, they swarmed from their helos and quickly assaulted the main building. As luck would have it, the first door they took led to an empty room, a blind alley. They had to back out and move to a second entrance—one that led to the main interior. Now the insurgents inside were more than ready for them. They had to take two more doors before they got to those inside waiting for them. The first Iraqi through this last door was shot and killed, and the SEAL behind him was wounded. Close behind in the stack was Senior Chief Matt Dale and Petty Officer Clark Schwedler. The two had no option but to move into the building and return fire. Inside, Chief Dale took the room to the left and Clark Schwedler the room up the hall and to the right. The interior was dimly lit, and the SEALs had their night optics in place. But so did the insurgents, and these insurgents were very well armed. Dale stepped inside and was confronted by three insurgents at close range with automatic weapons. The fight was on as the three muj took Dale under fire. A stray round from one of the insurgents flew across the hall and caught Clark Schwedler under the helmet in the back of the head. He died instantly. Chief Matt Dale was still standing, but in mortal danger.

SEALs train incessantly for this kind of confrontation—up-close shooting, engaging multiple targets, shifting from their primary weapon, a rifle or submachine gun, to their secondary weapon, a pistol sidearm. They drill in these shooting situations in different scenarios and situations, shifting from primary to secondary and back, over and over. Few ever have to put these skills, or the muscle memory developed in these drills, to use in extremis. On this day, Senior Chief Dale needed all of that and more.

The three insurgents focused their attention and guns on Matt Dale. One of their initial bursts took off a part of his thumb and knocked away his rifle. As he had done so often in simulation, Chief Dale reached for the pistol on his hip, a Sig Saur 9 millimeter, and brought the weapon level. Then he began to shoot—sight picture and squeeze; sight picture and squeeze. While Dale was shooting them, they were shooting him. The senior chief was hit an astonishing *twenty-seven times*. Eleven of those rounds were stopped by his body-armor plates. Sixteen of those rounds went through *him*. "It was easier to say where I wasn't hit than where I was. But it all happened very quickly." When it was over, the three insurgents were dead and Matt Dale was still standing.

"I didn't have time to think about it," Chief Dale told me. "My primary was gone before I got a round off. The rest was instinct and training. I knew I had to get to my pistol and there it was, in my hand and I was shooting." I asked him what he was thinking—feeling. "Pure anger," he said. "I don't remember much other than I was incredibly pissed off—that they had shot away my rifle and that they were shooting at me. I guess I was able to focus all my anger on the muj and stay in the fight. I didn't stop shooting until the slide on that pistol locked in the rear position and they were all down." Senior Chief Matt Dale graduated with BUD/S Class 169. He was on his seventh deployment.

The death of Clark Schwedler, like that of Mike Monsoor, came barely a week before his squadron was to be relieved by the next incoming squadron. Schwedler was twenty-seven and from the town of Crystal Falls, a small community in Michigan's Upper Peninsula. He attended Michigan State for two years before joining the Navy to fulfill his ambition to become a Navy SEAL. He graduated with SEAL Class 246 and was on his second combat rotation. Both Clark Schwedler and Matt Dale were from the East Coast–based SEAL Team Four.

"Clark was one of our best," Senior Chief Dale said of his fallen teammate. "He was a quiet leader and he understood the mission. Not all SEALs do. We were there to train the Iraqi soldiers to be the best counterinsurgent fighters they could be. He was very good with the Iraqis. He personally took charge of thirty of our scouts and looked after them—during training, during operations, and seeing to their personal needs. Clark was good at building their trust and getting our Iraqi soldiers to perform at a higher level. He was a great Navy SEAL."

Your turn; your shot. A SEAL from Team Seven offers pointers as an Iraqi scout takes a training target under fire. The Iraqi soldiers' marksmanship rose dramatically under SEAL instruction. *Photo by Dick Couch*

The Last Ramadi
Task Unit

Unless there's a reason or an operational necessity, most helicopters in Iraq fly at night. It's safer for those flying and marginally better for the machines in the air, as it's a little cooler. After three days and two helicopters—one an Army H-60 Blackhawk and the second a Marine CH-46 Sea Knight—we finally touched down at the helicopter landing zone at Camp Fallujah. It was just before midnight of 18 August. I was traveling with Lieutenant Steve Ruh, assistant public affairs officer for Naval Special Warfare Command. Without his help, the trip into al-Anbar province might have taken twice as long. Finding ground transportation and arranging space-available flights is a chancy and frustrating business in Iraq. It's often best for a writer in the battlespace to take the Arab approach: *Insha Allah*—as God wills it. But Steve Ruh didn't see it that way and managed to keep us moving, especially through the bureaucratic blight that is wartime Baghdad. He worked the issues like a border collie, and I was his flock of one.

In addition to the mandatory visa delays coming through Kuwait, there was the press-credential process in Baghdad. This was not my first trip into Iraq or al-Anbar, but it was the first time I had to get a press credential. On my last trip, the Army had moved me directly from Qatar through Balad Air Base and into western Iraq to the Special Forces advance operating base at Al Asad. They sort of smuggled me into the country—along with official permissions. Not this time. There is a remote and well-disguised office in the Green Zone that issues folks like me in-country orders and a press pass that allow us to move about military facilities in Iraq. It's a curious process, one almost designed to restrict the flow of journalists into theater, at least to where the war is being fought outside Baghdad. Fortunately, the farther one gets from Baghdad, the easier it is to move about. The process did give me a chance to wander about our embassy in Baghdad; we were trapped there for almost a day. It was by far the most depressing experience during this visit or my previous one. Our embassy was still housed in one of Saddam's minor palaces. Amid the vaulted ceilings and garish facades, there was an air of bustle and official imperative that seemed forced and synthetic. It reminded me of our embassy in Saigon, back when it was called Saigon. From the keep-off-the-grass signs where there is no grass to the Peruvian security guards (under contract to Triple Canopy, a professional military company) to the basement theater where you could sleep through a movie, which we did, there's something all wrong about the place. I couldn't wait to get out of there. The best part of our embassy visit was slipping over to the transient quarters for a shower and a shave.

Camp Shane Patton, located at the U.S. base in Fallujah, is head-quarters for SOTF–West (Special Operations Task Force–West). Petty Officer Shane Patton was a SEAL killed in action in Afghanistan in late June 2005. SOTF–West has tactical command of all special operations forces operating in al-Anbar province. The only exception to this is the SOF special missions units, which follow other rules. The "task force west" title indicates they are an extension of the Joint Special Operations Task Force headquartered at Balad Air Force Base. In composition they are a task group subordinate to the JSOTF. By the time we got to the compound, it was close to 1:00 AM. I had assumed that things would be quiet that time of the morning, but not so. The task group mans a small tactical operations center, 24/7, and most of the headquarters personnel were up and about. The majority of the operations conducted by SOF forces assigned to SOTF–West take place at night, so the task group and the task units scattered across al-Anbar are on a sleep-by-day, work-by-night cycle. They call them vampire hours. Working in the TOC and in other task group support roles were female sailors assigned to the squadron. Female soldiers are common on most bases in Iraq; within the deployed SEAL squadrons, they serve primarily at the squadron task group headquarters, usually not out with the task units. Other than the petty officers and the operations watch team, the TOC was also manned that night by a new SEAL ensign. New SEAL officers—that is, officers who have just graduated from SEAL Qualification Training and have recently been awarded their Trident pin—are immediately sent to Iraq. They're assigned to the SOTF–West commander and scattered about the battlespace for routine duties as

TOC watch standers and selected SEAL operations at the discretion of the task unit commanders. With the current deployment of Squadron Seven, this included all new SEAL officers and those new enlisted SEALs with orders to SEAL Team Seven. Following the redeployment of the squadron in October 2007, the officers will head off for their respective team assignments (for some of them, that will be Team Seven) and the enlisted men will join a platoon at Team Seven to begin preparation for the next deployment rotation. This brief stint in the battlespace means that when they make their first full rotation, they'll have some idea of what's ahead for them as operational platoon SEALs.

Down the hall from the TOC, I found Commander Tad Tierney at his desk, hunched over his computer. The various elements of the deployed squadron are linked by dedicated satellite voice and online capability. Communications and message traffic is handled on SupraNet, a secure, Web-based communications network capable of handling classified material. Tad Tierney, like his predecessor from Squadron Five, is a former enlisted sailor. He's a stocky, sandy-haired former college wrestler from Iowa. When I met him in San Diego prior to his squadron's deployment, he candidly told me, "I love the Navy. The U.S. Navy has given me everything and provided me every opportunity. I'm proud of the men and women I'm privileged to lead here. I'm very fortunate."

"Our force structure out in al-Anbar is pretty much what was in place when Squadron Five left," Tierney said of the current disposition of his task group. "We have task units in Fallujah, Ramadi, Habbaniyah, and Al Asad, with a detachment in Rawah." The Fallujah task unit with two SEAL platoons is colocated in the same compound as the task group—separate but only about fifty yards away. "We pulled one of the platoons out of Habbaniyah and moved them up to Rawah, where they're colocated with a Marine light armored reconnaissance unit." Rawah is a small city on the Euphrates just west of Al Qa'im. "They're a stand-alone platoon with a support element, and they report to the task unit commander in Ramadi. In Al Asad, we have four Special Forces teams operating out of Al Qa'im, Hadithah, Hit, and one with the headquarters element in Al Asad. As you know, things have quieted down quite a bit out here in al-Anbar. Nevertheless, AQI is doing their best to reinsert themselves back into the picture. Our job is to see that they don't do that. We know they're out there, but they're lying low."

"The only real change came with the move to Rawah," Commander Tierney said of this platoon's remote location. "The previous squadron commander detailed a few of his people from Fallujah and Ramadi to Rawah to make a site survey. We decided to put a full platoon up there. That's one of the benefits of Naval Special Warfare. If we see better opportunity to contribute to success in the battlespace, we can move fairly quickly. The Marines have done a great job of supporting us there, and we have a smooth working relationship with them."

I was in Fallujah only a short while, but I was able to spend a few minutes with the task group executive officer. He's a lanky lieutenant commander on his third trip to Iraq. "What we're seeing now is a circle of events that include lethal operations, nonlethal operations—operations that include civil-affairs projects and information operations—and the training of the Iraqi army scouts and the Iraqi police. We have to take these as they come—not force any one of them but be ready to move when there is opportunity. We also have to be ready to go on the offensive instantly if al-Qaeda makes a move back into one of the areas where we now have the upper hand. Our forces finally have them on the run here in al-Anbar, but we can't be complacent."

I asked him if he and the task force commander were getting time in the battlespace.

He smiled. "We try to get out from behind the desk as much as possible. The skipper's good about getting around to see the units of his task group, but they're pretty independent—they know what has to be done and they're doing it. Both of us try to get out with the operators in the battlespace, with the kinetic and the nonkinetic missions. It's good for people like myself and the skipper to put boots on the ground. It's also good for the troops to see us out there. If it's a combat operation, we usually become just another gun in the support element, one that keeps us out of the patrol leader's way, so that usually means we're in a security role or part of the blocking force. It's helpful to stay in touch with what's taking place on the ground without making ourselves a burden on the element leaders." He smiled again. "And it's a little reward for being chained to this desk.

"Another thing these deployments have done for us internally is to put the East Coast–West Coast thing behind us." Since my time in the teams in the late 1960s and early 1970s, there was always a running issue between the UDT and SEAL teams on either coast. At best, it's been an easygoing but competitive rivalry. At worst, it's been a difference in standard operating procedures and tactics, and, at times, almost a different culture. The recent mix and match of SEAL elements and platoons from both coasts in Iraq seems to have blurred these coastal differences. "We all now pretty much operate off the same sheet of music," the exec said. "What counts is the reputation and performance of the individual SEAL operator, not which coast he comes from." Since our time was short in Fallujah, he suggested I visit with Lieutenant Garner in the intel section before I moved on to Ramadi.

Lieutenant Dave Garner was an individual augmentee—one of the Tactical Intelligence Support Team members from the ONI Trident group. Garner is an example of the talent and diversity that deployed SEAL squadrons are able to bring to the battlespace. I'm sure the Marine commanders in Fallujah wonder just where the SEALs come up with some of this expertise. Garner had worked on President Bush's first campaign, which earned him a political appointment to the State Department. Once at State, he made his way to the section that deals with terrorism and counterterrorism. While at State, he continued working on his PhD in international relations at George Washington University. He also obtained a direct commission in the Naval Reserve. The latter made him a weekend warrior and eligible for active-duty wartime recall, something he welcomed. Captain Pete Wikul spotted him and recruited him into the Trident program.

Garner is a tall, genial, thirty-something officer with an easy smile and lively, intelligent eyes—the kind of officer one might not expect to find in a deployed SEAL squadron. His first deployment was to Afghanistan, where he ran one of the provincial reconstruction teams near the Afghan-Pakistani border for close to a year. He was back at the State Department for a little more than a year when he was again recalled and assigned to Naval Special Warfare Squadron Seven for a rotation to Iraq. I told him of my dismal experience at the embassy in Baghdad, and he nodded sadly.

"It's the Green Zone mentality. Many staffers there have never been out here—maybe never away from the embassy grounds. They see the big picture and maybe even the Baghdad picture, but they have no idea what we do out here or how important our noncombat operations are to putting this country back together. Sorry to say this, but they're very out of touch with what's going on here on the ground."

Garner's main job, as I came to learn, was principal American adviser to the mayor of Fallujah. As a part of the task force's tribal-engagement and civil-affairs efforts, Garner became aware that the mayor was having a difficult time of it, so he offered to help.

"Helping these people takes a little bit of finesse," he said. "The job and role of the mayor here is nontraditional, even ambiguous. In many ways he's typical of how leaders surface and attain positions of civic responsibility in a tribal culture. I'm sure he has no standing in Baghdad, yet he's very important here. The mayor is a relatively young man, but he has the blessing of the tribal elders in the city. He wasn't elected to the job; he just sort of took on the job and continues in the position with the support of the people—by way of the tribal sheikhs. Since he's an unelected official, he isn't paid, but he's a strong leader and has been a key player in keeping insurgents from reentering the city. We can't really pay him, and even if we could, he wouldn't take money from us. He has to show his independence from the Americans. So we help him with support for the local schools in the way of books and classroom equipment, and with civil-affairs projects such as wells, generators, and construction projects that support the people who live in Fallujah. This support is made available on his recommendation, and these civil projects reflect well on him. We think this patronage leads to some form of compensation from the people and the tribal leaders, but we don't really know—don't want to know. He has a police background, so he understands the security issues."

Right after SEAL Squadron Seven arrived in April 2007, one of the mayor's bodyguards was shot and killed. The mayor is a priority target for AQI, and there have been several attempts on his life. His car has been shot at often. In light of the bureaucracy that is the new government of Iraq, along with the restrictive role that coalition forces can play in internal Iraqi affairs, there seemed to be little that could be done to protect this important nonofficial. In a round-robin vehicle swap that *I* couldn't follow when they explained it to me, Dave Garner managed to get the mayor an armored SUV for his personal use. He also sent back to the States for two boxes of office supplies from Staples for the mayor's office—paid for out of his own pocket.

"This guy is important to us and to the future of Fallujah. He's his own man, but he's willing to listen to us on issues of good governance and the organization of his mayoral duties. Fallujah has suffered with a series of ineffective and corrupt mayors, men who eventually found themselves at odds with the tribal sheikhs. This fellow is a good leader, and he has the backing of the tribes—very important out here. It's in our interest to do all that we can to support him inasmuch as our goals for the city are consistent with his goals for the city. He's been a great ally in keeping AQI and their followers at bay and out of the city."

Just before I left Fallujah, I spent a few minutes with the senior enlisted leadership, the squadron/task group command master chief and the task group operations chief. Normally, the squadron commanding officer and command master chief will leave the command when they return from deployment. When possible, the operations chief moves up to the role of command master chief—the senior enlisted adviser. This orderly passing of the torch from one command master chief to the next is as important as the relief of the commanding officer, perhaps more so. At Squadron Seven, both these enlisted leaders were E-9 master chiefs.

"The key to keeping the peace in al-Anbar is the growth and maturity of the Iraqi police," the command master chief told me. "We need the Iraqi army and we're proud of our training with the scouts, but the role of the police is what is going to carry the day and allow us to leave. We're winning the battle here, but it takes time. Time and our continued presence here will equal success on the ground."

The operations chief echoed these remarks. "We've trained between seven hundred and eight hundred scouts and policemen in all of al-Anbar on this deployment, many of them to a level where they can go out and become the trainers for their units. As long as we're here, we can be a resource for them. I just hope we can stay long enough so they can stand alone, because al-Qaeda hasn't given up. Given the chance, they'll come back and reassert control of the population centers."

I then watched as these two went out for a midmorning run. We're talking summertime in Fallujah with temperatures well north of 110°. They were back forty-five minutes later, drenched in sweat and grinning from ear to ear. They have more than fifty years of experience between them, but they still go out and "pay the man" for the privilege of calling themselves Navy SEALs. The running of these two old goats was not lost on the new SEALs who just arrived at the task group.

Throughout the rest of my day at the task force, I visited with those assigned to the headquarters element. There was a constant level of quiet activity as they went about the business of monitoring the special operations and other military activity in al-Anbar province.

———

It was again another evening flight, this time a big CH-47 Chinook. The flight to Ramadi was a short one, only about twenty minutes, but waiting at the terminal often takes several hours. Helicopters have always scared me a little, as does night flying. I drew little comfort from the fact that the Chinooks and the Sea Knights that ferried me around Vietnam and Southeast Asia some forty years ago are the same airframes still flying today. Well, maybe not the same airframe, but the same type of helicopter. I arrived at Ramadi just before midnight on 19 August.

The trip from the helo pad on Camp Ramadi proper over to Camp Marc Lee is an easy ten-minute drive. We left Camp Ramadi through what can only be called a section cut into the wall that surrounds the camp. Driving past the checkpoints and the other former Shark Base dwellings—the Ranger compound and the "OGA" house—I finally arrived at Camp Lee. A single paved lane runs through the camp, with the team house, the platoon hut, the mess hall, the maintenance buildings, and the terp quarters on one side and the sleeping quarters—a mix of tents and module housing units—and shower trailers on the other. Unlike when the first task unit arrived in the fall of 2005, the showers and latrines were up-to-date, for Iraq, and there was plenty of hot water. A continuous blended drone of multiple generators carried across the camp. We dumped our gear at our assigned billets and headed for the TOC in the team house.

Lieutenant Commander Ron Roberts was the Ramadi task unit commander. His duties included the two platoons at Camp Lee and the platoon at Rawah. He was responsible for just under 150 souls in the Ramadi-Rawah battlespace. Roberts is an imposing 220 pounds and close to six feet tall. He is yet another graduate of the Seaman to Admiral program. Like Jack Williams, his predecessor once removed, he earned a four-year degree in three years from the University of San Diego. They were there at the same time, and it's almost scary to imagine those two imposing warriors prowling that sun-drenched campus in tandem—two SEAL veterans reluctantly away from the fight amid coeds in sundresses. Roberts majored in computer engineering, and when he's not deployed, he has a small side business building computers in his garage for pocket money. He has a wife and two children, and they plan to adopt two more when he returns from this deployment. Roberts wrestled and played football in high school, and is a committed Chicago Bears fan.

Ron Roberts is a genial man, but he was all business when I briefed him on why I was there and what I hoped to accomplish. He listened carefully and asked some very pointed questions before outlining how he could help me, and the access I was to have to his command. Roberts certainly knew of my visit and my project, but he wanted to hear it from me personally before allowing me to speak with the members of his task unit.

Also sitting in on this first meeting was Senior Chief Don Salinger, the task unit senior enlisted adviser. Salinger is perhaps five eight with a wiry, muscular build and quiet manner. Both the TU commander and the TU chief are multiple-tour veterans. Salinger and Roberts had met when they were both young sailors fresh out of boot camp. They attended "A" school together. And they were classmates in BUD/S Class 172. Together these two veterans manage the largest, and arguably the most important, SEAL task unit in Iraq.

Ron Roberts and Don Salinger share an office that was right off the tactical operations center in the team house. While we were talking, sometime shortly after 1:00 AM, one of the TOC watch standers stuck his head in the door.

"Sir, the helos are about five minutes out."

"Roger that," Roberts replied, "I'll be right there." Then he said to me, "I've got a team about to insert on target, and I'll need to pay attention to this. Let's go into the TOC."

The Ramadi tactical operations center is a plywood-wall-and-floor construction with three tiers of workstations facing several flat-plasma, wall-mounted screens at the front of the room. An array of status boards support these displays. Laptop computers litter the room. A small crowd had gathered, and the central plasma screen held everyone's attention.

"Alpha Platoon is out tonight," Roberts explained, "and they're due on target anytime now. They will be inserting on a compound out to the northeast of the city. As you know, things have really quieted down in Ramadi since we arrived last April, and there's not much work for the platoons out in the city. So, more recently, we've focused our efforts outside the city. The muj have moved out into the desert and the sparsely populated areas, and we've followed them out there. It's not that we've totally abandoned urban operations, but the Iraqi police have things pretty well in hand. There's still some work for us out in town, but the police and their Army and Marine advisers, the police training teams, don't really want us conducting kinetic operations in the city. The same goes for the Army and Marine battalions still responsible for the battlespace.

"It seems no one wants to disturb the peace that's descended on the city, and I can't say I blame them. Some of them have been here a lot longer than we have, and they've seen Ramadi when it wasn't so peaceful. As for the Iraqi police, I think it's a matter of turf and pride. They've taken ownership of the streets. For the task unit, it's a little frustrating as the op tempo is not what we expected or even hoped for. When I say 'hoped for,' I mean we trained hard for this deployment, and we want to be more involved. Yet one of the reasons for our presence here is to end the violence. It's a tribute to the sacrifices of those soldiers and marines who've been fighting here for the last few years that things have settled down in Ramadi. Credit them, as well as Squadrons Three and Five, that the insurgents have pretty much left the city—left the city or been killed off. Now it's our job to make sure they don't come back, and that's why we have a team out hunting for bad guys hiding in the desert."

"Helos on final, sir."

"Roger that." Everyone quieted down as we watched the wall-mounted display.

The presentation was a low-resolution, black-and-white overhead shot of a compound with a main building, several smaller outbuildings, and what appeared to be fifty meters of desert around the structures. The presentation was revolving very slowly in a counterclockwise direction as the unmanned aerial vehicle orbited the target. I could only assume it was a Predator drone, as they're the most common UAVs (unmanned aerial vehicles) flying in Iraq. I was told there was also an AC-130 orbiting above in case the ground element needed air support. Moments later, two clearly defined H-60 Blackhawks approached from the south. Tiny figures poured from either side of both helos and swarmed into the compound. Some took security positions while others moved to the buildings in assault formation. As the figures entered the compound, the image zoomed in. The compound filled the screen, and we lost the helos.

"Are those sheep or dogs?" I asked the SEAL who was watching next to me.

"Dogs, sir," he replied, without taking his eyes from the screen.

The operation unfolded, and a short time later, the ground force redeployed to the helos, and we watched them take off. I later learned that there were no detainees brought out by the assault teams. Later I spoke with one of the SEALs who was on the operation.

"Things weren't quite right in that compound, but there was nothing terribly wrong, either. We found some evidence that the muj had been there, but nothing of hard intelligence value. The fact that there were no men, just women and kids, was suspicious. Sometimes we get lucky and sometimes not. At the very least it keeps us busy, and it keeps the muj on the move, probably sleeping in the open desert to be safe. They have to know that if they stay in one place too long, we'll come for them."

During this ground action, most in the TOC were observers, but for one lieutenant who was fully engaged. He was camped behind a laptop and periodically spoke into a radio handset near his keyboard. This officer seemed to be the only one in the TOC directly connected to what was happening out in the desert.

Lieutenant Clark Gannon was an F/A-18 pilot attached to the task unit. Each of the Ramadi task units had one of these naval aviators detailed to them. They were assigned as task unit air operations officers, and their duties ranged from passenger service to on-call air support. These individual augmentees are yet another example of the Navy's effort to help with the ground war in Iraq and Afghanistan. Clark Gannon was a carrier pilot who recently completed a tour with the fleet. He was en route to shore duty as a replacement air group instructor at Lemoore Naval Air Station—by way of Iraq.

Gannon is from Oklahoma, a 2000 graduate of the Naval Academy, and a classmate of the Bravo Platoon SEAL OIC. He's short and blond, and he looked very fit as he took his workouts with the task unit SEALs. He looked barely old enough to drive, let alone bring a modern jet fighter on board an aircraft carrier or manage the air assets for a SEAL operation.

"We all have to do one of these tours," Gannon said of his individual augmentee assignment with the Ramadi task unit, "and it could be just about anywhere—here, Afghanistan, with the Marines, whatever. This is my IA duty, and I couldn't have had a better experience than being here with the SEALs. Great bunch of guys. And it's good for me as an attack pilot to learn as much as I can about what takes place on the ground."

I asked about the radio he was manning.

"It's an airborne relay to the SEAL element on the ground. He can talk to us if he needs to, and I can pass traffic from the TOC to him. Unless something unusual comes up, there's very little chatter between the TOC and the ground element. Commander Roberts doesn't micromanage his teams in the field. Of course, if we see something from the drone imagery, we'll pass it along to the team."

"And the computer?" I asked. "Are you flying the UAV from here?"
"Not really," Gannon replied. "I have some control of the images, but I'm online with the controller. It's with this computer link that I control the controller. I tell the controller what we want and he positions the drone accordingly."

"So where's the guy flying the UAV?" I ask.

"I don't know. Could be a base in Iraq or in Germany or Nevada for that matter. Just about anywhere."

"It must seem a little strange, directing the drone from here in the TOC."

"It does and it doesn't. I've flown a lot of these same missions in the F/A-18. We'd launch from a carrier in the Indian Ocean and take station over the target. Then we'd orbit the target, just like the UAV is doing right now, only I'd have to leave station every hour or so to find a tanker and take on fuel. Some of those missions could last for six or seven hours. This is a good mission for a UAV, and it's a lot cheaper than parking a section of F/A-18s over the target."

"Can the men on the ground see this?"

"They could if they had the rover, a field-portable monitor they can carry, but they seldom take one along for this kind of mission. They rely on us to let them know if there's a threat in the area. There's also an AC-130 gunship orbiting the target, and they're watching things with their own suite of sensors."

It seemed to me that we were only a step away from SOF ground controllers piloting their drones, with JDAMs and missiles aboard and calling in air strikes from their own UAVs. I said as much to Lieutenant Gannon.

"Hold on there, sir. I'm an attack pilot; I drop bombs for a living. You're not trying to put me out of a job are you?" But he said it with an easy smile.

After the extraction of the assault teams, the TOC cleared out with only a few TU members remaining. One of them was a first class petty officer— a master-at-arms, or MA. He was yet another of the individual augmentees assigned to the task unit. Within the Navy, the master-at-arms force has grown dramatically since 9/11. They're responsible for force security and force protection for U.S. naval bases and for units of the fleet, both domestically and in foreign ports. Sixteen MAs from the Naval Security Forces Detachment in Guam were assigned to Squadron Seven. Three of those master-at-arms augmentees were with the task unit in Ramadi.

"We're responsible for the physical security of the camp and for managing the marines who man our guard post and the camp entrance," the petty officer told me as he explained the master-at-arms function in the task unit. He was an affable black sailor from New York City. He'd just been selected for advancement to chief petty officer and currently served as the MA detachment leading petty officer. "We also secure and manage any detainees brought in by the operational elements."

I asked how that worked.

"When detainees are brought in, they are handled in a proscribed manner, one that keeps them safe and restrained. The process begins when we take them off the helo or from the Humvee. There are protocols we observe here at Camp Lee that I can't really go into. Then we take them to the ARDEF—the al-Ramadi Detention Facility on the main base. There we can hold them for up to three days, and our interrogators work with them at the ARDEF. After that time, they're released or put into the Iraqi judicial system. Our job is to see that they are safe and properly cared for, and that there is a chain of custody for them personally, along with any documentation that may have been brought in with them. We take care of everything but the interrogations."

A great deal of the essential, nonoperational business of the task unit is carried out by these individual augmentees. Another I met was one of the linguists assigned to the intelligence section. He was a first class petty officer from Chicago who received his training at the Defense Language Institute in Monterey, California. Normally, his duties took him aboard ship, where he provided a bridge-to-bridge Arabic capability for American warships on the high seas. Now he was assigned to the Ramadi task unit, more in the role of a translator than an interpreter. "I have my limitations," he told me, referring to his work. "As a nonnative speaker, my training is in modern standard Arabic. The Iraqi dialect is very different, almost like a separate language. So I work closely with our interpreters who have the native abilities I will never master. I don't have their skill with the language, but I understand the English usages and format that sometimes give them trouble. We work together to get the job done. I help them and they help me."

I asked him if this was his first nonshipboard tour.

"I was in Fallujah with the Marines last year for a six-month stint. It was different working with the Marines. They're a lot more regimented. In their intelligence or G2/S2 sections, they do the work as it's assigned from higher up, and they do it well. SEALs are different. They do the work, but they're always looking for better work. Much of the intelligence product is generated from the bottom up, from the interrogators and enlisted analysts. What I mean to say is that in the task unit here, they're always trying to figure a way to do it better. If a task or an intelligence lead isn't working or is unproductive, they're quick to put it aside and look for a different avenue. There's good communication up and down the line for what's working and what isn't. The intel shop here has a lot of latitude to do what it thinks is right."

For most of my first day at Camp Lee I moved about the area and got the feel for life at this small SEAL base. As in Fallujah, the SEAL operators observe vampire hours, but life went on 24/7. Most slept from 4:00 AM to noon or thereabouts. The two platoons shared a large Southwest Asia hut, walled off in the center, where they stored their gear and planned their operations. Inside, as out, the SWA huts were all plywood and two-by-fours. There were lots of whiteboards for briefing, a sand table for terrain modeling, and several laptop computers. For the platoons, this was their place of work and their hangout—it was home. It wasn't much different, except for the laptop computers, than my hut in the Mekong Delta—except, of course, for the air-conditioning.

For most of the task unit, the hub of camp life was the mess hall, yet another SWA hut with a long table for eating and another for food service. Chow arrived three times a day: noon, early evening, and at midnight. A detail from the task unit drove over to the mess hall on Camp Ramadi and brought back food in the insulated thermidor-type serving containers. No salads and very few desserts—just five or six bins of starch, meat, and overcooked vegetables. Along one wall were a row of nine refrigerators with water, Gatorade, milk, sodas, and frozen burritos. The burritos were decent. Along the other side there was shelving for consumables—potato chips, instant oatmeal, PowerBars, beef jerky, muffins, cereals, soups, crackers, assorted snacks, and every condiment in the world. One corner held a large-screen TV for movies, but the set was usually tuned to a satellite sports channel. The opposite corner held three plywood computer bays with WiFi access. These computer bays were usually busy, while the men watching TV were usually eating. No one simply just sat and watched TV. The platoon SEALs took their meals in the mess hall along with the task unit support staff. I noticed a nice mix of SEAL and non-SEALs eating together.

One SEAL I met over a burrito had just been honored as the Navy's Pacific Fleet Sailor of the Year, which meant he had been meritoriously advanced from first class petty officer to chief petty officer. He was high on the current deployment and high on life. He'd graduated with BUD/S Class 226 in 1999 and was on his fourth combat rotation. He had a solid reputation as a combat SEAL operator. At home he had four children, one of them adopted, and a fifth on the way.

"Life is good," he told me. This new SEAL chief grew up in the Bronx. He was a fit-looking six-three, with a huge smile and movie-star good looks. "I'm blessed with a wonderful family. If I could, I'd want a dozen kids, but there's the reality that I'm gone from home a lot. These deployments are personally and professionally rewarding, each one more so than the last. But it's time that I spent a little more time at home, and that's about to happen."

"How so?" I asked.

"This is my last rotation, or at least my last rotation with Team Seven for a while. I have orders to the Center [the Naval Special Warfare Center at Coronado]. I'm going to be a BUD/S First Phase instructor."

In the course of writing this book I've had the pleasure of interviewing and breaking bread with dozens of Navy SEALs—all combat veterans, all either coming from or going to the fight. My sampling may be too small for a broad generalization, but it seemed to me that the men who wanted to tell me about their families were also among those most respected by their peers as SEAL operators—those with the best reputations in combat. In my small census, it appeared that the premier operators were also premier family men.

The Camp Lee I experienced was much more built up than in the early days of the first task unit. Only the meal arrangements seemed to be the same. On occasion members of the task unit would go over to the main base for a meal or to visit the small post exchange, but for the most part, they stayed on Camp Lee. Aside from seeing the camp and spending time with members of the task unit, I had two goals on this brief visit. One of them was to see Camp Corregidor.

The visit to Corregidor came about by way of a scheduled operation to support a CME—a combined medical engagement, an operation whereby U.S. medical personnel could treat Iraqi civilians. Early during my second day in Ramadi, we met in one of the platoon spaces for the convoy briefing. Along with the platoon veterans supporting this operation there were two of the new SEALs, men who had only recently completed their training. This was their first venture into the battlespace. Regarding the participation of these new SEALs in task unit operations, Commander Roberts had this to say about the new arrivals:

"I tell the men who have just earned their Trident that your reputation in the teams begins here, right now. We're all watching and will judge you by your actions. You can go outside the wire when my senior enlisted SEALs say you're ready to go outside the wire. Show us you're ready to conduct yourself as a professional, and we'll give you the opportunity to do more. The only limitation is your own performance."

This CME was an Alpha Platoon operation, and as a noncombat evolution, a good chance for a few of the new SEALs to see Ramadi.

"OK, listen up. It's now 0630 and we'll leave for Corregidor at 0730 sharp," said Lieutenant Ned Hurt. "We'll be moving in three Humvees and the armored flatbed [truck] in convoy formation as indicated."

On the whiteboard were the vehicle file order and the individual assignments in the vehicles. Each Humvee had four seated riders and a ring-turret gunner manning the .50-caliber heavy machine gun. The briefing covered the route to Camp Corregidor, possible danger crossings, hand-and-arm signals, and rules of engagement.

"Things are quiet out there," Hurt continued, "but that's no reason for us to be complacent. All our standard convoy procedures remain in effect. Our biggest problem remains that some truck driver or private auto will pull into our line of vehicles. They're getting used to us and getting used to driving on the roads. Yet we still have to maintain convoy integrity and keep these civilian vehicles away from us. If they don't respond to the horn or arm signals, you might want to use a pencil flare. That's been working pretty well. Past that, you all know the steps for the escalation of force when it becomes necessary—tires, engine block, then passenger compartment. Above all we need to be situationally aware and anticipate worst-case scenarios. On this trip we'll have Mister Couch and Lieutenant Ruh with us, so stay sharp. We want to take good care of them."

Lieutenant Ned Hurt, Alpha Platoon's OIC, brought a great deal of recent experience and local knowledge to Squadron Seven's deployment. He was a platoon AOIC with Squadron Three and a veteran of the recent heavy fighting in the battle for the city. After barely five months in Coronado, he was back at Camp Lee. Ned Hurt's sojourn to the SEAL teams was an interesting one. He was a high school all-American water polo goalie and was recruited by UCLA, a perennial national powerhouse in the sport. Finding college not to his liking, he enlisted in the Navy to become a SEAL. However, shortly after beginning BUD/S training, he developed severe stress fractures in his legs and was medically dropped from the program. As with most BUD/S dropouts, Seaman Hurt was given orders to a warship. Then the Naval Academy water polo coach learned that one of the nation's premier players was in a Navy uniform, getting ready to ship out. The coach intervened. Hurt made the transition from seaman to midshipmen and graduated from Annapolis, Class of 2003, where he was a consensus collegiate all-American for three years.

He then graduated with BUD/S Class 248 and was assigned to SEAL Team Three. During his previous tour in Ramadi, he served as a platoon assistant working out of Camp Lee. On this current rotation, Hurt and his platoon had initially operated out of Camp Corregidor. Owing to operational inactivity at Corregidor, Ned Hurt and Alpha Platoon were moved back to Camp Lee midway through the tour.

We drove past the Camp Lee guard shack just after 7:30 AM, across Camp Ramadi, and out the main gate. Once we were clear of Camp Ramadi, I heard Ned Hurt pass along the command to activate the radio emitters. This reminded the men in each vehicle to turn on their frequency jammer, a device most vehicles in Iraq carry to defeat cell-phone-detonated and remotely detonated IEDs. The little convoy took Baseline Road past the glass factory, and we were soon on Route Michigan heading east toward Corregidor. Driving through Ramadi along this particular route was like a tour of Stalingrad in 1944 or the outskirts of Dresden. We passed a few structures that were intact, but I saw none without broken windows and chips in the exterior, the result of small-arms fire. There were people on the streets—some waved and some didn't. Children shyly approached with their hands over their heads, a universal sign for kids looking for the gift of a soccer ball. Occasionally, there were modest signs of commerce, but the buildings along Route Michigan were devastated. Lieutenant Hurt was on the radio clearing our crossing of one Army or Marine battalion battlespace to the next. We crossed three of them.

"I'm continually amazed at how much things have changed—how they are now compared to when I was here a year ago," Ned Hurt said of the conditions. "Now it looks as if we're presiding over quiet rubble. Like after the Battle of Fallujah, parts of the city are simply trashed. This place will come back if the Iraqis, with our help, can maintain this level of security—keep things this quiet. Yet nothing is going to get done unless the police and the locals can keep the city safe. We'll be around for a while, but it's up to them now."

As with many combat outposts around Ramadi, the activity at and strategic value of Camp Corregidor had all but disappeared. Gone are the days when insurgents from the sanctuary of the Mala'ab and Sufia districts launched mortars and RPGs at Corregidor on a daily basis. Also gone are the days when going twenty-four hours without a casualty was celebrated. Weeks now go by without incident. At the entrance to Camp Corregidor, a M113 armored personnel carrier still blocked the main entrance to the camp. It chugged aside for our little convoy to enter. Nothing like a piece of armor to discourage a vehicle-borne suicide bomber. The Army 1-9 infantry battalion was still stationed at Corregidor in support of the three Iraqi army battalions of the Iraqi 1-1 brigade, located just across Route Michigan. Like the city around it, Camp Corregidor was very quiet.

The Full Metal Jacket compound was still standing, but mostly deserted. Only the Marine ANGLICO team and an Army EOD contingent remained in residence. The building itself was a dirty, three-story structure with an open courtyard. Ned took me on a tour of the SEAL platoon spaces. Save for a recent layer of dust, they were much as they were when Squadron Three built them just over a year before. They were kept under lock and key, and the Marines kept an eye on them in case there was a need for the platoon to return. We had breakfast at the Corregidor mess hall, which carried a reputation for having the best chow in Ramadi.

"The hair on the back of my neck still stands up when I come back here," Ned Hurt admitted. "Not so much from when we were here a few months back, but from last year. We came here once or twice for operations, and it was a compound under siege. My chief stepped out of the building to make a satellite phone call to his wife. He was talking to her when a marine not five feet away took a round in his collarbone. He had to quickly hang up and give the guy first aid. And see that empty parking lot over there? Last year it was full of M1 Abrams tanks and Bradley Fighting Vehicles, all in various states of disrepair. Those brave Army mechanics worked on them day and night, under fire, to get them back in the fight. There were a lot of heroes living here when we fought for control of the city, including my brother SEALs from Team Three and Five. It's almost surreal now—so quiet. What a difference."

Hurt went on to explain why they had spent only three months at Corregidor on this rotation. The tempo of operations had fallen so dramatically that there was no need for them to remain. They did conduct ongoing training for the scout elements with the Iraqi brigade and for the local police in the area. However, the scouts, after more than a year of fighting with Squadron Three and Squadron Five SEALs at Corregidor, didn't need much work. There was no longer a need to train at Corregidor. Now that military vehicles and the police pickup trucks could move about the city without being shot at, both Iraqi army and Iraqi police training could be conducted at the ranges on Camp Ramadi. When Ned Hurt and his platoon left Camp Corregidor, the scout and police training programs were turned over to the 1-9 infantry battalion.

One of the reasons for this run from Camp Lee to Camp Corregidor was to retrieve a container of equipment left behind from the SEAL occupation of Corregidor. While I toured the camp, the SEALs set about getting the container onto the flatbed truck. The other reason was to drop off the medical team that was to remain for the day to conduct the combined medical engagement. This involved the platoon corpsman and two platoon SEALs, who would help with security. The engagement was to be "combined" in that it involved SEALs and marines from the ANGLICO detachment and a detachment from the Iraqi army brigade. In addition to a Marine security element, there was a Navy hospital corpsman from the ANGLICO unit. This medical team had no doctors, but there was considerable talent in these two enlisted "docs." The SEAL was an 18 Delta–trained combat medic and the ANGLICO corpsman was certified as an independent-duty Navy corpsmen. That evening I found the SEAL medic and asked him about this engagement.

"It's one of the positive things we can do for the Iraqis here in Ramadi," he told me. He looked very tired. "This time we set up in the home compound of a minor sheikh. We don't publicize these engagements, but the people somehow know we'll be there and the crowds gather well before we arrive. Security is a big thing with us, and the security teams all but strip-search those entering the compound for treatment. In addition to a few marines and SEALs, there's an Iraqi army security element standing by to help manage the crowds. AQI would love nothing better than to get to us or to the people who come to us for help. We're always on the lookout for suicide bombers, and the suicide bombers are always looking for crowds of civilians. For some folks we see, it's maybe the only medical care they've had in their lives. This time we had two corpsmen from the hospital there to help us. These two medics set up a triage room to screen those coming to see me or the ANGLICO corpsman.

"As for treatment, we deal with infections, disease, respiratory problems, problems from malnutrition, dental problems, you name it. Still, we can do only so much. We dispense meds like penicillin and antibiotics and topical ointments, dress wounds, and sew up cuts. Occasionally, we'll do an IV with antibiotics. On occasion we set bones, but only if there is no pulse in the extremity, which means that they'll lose the limb if we don't do something. For things that are well out of our expertise, we send them to a civilian hospital, but often there's little help for them there. Ramadi General is not the Scripps medical center. It's short of doctors and medicines. In some rare, life-threatening cases, especially with children, we get them to the hospital at Camp Ramadi."

"You look beat," I observed. "I can only guess that it's hard duty."

"Tell me about it," he said wearily. "We stay at it for about four hours. That's about when we run out of meds. It's hard on us and hard on our interpreters. The terps work as hard as we do. We try to do at least two of these a month. It's not always possible, but we try. It connects us with the people in a positive way. I happen to like Iraqis. They're different from us, but in their own way they're very special. They're worth everything we can do for them."

These medical engagements began with the Squadron Five task unit and have been continued with Squadron Seven. The previous TUs had no opportunity for medical outreach owing to security conditions. My final question for the corpsman: "Are the Iraqis grateful for this; do they thank you?"

"I know they appreciate it, but their gratitude is restrained. After all, their war began when we arrived; when we came, things got worse. The women will nod as they leave, and sometimes the men will hold a hand over their heart and say, '*Insha Allah.*' One of the sheikhs who spoke English did thank us for helping his people. It's enough. We know we're making a difference. Professionally, it's rewarding. Few doctors practicing in America treat as many patients as I did today. I know none of them see the range of maladies."

The trip from Corregidor back to Camp Lee was another uneventful tour of the rubble that is now this part of Ramadi. On our return trip, as it was later in the day, I did begin to see signs of progress. A few earthmovers were clearing debris from around crumpled buildings. There were a few taxis out and some sidewalk merchants. Blue and white Iraqi police pickup trucks weren't far from the clearing operations, and there were police on most street corners. More important, Anbaris were out on the street about their business. I asked about the future of Camp Corregidor and was told that there are plans to return it to what it was before the war—an agricultural college. As for the battalion stationed there, it was my understanding that they planned to leave behind only a military transition team to work with the Iraqi 1-1 brigade.

The following morning I made my final sortie from Camp Lee. This was a trip I'd asked to make and Ron Roberts made it happen—a visit to COP Falcon. Given all I'd learned from those who fought for this COP and those who defended it, I was anxious to see it for myself. Again, the trip was preceded by a convoy briefing. Again, we drove through very battered streets. This time I was with SEALs from Bravo Platoon. The streets and arterials that connect Camp Ramadi to the outposts had once been shooting galleries, and had seen the worst of the fighting. The aftermath of battle was evident all along these routes. We began on Route Michigan and turned south on Baseline Road for COP Falcon. A year ago this same drive could not have been made without drawing small-arms fire and with a better than even bet to be hit with an IED. The entrance to the COP was manned by Iraqi police; they raised a wooden cantilevered pole to let us into the outpost. There was a five-ton truck parked across the entryway for good measure. The additional security was there to protect the police station colocated at the COP. Just outside, a dozen or more women in full burkas sat in a group and gossiped. I could see a few food stands in operation. The outpost was now manned by a Marine police training team that supported the Iraqi police station. We were greeted by a very sharp Marine first lieutenant and his gunnery sergeant, and allowed to walk about the facility on our own. Again, all was quiet. Like Corregidor, it was mostly deserted—the gun positions and sandbagged observation points that dominated the rooftops were vacant. Plans were under way to return most of the commandeered buildings to their owners; the police station would remain. Having written about, but never experienced, the tension and fighting that went on here, I found the quiet emptiness almost unnerving. Perhaps I was feeling the spirits of Mike Bajema and his Bulldogs that still lingered in this mostly abandoned outpost.

Following the convoy runs to Camp Corregidor and COP Falcon, I spent the rest of my time at Camp Lee and Camp Ramadi moving about the camps and speaking with SEALs and other members of the task unit. As with the task group in Fallujah, activity at the Ramadi task unit goes on day and night, 24/7. In that there is a discernable daily pattern with the SEALs and the TU operational support staff, their workday began early in the afternoon. The platoons muster in their platoon spaces for quarters and work assignments at 1:00 PM. At 2:00 PM there's the daily staff meeting in the TOC, attended by representatives of the various task unit departments and the platoons. The format for this gathering was the same as at staff meetings that take place in U.S. military headquarters and battle staffs everywhere, only those gathered at the Ramadi TOC were in T-shirts, shorts, and sneakers. Yet the meeting itself was highly organized and professional. Ron Roberts had his agenda itemized on PowerPoint and displayed on one of the large TOC plasma screens. He moved through it quickly and efficiently, beginning with the quote of the day:

Every time we insert SEALs, something catches on fire.

—QRF pilot

The N1 gave a quick overview of the task unit manning levels, with a reminder to all to stay on top of personnel evaluations and administrative deadlines. This N1 rep was a huge black petty officer with a kind, affable smile. He managed the task unit administration, and everyone took note of his requirements. The N2 reported that the Ramadi battlespace was again quiet for the last twenty-four hours, then followed with a quick summation of a new type of unexploded ordnance. The intelligence outlook was cautious but optimistic.

"It seems that the weapons caches we uncovered in June and July are beginning to have some effect. There are indications that AQI is experiencing some ordnance shortages. There are no indications of new threats to the city, but we have to expect some increased enemy activity as we get closer to Ramadan [13 September to 13 October in 2007]. Across the Ramadi battlespace and farther west to the border regions, things are pretty quiet."

The N3 quickly summarized convoy runs to Corregidor and to COP Falcon the previous day. Going forward, the task unit training cell would be conducting a live-fire exercise on Camp Ramadi that afternoon for scouts from the 1-1-7. No operations were scheduled for that night. From the N4 came an overview of funds committed to camp improvement, particularly the small firing range on Camp Lee. The N5 is not staffed at the TU level. The N6 reviewed what communications links were up and which ones were down, but most of the comms were up. He followed this by a reminder that laptop computers have a hard life in Iraq and that everyone should back up their data to an external source. I took note of this and immediately dumped my trip notes onto my thumb drive. Ron Roberts brought the twenty-minute meeting to a close with a final comment.

"We're scheduled to redeploy sometime in October. I stress the word 'sometime.' Much as we want to get home, we don't leave until the task unit from Squadron One says, 'We got it.' Don't make plans and promises back home that I can't keep. Most of you will be able to have Halloween with your kids. Now's the time to stay focused and make sure nothing falls between the cracks. We've got a good deployment going, but we're not done yet. Again, I want everyone to stay focused."

Shortly after the staff meeting I caught a ride over to the firing range on Camp Ramadi, where the task unit training cadre was working with the scouts from the 1st Battalion, 1st Brigade of the 7th Division of the Iraqi army. The range was a flat piece of dirt some one hundred by two hundred yards with high, bulldozed berms on three sides. There, a half dozen SEALs were putting some thirty Iraqi scouts through fire-and-movement drills. Overseeing this training was the Bravo Platoon AOIC, Lieutenant (junior grade) Kyle Peters. This was Peters' first SEAL deployment. In addition to his platoon operational duties, he was assigned the lead role in the task unit's training responsibilities. Early in the tour, he had been responsible for the training of the Iraqi police. Now he and the task unit were back to training *jundi* scouts.

"We picked up our training duties from Squadron Five where they left off last April, which was the training of the Iraqi police. When we got here, it was all about training new Iraqi policemen and getting them on the street. Our training of the police at the time focused on teaching them to move safely in the streets, room entry, and the management of detainees." Kyle Peters graduated from the Naval Academy in 2004 with a degree in physics. He went straight to BUD/S, where he graduated with Class 242. "The police were doing pretty well when we arrived, so we continued with the work Five had started. They had just begun working with the Army and Marine police training teams to create a citywide police SWAT element that could fight and win against a band of a dozen or so insurgents. The U.S. advisers rounded up about sixty policemen from stations across Ramadi, and we put them in a three-week course. Most of them had already had the basic one-week police training course. This new course was heavy on close-quarter combat and room-clearing skills that the police need to know to take AQI fighters out of a building. We graduated thirty-one. The course drops were due to attitude, safety violations, and maturity issues, mostly with the younger trainees. The Iraqi police officers agreed with and supported dropping those trainees from this program. In the final analysis the idea of a citywide special team was not such a good idea. The Iraqi policemen are most comfortable in their own neighborhoods and patrolling their own turf. They didn't seem too eager to drive across town to take up another tribe's fight in another tribe's neighborhood. However, we did train them to a level so they can now go back to their own police stations and train other police. It was a good learning experience for us, and the police are now better able to defend their city.

"When we shifted operations away from the city, we needed to reconnect with the Iraqi army scouts—the *jundis* whom the previous task units had trained. We needed an Iraqi army presence on these operations outside Ramadi, but we had yet to work with them. These were the three battalion scout elements from the Iraqi 1-7 brigade and the brigade special missions platoon. SEALs hadn't trained with them since December 2006. The Army and Marine training team advisers hooked us back up with them, and I think they were glad to be back having us train with them. Partly because they like working with SEALs, which reflects well on the guys from Five, but also because we have lots of ammo. The Iraqi battalions don't have all that much ammunition for training, maybe a dozen rounds per man when they come to the range. When they're on the range with us, they get to shoot a lot. We try to get them somewhere between 250 and 300 rounds per man. This shift back to working with the scouts began last June. I think they were a little surprised to see us again, as for close to seven months we did nothing but train the police. Yet they seemed to be happy when we resumed the training and got them ready to operate outside the city. There were new *jundis* in the scout elements who had yet to receive our training, but many of the veteran scouts who had been around for a while were glad see us—they remembered the SEALs from Three and Five. They have assigned duties within their brigade, but they always seemed willing to break away to train or operate with us."

One of the SEALs filled me in on their recent training history. The range drills began with precision shooting. When the *jundi* scout trainees began to shoot tight groups, they moved on to patrolling, room clearing, prisoner handling, and fire-and-movement drills. The particular fire-and-movement drill that I observed had the trainees working in pairs. One *jundi* would shoot at some target silhouettes, downrange and to the left of range center, while his shooting partner would sprint downrange to the right of center. This second *jundi* would stop and take up the firing while the first would sprint downrange, keeping to the left. Using this fire-and-run, leapfrog maneuver, they advanced down the firing range and back again, with each scout providing covering fire while the other moved—just as they would do in combat.

"The final evolution for them here today is a mini stress course," the lead instructor told me of the drills. "It's the kind of thing we do during our own predeployment training, although the distance between those shooting and those moving is a lot closer when we do it. But then we have shooting discipline and safety awareness that these soldiers don't yet have." I'd met this instructor in 2002 when I was researching *The Finishing School,* the book on SEAL Qualification Training. Then he was a young petty officer and aspiring SEAL trainee, and I remembered him as quiet and serious. Now he was a first class petty officer and a multitour veteran, teaching combat tactics to the Iraqi scouts. He was also an enthusiastic, natural teacher—very take-charge and animated as he ran the training range. It was gratifying for me to see the professionalism and maturity with which he put his *jundis* through their drills. His father is a master chief in the SEAL teams. Just imagine how proud he is of his warrior son.

"All our teaching methodology during this training is the same," this instructor told me. "First, I explain the drill to them through the interpreter. I speak for a sentence or two, then the terp translates. We talk it through, start to finish. Then we show them the drill. I talk, the terp translates, and one or two of my instructors execute the drill. Only then do we put them through the drill, first at a walk and then full speed. It's just like SEAL training—crawl, walk, run—only here I need a good interpreter."

The role of the interpreter in this kind of training can't be underestimated. I watched closely as the instructor spoke; he gave clear, simple instructions, but he was animated with lots of movement and arm gestures. When the terp made the translation, he was just as lively. They were like two Italian drivers after a collision with all the expressive body language going on between them.

"When you come off line," the instructor said as he demonstrated a particular move, "keep the muzzle of your weapon pointed up and turn, don't spin. This is not a ballet; you're not ballerinas."

As the terp made the translation, I looked at one of the other interpreters who was watching the drills with me. "He told the *jundis,* 'Make the turn slowly with the barrel pointed to the heavens. Do not whirl; you are not dancers.'" We both chuckled and turned back to the training.

I watched several iterations of the mini stress course. The drill began with the *jundi* shooting pair doing ten push-ups—not all that easy in the heat and with their full combat load of helmet, body armor, water, and ammunition. Iraqis tend to resist all forms of regimented physical exercise, but they knew the push-ups in this case were to simulate the stress and exertion of combat. They also knew it was part of the game—the competition. They do respond to competition, and the stress course was a timed evolution. Following the push-ups, they moved to the firing line. Then they began their leapfrog, fire-and-movement drill downrange to the far target and back. As each scout raced from one firing position to another, a SEAL instructor ran alongside and slightly behind the shooter. They were there to offer encouragement and correction, as well as to serve as safety observers. I was very impressed with both the SEAL trainers and their Iraqi scout trainees.

"They're good soldiers, but they're not like us," the lead instructor said during a break in the training. "They can learn what we have to teach them, but we have to bring the information to them within the norms of their culture. We have to understand technically what they can and cannot do, and how to keep them safe. We also have to learn how to motivate them, without giving offense or embarrassing them. They typically don't like to stand out in a group or call attention to themselves, so they'll do only what they're told and hope to get by. Praise goes a long way. Praise one guy for shooting a tight group, and pretty soon all of them are shooting tight groups. We also have to be careful with censuring them. When we give them some push-ups for a safety violation, most of the time we do the push-ups with them. We say, 'Your mistake also my mistake—we do penalty together.' All this has to be done with some care and attention as to how this makes them appear to the group."

"Most of these scouts were pretty well trained when we began working with them a few months back," Lieutenant Peters explained, "so much what we're doing is sustainment training. The only new things we taught them relate to operations from helicopters. They know how to do assaults and to make the transition from a foot patrol or a Humvee to an assault formation for a fixed target. Since most of our operations are now outside the city, many of them are insertion by helo. We had to work with them on airborne assault tactics, getting on and off the helo in a tactical manner—that kind of thing. Weapons safety and discipline are also very important in helicopter operations. We all have to work together as we never go into the battlespace without a contingent of Iraqis with us. They're still learning on the job, even out in the battlespace, so I guess this is technically still combat FID."

I was interested in how this recent shift back to working with the scouts translated to operations, both in and out of Ramadi. With the police now on the streets in force, how did this affect the SEAL–Iraqi army scout operations when there was a mission in the city? The transition that the Squadron Five task unit made to begin working with the police seemed to have supported the intent of the local sheikhs, and helped to bring about the recent and much-welcomed calm that had descended on the city. Currently, the training of policemen had become more formalized, and in the hands of the military police transition teams. The SEALs were now back with their *jundi* scouts.

The Bravo Platoon OIC told me an interesting story that illustrated what was taking place on the streets when American or Iraqi army units did venture into Ramadi. After the shift back to training with the Iraqi army scouts, the officer in charge of the special missions platoon sought out the SEALs with a target the Iraqi brigade intelligence staff had worked up. He said they had learned of two insurgent fighters hiding in town, and they wanted to mount an operation to go into the city and pick them up. What he was saying was that he wanted to go into a local neighborhood, controlled by the local police, and get these two enemy fighters. What he was also saying was that he wanted a SEAL element to go with him to "legitimize" his entry into this area. The SEALs agreed to support the mission and obtained the operational clearances for the operation.

"In many ways, this was a validation of the progress made by the three previous task units in training the Iraqi army scouts," the platoon leading petty officer told me. "The two insurgents they were after were known to have worked with AQI and had planted IEDs that had killed Iraqi soldiers. Once the scouts told us where they were living, we showed them how to use Google Earth to get an image of the target house. Some of the sharper scouts learned to make the jump from an overhead image to a street-level perspective—they were able to pick up on known landmarks like intersections, water towers, and walled compounds. They worked up the operation, and when we got on target, they did the breaching and made the assault with very little help from us. Think about it," the petty officer said. "A year ago, we took these scouts into the streets and we made all the decisions; now it's the other way around. And the ratio of them to us is changing. On this operation there were six SEALs and an EOD guy with fourteen scouts. We were along in a true advisory role."

The combined SEAL–Iraqi scout force moved into the area at night, first by Humvee and then on foot patrol. The scouts' information proved accurate; they entered the house and found the two men they were looking for. By the time they had searched the house and brought out the suspects, the local Iraqi police had gathered.

"I found myself in a bit of a turf war," the SEAL platoon officer said. "These were clearly the insurgents we were looking for and, according to our intelligence, they had established ties to the insurgency—they had rap sheets. However, the local police chief claimed they were *not* insurgents and vouched for them. We had something of a jurisdictional issue. No one was going for their guns, but clearly the police did not want us to detain these guys and the scouts wanted to take them back with us. I could see that if I insisted, it would cost this police chief stature—some *wasta*."

"So what did you do?"

"I decided to side with the police. We really had no choice—it was their neighborhood, their turf. I told the police chief that I was going to release the suspects—these two insurgents—into his custody. I also told him that if they caused any trouble in the future that I was going to hold him personally responsible for their conduct. I later told the Iraqi scout leader that they'd done a good job in finding these insurgents, but that we had no choice but to respect the local police in this matter. After all, the Iraqi army is like us; they're outsiders here in Ramadi. A year ago, maybe even six months ago, something like this would have been unthinkable. It was a little frustrating, finding men with known insurgent ties and not being able to bring them in, but it also shows how far we've come in gaining control of the city. And how far the Anbaris have come in taking responsibility for security in their neighborhoods. My guess is that these insurgents have been 'converted' by their tribal leaders and will give us no more trouble."

During my final day at Camp Lee, I spent as much time as I could with the SEALs and other members of the task unit. As for the SEALs, the pace of operations simply hadn't been what it was for the Squadron Three or Squadron Five task units—certainly not the pace of active combat engagements. I sensed a bittersweet reaction among these warriors about this relative inactivity. They understood that AQI had been largely driven from their operational area, and there was little they could do to engage an enemy who wasn't there. They had trained for battle, and wanted to put that training to good use. When they were not in the field or training Iraqis, life at Camp Lee was all about eating, sleeping, and working at their assigned platoon duties, including reviewing target folders, working out, and shooting. Regarding the latter, there was a small shooting range on the northern tip of the Camp Lee compound. It was adequate for sighting in an M4 rifle on the 1,000-inch range and for pistol drills. There was a shooting station on top of the team building with what I estimated was 150 yards to the target berm. Any long-distance shooting or the calibration of a sniper rifle would have to be done on the ranges at Camp Ramadi.

The SEALs work out on a daily basis. For a Navy SEAL exercise is, to some degree, a form of recreation. There were two weight-training facilities at Camp Lee. A few of the SEALs I spoke with lifted weights every other day and blended the lifting with some form of CrossFit training. Many took weight training for three days and then took a day off. Some of them did the CrossFit training individually, but most of them worked in groups; the group dynamic seemed to make for a more strenuous workout. A few times each week they took a long run or played a game called speedball. The runs or the games took place in the evening when the temperature came down to 105° or so. These speedball games were not restricted to SEALs, and many task unit members joined in.

Speedball is like ultimate Frisbee played with a football, only you can run with the ball. A two-handed touch by the opposition means the ball carrier has to give the ball over to the other team. No referees are needed because there are no rules. If a guy is out for a pass and there are two defenders, one just grabs the receiver and throws him to the ground while the other defender goes for the ball. Any player can be as rough as he likes on offense or defense. And you can pass it to yourself. If someone is about to tag you, you can toss the ball in the air, get away, and catch the ball yourself.

"There's always lots of pushing and shoving, and it can get very physical," one of the platoon SEALs told me. "Given the temperature, you sweat like a pig. Forty-five minutes of speedball can really trash you. And you drink gallons of water."

After one of the speedball games, I saw a few of the SEALs taking their turn with the tire. A few of the platoon SEALs brought back a two-hundred-pound heavy-equipment tire from the dump on Camp Ramadi. They used it in two ways. One was to get into a harness and pull the tire on the paved road the length of Camp Lee and back. The other was to flip it over like a coin, squatting to lift it over, again and again. These are squat lifts of one-hundred-plus pounds. The men were not only covered with sweat, but they were incredibly dirty from the tire. But with this kind of conditioning and acclimatization to the heat, it's easy to see how they can carry a combat load of fifty pounds or more at a dead sprint. It was yet another reminder for me that there's quite a difference between being in shape and being in SEAL shape. I'd like to say that the SEALs of my era worked that hard and that consistently at our physical conditioning, but that was not the case. This extreme approach to physical conditioning is a whole new evolution of our warrior culture.

During that final day I learned a great deal about the nature and scope of SEAL and SOF operations in Ramadi and was privileged to hear about many of the task unit's operational successes. Among them, two stand out as representative of the mission and reach of the Ramadi task unit, as practiced by this task unit from Squadron Seven. One of them was the SEAL participation in what MSNBC called the Battle of Donkey Island. The *Washington Post* also reported this engagement in an article on 19 August 2007 entitled "A Deadly Clash at Donkey Island." The battle actually took place some six weeks earlier.

The AQI, having been pushed out of Ramadi, had been doing all they could to reenter the city and reassert their control over the population. By necessity, their efforts to mount a return to the city had to be organized and staged *outside* the city. Late in the evening on 30 June, during a routine patrol along the Habbaniyah Canal southwest of the city center, an element of the 1-77 infantry battalion came across an AQI force preparing to move into the city. This was a well-planned and well-orchestrated effort by al-Qaeda to reestablish a presence in Ramadi. There were seventy-some insurgents marshaled at a bivouac area some seven miles outside the city. Their camp was near an island in the Habbaniyah Canal called Donkey Island. Along with these fighters were two semitrailers that served as their transport and to smuggle in a large quantity of weapons, ammunition, explosives, IED materials, sniper rifles, and explosive-laden suicide vests. It was a chance encounter by the patrol—one totally unanticipated. These routine patrols had encountered no resistance or insurgent activity in several months, which speaks to the sudden reversal of fortune for AQI in Ramadi and al-Anbar. Yet this preplanned incursion was a sudden reminder that the insurgents had not given up.

"These guys were organized and trained to try to retake Ramadi," one of the SEALs told me. "I don't think they'd have succeeded, but they would have caused a lot of civilian casualties and upset the current level of security in the city. The uniformity of their equipment was unbelievable. They had the same clothes, same sandals, and same weapons. Their backpacks, first-aid kits, scarves, rations, and ammunition vests were all of the same standard. They had been trained and outfitted at some secure location and were carefully making their way back into the city. It's a good thing for all of us that the Army patrol stumbled onto them."

The details of this engagement are well documented in the *Washington Post* article. The Army patrol from the 1-77 was heavily outnumbered, but they tore into the AQI force with great courage and tenacity and, with reinforcements, were able to kill close to half the insurgent force and scatter the rest. Throughout the night and into the early morning hours, they battled the enemy. For their part, individual fighters resisted fanatically, with the wounded clutching grenades or pistols, waiting for the Americans to approach for one last chance to kill an infidel. The enemy fighters, or an advanced element of this group, had prepared this staging area for defense. There were fifty-five-gallon barrels sunk into the ground as fighting holes, affording enemy marksmen good cover and concealment. The battle continued throughout the night, and the engaged Army elements suffered close to a dozen wounded. In one particularly courageous act, an Apache attack helicopter pilot helped a badly wounded soldier into his seat in the helo and clung to the side of the aircraft while the other pilot flew the helo and the wounded man to the hospital on Camp Ramadi.

This battle was as unexpected as it was vicious. Ramadi had become so quiet and uneventful, routine patrols had become the norm for Army and Marine elements moving about Ramadi. For most of those brave Army soldiers, this was their first combat action, and they fought well.

The following morning at daybreak, a SEAL element from the task unit's Bravo Platoon was sent to the battle site to help with the mop-up. Sandals were found along the bank, and a rope had been strung from the bank of the canal to Donkey Island. Donkey Island was a flat, barren island ringed with a thick crown of reeds. Lying in the middle of the canal, it was a natural hiding place for enemy refugees from the battle. The SEALs arrived and began to inflate their Zodiac-type boats. Their assignment was to cross to the island and clear it of any AQI stragglers.

"It was quiet, and there were bodies and body parts everywhere along the canal," Chief Todd Day told me. Day was the Bravo Platoon chief petty officer. He was on his fourth combat rotation and a familiar face. I'd met him when he was a Third Phase instructor at BUD/S and I was working on *The Warrior Elite*. "It was a pretty gristly scene. While we pumped up the boats and motored over to the island, a squad of soldiers began to check out the banks along the canal. We'd just beached the boat and were starting to clear the island when a firefight broke out along the bank of the canal. Some muj hiding in a clump of bushes behind a berm had suddenly opened fire and pinned the Army soldiers down."

The SEALs quickly recrossed the canal and moved in to help. "Two muj had been hiding in this thicket or dense brush in a ditch above and parallel to the canal," Chief Day recalled. "They had good cover canal-side and away from the canal as well. Two of the soldiers were down. We moved one of our Humvees to a position to cover the downed men while the Boss [the Bravo Platoon OIC] and another SEAL flanked the muj and came up the ditch at them. They did a good job of maneuvering under fire to get into position. They closed in and were shooting them up pretty well, but I guess not well enough. When they got close, the muj blew themselves up."

About half of these AQI fighters had suicide belts. These belts were not the kind designed to create mass casualties in a marketplace, but were part of their individual kit, to be used to kill themselves and any nearby enemy rather than be taken alive. In this skirmish with the SEALs, that's exactly what they tried to do. These belts are bands of high explosives imbedded with ball bearings. Both SEALs who had flanked the enemy position were wounded by these explosive vests. Two soldiers who had gone down at the beginning of the skirmish died, one instantly and the other as he was evacuated. They were the only American fatalities in the battle.

"It goes to show how committed these insurgents are," said Lieutenant John Hite. Hite was the Bravo Platoon OIC and one of the SEALs wounded in the skirmish. A 2000 Naval Academy graduate, he was on his third combat tour. During his previous rotation, he managed to acquire a conversational ability in Arabic. This was his first Purple Heart. "We learned a lesson on this operation: we were just too complacent. It's been so quiet in and around the city that we let our guard down. We walked right by where those guys were hiding. They could have taken out two of us just as easily as they did those two soldiers. In this game you have to always be on the alert. You can take nothing for granted, and you have to be professional at all times."

I asked why the SEALs had to come back across the canal to make the assault on the AQI hiding in the ditch. Where were the other soldiers who were with the two who went down? I could see Lieutenant Hite and Chief Day were a little hesitant to reply. It was the chief who spoke for both of them.

"That element of the 1-77 hadn't been here all that long, and this was the first combat some of those young soldiers had seen. Don't forget, some of those soldiers were still in high school when we began preparing for this deployment. Everyone in the platoon element out there that day was a veteran. SEALs are aggressive; it's how we train, and it's how we fight. Those two AQI were probably veteran fighters as well, and they kept up a good volume of fire. While the soldiers were figuring out what was going on and what to do, we just did it. It takes a few firefights before you learn to respond quickly. The Army guys are all right; they just don't get the training we do. It was still a tragedy. Army, Navy, Marine—it doesn't matter. We lost two brother warriors that day."

A few days after the battle, the task unit turned out en masse for the service held on Camp Ramadi to honor the two soldiers killed near Donkey Island.

One of the least visible and most important elements of the task unit is a small group that works within, and is closely aligned with, the task unit intelligence department. This is the Advanced Special Operations group, usually referred to as the ASO. In Ramadi as in the other task force TUs, what they do and even who they are is classified. In the team house in Ramadi, behind closed doors, the ASO intelligence specialists, linguists, analysts, technicians, and senior SEAL operations cadre are working to defeat AQI operations and target AQI leaders. Their human and technical information-collection tentacles reach well into the battlespace. These ASO intelligence and targeting capabilities benefit both the special operators and the conventional forces in the field. While their mission responsibilities focus on the development of tactical operational intelligence, sometimes this group conducts operations of its own. The men seldom talk about what they do. I asked for permission to document one of their operations in Ramadi for this book, and I was told of one they had conducted a few weeks before my arrival. As with the engagement at Donkey Island, it shows the length to which AQI will go to get back into Ramadi, and the resources at their disposal. This story is also an indictment of the deadly and ruthless enemy that wants to exert control over the people of Iraq.

The SEAL who told me about this operation remembered me from fifteen years before. I had the high honor to be the graduation speaker for his BUD/S class (Class 182) in July 1992. Then he was a seaman with less than a year in the Navy. Now, fifteen years later, he was a senior chief petty officer. His hair was slightly longer than regulation and he had a beard. He was dressed in tan slacks, an open-collar shirt, and sneakers. Behind all this was a very resourceful and experienced SEAL operator.

"As much as we'd like to think all the insurgents have left town," he began, "that's not so. Maybe all the stupid ones left or have been killed, but the survivors are very smart and very committed. These few that remain may be the ultimate survivors. They know how to beat our intel nets with strict compartmentalization. They watch the sky constantly for UAVs, and they've learned to be careful with cell phones. Most are not highly educated, but well schooled in insurgent survival skills. They're almost like a cult. Our best chance to catch the last and most talented of these insurgents is working closely with the people.

"We have a lot of contacts out in the city and the province. They run the gamut from shopkeepers to policemen to taxi drivers—from tribal elders to burka-clad grandmothers. These contacts provide us a mosaic of what's going on out there. We track all of it. If a source is telling us about a potential target, we always try to confirm it with another source. We knew that AQI was trying to target the police in Ramadi with suicide bombers. We had confirmation of this from our sources and sources well outside our own organization. The police are a big problem for AQI. Since the police took back to the streets of Ramadi, or"—he said this with a grim smile—"since the Army and the Marines gave them back the streets, the insurgents have come after them. Their plan was to bring in four bombers dressed like the Iraqi policemen. Most of the police wear light-blue shirts with dark-blue armored vests and dark trousers." I nodded; I'd seen them out in Ramadi, patrolling the streets in their blue-and-white pickups and smoking cigarettes on street corners. "Well, these insurgents were going to be wearing dark-blue vests packed with explosives. Their intent was to walk into police stations, kill themselves, and kill as many policemen as they could.

"The AQI plan was to move these suicide bombers from a safe house well outside Ramadi into the city. Since the people, at the urging of the tribal leaders, have nearly all turned against al-Qaeda, it's hard for them to mount any kind of offensive here. The people rat them out. So they had no choice but to move these bombers along one of their infiltration routes to the city. These routes are very much like what the drug smugglers use. One person takes them from A to B—perhaps two or three miles, or maybe two or three blocks. Then another escort takes them from B to C, and so on. The individual bombers themselves may or may not know their ultimate target, and they're kept blindfolded during most of their journey."

As he explained it, they're kept hooded during transit so that if they're captured, they can't reveal who transported them or along which route they traveled. I was curious about these links in the chain and the people who do this for al-Qaeda. Why do they do it, or why don't they go to the authorities?

"They do it because they aren't given a choice," the senior chief explained. "If you're some goat herder and al-Qaeda says to move people from one place to another, or to keep them in your home for a day or two, you do it. If you refuse, they kill you. If you go the police, they kill all of your family in front of you, then they kill you. This is not a threat and it's not unusual—the AQI and their foot soldiers do this on a regular basis. Goat herders, schoolteachers, merchants, taxi drivers, clerics—it doesn't matter: cooperate or risk torture and death. It's an act of great courage when one of these people comes forward and drops a dime on them. Now that the tribes have turned on al-Qaeda, we're seeing a lot more of that. That's what happened in this incident. One of those links in the chain here in Ramadi was working with us. In this case, we knew these four suicide bombers were coming, and we were able to learn how and when they were coming."

As explained to me, this was a major operation for AQI, and one that could have caused a great deal of damage. At the urging of the tribal sheikhs, large numbers of Iraqis had volunteered for police training and police duty. The Americans and the Iraqi army may have taken back the streets of Ramadi, but they were now held by the local Iraqi police—the Ramadi police. A year earlier there were few to be seen; now there were more than *five thousand* of them. Their presence on the streets was one of the keys to keeping AQI out of Ramadi and the surrounding area. Their presence also encouraged citizens to report on insurgent activities, from planting IEDs to bringing in suicide bombers. With the police on the streets, the task unit intelligence section was able to greatly expand its human intelligence-collection efforts. In counterinsurgency warfare, the people are always the prize—they are everything. With the police on the streets, AQI could no longer hide among the people, and we began to win. So the ability of the task unit and its intelligence component to smell out this attack on police stations was a huge victory.

"This was also a big setback for AQI," the senior chief said. "We were able to intercept these four bombers, and since they were hooded and had been told little about their journey, we had them in custody and they didn't even know it. We simply led them to a safe house, and they were none the wiser. 'I will soon take you to kill the infidels,' our agent said to them. 'Are you ready to die for Allah?' 'Oh, yes,' they all replied. 'We are ready; we are ready now!' They were disarmed and put at ease, still thinking that they were in insurgent hands. It wasn't until their hoods were pulled off and they saw us all standing around that they knew they were busted."

"Who were these guys?" I asked, anxious to know. "Where did they come from?"

"One of them was a Saudi, a Wahhabi," the senior chief replied, "so who knows how long he was trained in some madrassa for this kind of death. The other three were young Iraqis—the youngest only fourteen." For the first time the senior chief showed strong emotion. "Those SOBs go out and recruit kids to do this. Our interrogators were able to get the whole story from them. One of them had been sexually abused as a young boy and was told the only way he could reclaim his family honor was to die for Allah in this manner. The others had similar issues of low self-esteem. The senior AQI leaders—the foreigners—won't do this themselves. They get others to do it. They prey upon kids, young boys and girls who are insecure or have some psychological disorder. Some of them have severe learning disabilities, just like kids in America, so they are easy prey for recruitment as martyrs; they're promised things will be better in the next life. That's why our work here is so important; that's why we have to beat these guys."

The explosive vests these suicide bombers wore spoke to the sophistication and relentlessness of AQI in their efforts to reenter Ramadi. The vests were identical to the vests worn by the Iraqi police in Ramadi. The detonation mechanics were simple but well designed, and they were packed with an effective balance of high explosives and ball bearings. No one said as much, but it seemed to me that the AQI efforts in Ramadi were down to the use of suicide bombers and suicide fighters as their principal weapon in al-Anbar. Few locally recruited insurgents—the AQI foot soldiers—were still on the streets. We'd won in that regard, and the citizens of Ramadi had won. Ramadi, the city itself, had taken a terrible beating and was in need of a massive reconstruction effort, but al-Qaeda had been driven out.

In late September 2007, elements of the advanced party from SEAL Squadron One began to filter into al-Anbar and relieve their brothers from Squadron Seven. The incoming task unit from Squadron One was slightly smaller in number than the Squadron Seven presence in Ramadi. They would have only one platoon of SEALs to work out of Camp Lee. As with all squadrons, it was designed around the current conditions of the battlespace and the disposition of the enemy across al-Anbar. The size of the intelligence section and Advanced Special Operations component was classified, but it was safe to say that it would remain robust and vigilant against future AQI penetrations. But for the moment, Ramadi was quiet.

My visit to Ramadi took place in late August 2007, and was largely confined to bases and outposts. I spent most of my time with the individual members of the SEAL task unit. It was a restricted snapshot of Ramadi; I met with the warriors and saw the aftermath of the fighting—mostly the rubble along Route Michigan. My travel in Ramadi was limited, so I did not get into the heart of the city, nor did I have a perspective on how bad the conditions were only a year before—in August 2006. Lieutenant Colonel Jim Lechner, who visited Ramadi early that same August, did. Lieutenant Colonel Lechner was the deputy brigade commander under Sean MacFarland. He was back in Ramadi for a short visit from his current job in Baghdad. After a luncheon with Sheikh Sattar, he toured the city he had known so well during the battle. These were his observations.

"We drove along Route Michigan to COP Firecracker, around the racetrack and visited the now-open Saddam Mosque. Then we stopped by the souk [the central market], drove down Central Street to Twentieth Street, onto Canal Road, and then all the way across Baseline. Continuing on from there, we passed through the neighborhoods in the city center, through small markets that had sprung up, and back up to the Government Center. As we drove along our route, there were literally thousands of people on all the streets and in outdoor cafés, and at least ten soccer games being played in an organized league. The people were deeply involved in cleanup and reconstruction. Streets were being swept, services installed, and rubble from buildings was being bulldozed. Every major intersection in the neighborhoods had police checkpoints with police sitting out on the street drinking chai. Not one shot fired and no IEDs.

"It's very difficult to comprehend that transformation unless you had experienced Ramadi over the past two years, when you were guaranteed to have been engaged by small arms, snipers, RPGs, and have at least one vehicle hit by an IED on any one of the above-mentioned roads. Pretty stunning and as clear a victory as can be gained in this insurgency. Not the end of the war but, at least for now, the end of the Battle of Ramadi and a tribute to those who died in the fighting there."

It is my observation that the people of Ramadi and the tribes seemed to be holding onto the victory that the soldiers, marines, and SEALs who fought the Battle of Ramadi handed them. In saying this, I don't mean to belittle what the people of Ramadi did in this fight; if nothing else, they endured. And I certainly don't mean to pass judgment on them for their collective role in the insurgency, whether active or passive, following the overthrow of Saddam Hussein. Amid the shifting allegiances that are a part of Anbari culture, they finally came to our side and against AQI, and that made all the difference. We must be very careful that as the influence of al-Qaeda wanes in Ramadi and al-Anbar, we do not again become the touchstone for insurgent activity there. This applies to our presence, as well as that of the Iraqi army. Having said that, it would seem that al-Qaeda is determined not to allow the tribes in al-Anbar to forget that it is around, nor has it abandoned its methodology in trying to assert control over tribal life. It is still a brutal and murderous influence in waiting. It's not just AQI; there's the lingering animosity between the Shiite militias and the Sunni insurgents.

On 25 June 2007 there was a meeting of Anbari tribal leaders in Baghdad at the Mansour Melia Hotel. General David Petraeus orchestrated this meeting, which was the culmination of an effort to get the Anbari tribal sheikhs to speak with representatives of the Baghdad government. The sheikhs arrived first. Among them were leading sheikhs of the Albu Nimr, Albu Fahad, and Khaza'a tribes, and leaders from other influential tribes. Many were members of the Anbar Salvation Council, the formal body that grew out of the Awakening. The Mansour is one of Baghdad's most prominent and secure hotels. Even so, shortly before noon, a well-placed bomb exploded and killed twelve Anbaris. Six of the slain leaders were members of the council. It has never been proved whether this was the work of AQI or Shiite militiamen. In Baghdad as in al-Anbar, assassination is a form of statecraft and political maneuvering. By any measure, it was a setback for the efforts of the tribes to resist al-Qaeda in al-Anbar, and a message to those Iraqi leaders who too closely ally themselves with the Americans.

Perhaps the most devastating attack on tribal leadership and a demonstration of AQI's persistent intentions came in early September with the assassination of Sheikh Abdul Sattar Abu Risha. A roadside bomb near his home in Ramadi killed the sheikh and two of his bodyguards. The death of Sheikh Sattar came only ten days after he met personally with George Bush on the president's visit to Al Asad Air Base. This assassination was clearly the work of AQI and a reminder to all Anbaris of the lengths to which al-Qaeda and its allies will go to achieve their ends. This charismatic and energetic leader met his end in the same manner as his father and three of his brothers—AQI killed all of them. Yet his death came too late to influence the Battle of Ramadi or to stop the spread of the Awakening across al-Anbar.

"If AQI wanted to stop the Awakening," Colonel Sean MacFarland told me following the death of Sattar, "they should have killed him about six months ago. Now it's too late." Following the burial of Sattar Abu Risha, his younger brother, Sheikh Ahmed al-Rishawi, was elected to lead the tribal coalition. "Al-Rishawi hasn't the charisma of Sattar," the former Sheriff of Ramadi said, "but then he doesn't need it. For now, the sheikhs are united behind him against AQI."

The Awakening and the revolt of the tribes against al-Qaeda is still an active movement, and the movement's legacy is the absence of violence in Ramadi and al-Anbar province. This tribal-centric revolt may even spread past the boundaries of al-Anbar. But how long will this last? In my opinion, as long as our interests are in keeping with *their* interests and our agenda there does not violate *their* cultural norms. This is true for the people of al-Anbar, and indeed, for all Iraqis. Perhaps Sean MacFarland said it best in an interview with *Time* magazine reporter Mark Kukis: "Tribes are like countries. They don't have friends, they have interests. Right now we're both to them. Down the road, would they fight us if we overstayed our welcome? They might very well."

Author's note: The deployment of the task unit from Squadron Seven did *not* technically comprise the last Ramadi task unit. It was, however, the last task unit to conduct ongoing operations in the city.

Two cultures, two generations. An American soldier on patrol pauses to speak with a young Iraqi boy. The Battle of Ramadi was for his future. *Courtesy of the U.S. Army.*

The Lessons of Ramadi

I learned a great deal in the writing of this book, perhaps more so than in any previous work. As with any writer, I began with my own opinions and biases. Some were based on previous experience with SOF operations, but much of what I thought I knew was colored by media-generated noise. Most of us in America wonder what's *really* going on over there. Are we winning? Can we win? What will it take to win? If you live in the United States of America, unless you live without electricity or contact with other people, it's hard not to be swayed by information peddlers, of which I am one. Furthermore, no matter what your perspective, experience, or political leaning may be, you can always find some pundit or talking head who not only holds those same views, but will also reinforce that opinion. I follow and write about national security affairs. When I began this project in the summer of 2006, I was growing pessimistic regarding our adventure in Iraq. Each night on *The NewsHour with Jim Lehrer,* the daily listing of Americans killed in action grew. My liberal friends, who are good and true Americans, lamented about a failed policy and advocated withdrawal. At that time, it was a $400 billion exercise—why, they said, throw good money after bad? I had few good answers for them. I had to sort through all this macro-chaff even as I was beginning to learn about al-Anbar, Ramadi, and Navy SEAL operations in Ramadi. Early on, I thought this would be a narrative of courage in a losing cause—the orchestra on the deck of the *Titanic.*

Still, I knew there was a good story here, and there were a few things that I knew to be true. One of them was that Ramadi and al-Anbar province were host to some of the most vicious fighting since the fall of Baghdad. Another was that the deployed SEALs in al-Anbar were committed to this fight. I knew I could count on the role of the SEALs to be central to the issues decided in al-Anbar, even if the prospect of a positive outcome seemed bleak. And finally, I knew there would be some interesting operational and personally courageous stories.

What I really didn't know or fully comprehend was the extended nature of the al-Qaeda-backed insurgency in al-Anbar and viciousness of the AQI operatives behind this movement. I knew little of the Iraqi culture in general and especially of the tribal lands in al-Anbar. In my research I was surprised, and more than a little appalled, at just how badly we had mismanaged this war owing to our lack of understanding, both of our enemy and the people we wanted to help. Yet I was pleasantly surprised at the maturity and capability of our conventional forces, and their ability, when given the chance, to operate effectively in a counterinsurgent environment. While the things we did wrong following the invasion of Iraq are legion, we finally got it right in al-Anbar. So what does this all mean, for the future of al-Anbar and the future of Iraq? What do we need to do to preserve the success in al-Anbar? There are lessons here, but just what are they? Ramadi and al-Anbar are unique. What can we *safely* learn from this experience and apply elsewhere—in Iraq and beyond?

Before looking ahead, let's take stock of exactly what happened. I'm not sure just how many Americans understand that we won one. The people of al-Anbar province, the Iraqi security forces, and the American military combined to win al-Anbar and the Battle of Ramadi. Al-Qaeda lost. Our media is quick to point out our shortcomings in Iraq, but it seemed to me that the winning of al-Anbar was underreported. To be sure, it was a single battle in this war. This is the first time in a long time that insurgents took control of an area—actually a population— and we took it back. Since an insurgency is a battle for the people, it's instructional that we fully understand what took place. It's also important that we don't try to apply the lessons of Ramadi and al-Anbar where they may not be appropriate.

Some may say that we got it wrong for so long that somewhere along the line we were bound to get it right. There may be something to that, but I'd like to believe that a part of this had to do with the talent on the ground. Don't forget that at this stage of the conflict, we had developed some very experienced and seasoned commanders, and we had a veteran force in place. This level of experience simply wasn't there in 2003 and 2004. First of all, we must never overlook the fact that this was bottom-up victory, both politically and militarily. Militarily, I think there were elements of frustration and failure that came into play. Prior to the summer of 2006, nothing we tried was working, or if it worked it seemed to be at best a temporary solution. We were frustrated that the insurgents, both the hard-core foreign fighters and the local foot soldiers, appeared to be deeply embedded in the population. There was, however, a growing awareness in the military that while we were losing ground, the people were not firmly in the enemy's grasp. Still, in Ramadi things were so bad that we were in danger of ceding the victory to the insurgents—bunkering down in our fortified bases and letting the insurgents have the rest. This was the stage onto which Colonel Sean MacFarland and his 1st Brigade Combat Team stepped. He was given a free hand to retake Ramadi. As brigade commander, he was cautioned against a sustained, pitched battle as happened in Fallujah, but then he really didn't have the resources for that kind of action. MacFarland was not given a battle plan, nor did his superior tell him how to proceed; his marching orders were simply to take Ramadi. "I was given very broad guidance," recalled MacFarland about May 2006, when the Sheriff and his 1st Brigade staff came to Ramadi from Tall 'Afar. "Fix Ramadi, but don't destroy it," he said of his orders. "You name it, I tried it. I had a lot of flexibility." This was a pivotal battle at a critical time in this conflict. His brigade staff developed the battle plan, and the forces in MacFarland's 1st Brigade Combat Team executed it. I don't believe this kind of broad mandate of freedom of action would have been granted to a commander earlier in the campaign. The lesson here: let the commanders on the ground make the tactical decisions. They, more than anyone up the chain of command, know the local dynamic. And if one approach doesn't work, they're the ones who will be quickest in shifting tactics to meet the local threat.

Politically, the Awakening and the revolt of the tribes were also bottom-up phenomena. The Baghdad government and the Iraqi army had been largely ineffective in bringing a national-security solution to the insurgency in al-Anbar. When the tribal leaders had finally had enough, things began to change. Al-Qaeda began to lose local support, and that's the death knell for an insurgency. Within the individual tribal lands and neighborhoods, AQI lost its sanctuary and its base of recruits. From the enemy military perspective and capability, it was worse than that. Local foot soldiers left the ranks of the insurgents and joined the police. The balance sheet tipped dramatically in our favor. In other local insurgent battles in Iraq, coalition firepower had often swept the streets clean of insurgents, only to have them return because they had sanctuary—we had won the streets but not the people. In Ramadi, the Army and the Marines systematically took back the streets. Then we won the people— or, rather, when the tribes turned against al-Qaeda, the people swung to our side. Sean MacFarland and his subordinate commanders had, by now, enough in cultural expertise and counterinsurgency talent to seize this unique opening. They were all over it. Earlier in the conflict, I'm not so sure we had commanders on the ground with the experience to see this kind of opportunity and exploit it. It made all the difference in winning the people.

And, of course, there was the brutish and arrogant nature of al-Qaeda in its attempt to control the people. From trying to force daughters of tribal leaders into marriages of convenience to the overt campaign of murder and intimidation, al-Qaeda could not have played its cards in worse fashion. Its claims that "We are Sunni and you are Sunni, and we are here to protect you from the Shia majority" finally fell on deaf ears. It takes a great deal of effort to get an Arab tribal region, even a secular one, to side *with* a Western army of occupation, but al-Qaeda did it in al-Anbar. I often wondered what would have happened in Ramadi had al-Qaeda been more like Hezbollah, with a more careful and thoughtful approach to local customs and the needs of the people. If AQI had shown some respect for the tribal leaders or been less insistent on a strict Islamist agenda, it might have won the people, which is the same as winning the battle.

Having prevailed, how do we preserve this hard-won victory in al-Anbar. Since the insurgent battleground is a human battleground, the victory is a fragile one, and the people, once won, can be lost. Our forces are still an army of occupation on foreign soil. Their role is necessary and important, but it must be subtle. In Ramadi the current peace and security are being preserved by the police. Going forward, our every action should be colored by how our presence and activity reinforce the security role of the local police. We should be asking, what can *we* do to support and preserve *their* victory? For the most part the Anbaris now appreciate our role in driving out al-Qaeda. Yet our mere presence is a reminder of Western occupation and a rallying point for the jihadists. For example, an American military convoy driving through the city has consequence. The new security conditions notwithstanding, it's an armed force that must take its own security measures and precautions.

It's a reminder to Iraqis that Crusaders are still among them. We are still needed in al-Anbar, but in what strength and what configuration? Clearly, we need to have a robust intelligence effort to guard against resurgent AQI efforts. We also need to make sure the Iraqi army does not exceed its mandate as a national, and overwhelmingly Shiite, presence. There are ongoing decisions regarding our direct and indirect efforts to promote the security of tribal leaders, the training of local security forces, and the need for reconstruction. I believe that we are approaching endgame in al-Anbar, and that our kinetic operations in the region must be judicious and well thought out. The role of the new Sheriff of Ramadi will be far different from Sean MacFarland's. In many ways it will be more difficult. Sean MacFarland, his conventional forces, and his SEALs won the peace. We now face the military, cultural, and political challenges of preserving that peace.

What could we have done better in Ramadi and al-Anbar? Or more pointedly, how did we drop the ball and why did it take so long to get it right? One of our shortcomings, in my opinion, has to do with our lack of cultural understanding and our inability to rapidly adapt to changes in the battlespace—both in al-Anbar and across Iraq. Democracy and federalism have limited application in Islamic nations and tribal societies. That is not to say they have no relevance; a democracy—specifically, an economic democracy—and federalism are bridges to modernity. But these ideas have to be applied in the context of a careful analysis of local customs and local politics. It's not easy, but it's doable. Regarding our inability to adapt, we paid dearly in terms of lives and treasury. This insurgency should never have been allowed to get to that stage. Junior battlefield commanders saw this insurgency coming well before it was given any credence by our senior military and political leadership—and before it became an issue in the media. How did this happen? Many junior military leaders I spoke with, many of them multitour veterans, lay the blame squarely on our senior military commanders. Senior military command in Iraq had been a path to promotion and more senior rank—that next star, perhaps two—unless things become worse. Those in senior command, junior leaders told me, never wanted to report that things were bad, or going from bad to worse, on their watch. Perhaps they were reporting these things up the chain of command, but our political leaders didn't want to hear those reports. Whatever the reasons, we were slow to react, and because of our poor understanding of the culture, we seemed not to know how to react. Those on the ground often see things clearly and early. There's a lesson here as well: listen to the junior commanders—the captains, the lieutenants, and the majors.

Simply stated, we have to be quicker—more responsive and nimble—on the insurgent battlefield. Colonel John Boyd, the legendary Air Force fighter pilot, developed tactics for air combat that proved to be highly adaptable for enterprises ranging from corporate management to maneuver warfare. Boyd's strategy, like that of Sun-tzu, is complex and worthy of study, but simply stated, the Boyd OODA (observe, orient, decide, act) Loop is an adaptive and responsive way to fight. As a fighter pilot, if you can always turn in inside your enemy, you can always bring your guns to bear on him, and he will never be able to put his guns on you. To "turn inside" means that you must outthink your enemy or confuse him so he cannot outthink you. *Then* you have him at your mercy. This has direct application for insurgency warfare. For most of our venture in Iraq, the al-Qaeda-led insurgency stayed ahead of us. The AQI were more nimble; they kept us off balance; *they turned inside us.* Only when we began to understand the nature of the AQI, their relation with the local population, and their vulnerabilities were we able to turn the tables. Using Boyd's wisdom in an insurgency begins with understanding the cultural and human terrain. How do we become quicker and more nimble than this mobile and adaptable insurgent enemy? Push the decision making down the chain of command. This is not the same as streamlining the chain of command. This means developing capable, culturally aware junior commanders, then empowering them—those captains, lieutenants, and majors—to make the decisions on the ground.

Perhaps the most important lesson to be learned is that when we invade and put our troops ashore in a foreign land, the clock starts ticking. No matter what our reasons for invasion or how benevolent or righteous the cause, our presence will be resented. And the strongest resistance will come from those most in opposition to our interests. They will use our presence to their advantage, and time is simply not on our side. The faster we can accomplish our goals and withdraw, the better. If our incursion is a high-visibility affair, as it was in Iraq, then our timeline is that much more restricted. A clear and accurate understanding of *their* culture and *our* limitations within that culture is essential to any endgame. Another important lesson is that there's always an endgame. We may leave a below-the-radar military or advisory presence, but whenever we go in with a visible, conventional presence, we must be seen to leave. We gave back Okinawa; we'll have to give back Iraq.

Regarding these lessons, if you think that my speaking to them here represents some kind of original thinking or novel insight on my part, you can put that notion aside. There are old counterinsurgency hands in the military, at the CIA, and at the State Department who knew this well before 9/11. Many of them stood up and said as much, but they were ignored. Imagine their dismay and frustration watching this play out—again. For my part, I'm not so sure I had a full understanding of these issues until I wrote this book.

Going forward, what are the implications of the success in al-Anbar for the rest of Iraq and beyond? First of all, Iraq. What worked in the Sunni tribal lands of al-Anbar may not be directly applicable in Shiite-dominated regions—in Baghdad and the southern provinces of Iraq. Iraqi culture and character are very complex. While it would be inadvisable to think that all of what worked in Ramadi will work in Basra, there are a few lessons that may be useful. Perhaps the most glaring is the "central-ness" of the people to any solution that involves local security. This applies to the problem of AQI-backed insurgents who threaten that security, and ultimately, our continued presence as guarantors of that security. Insurgents swim in the sea of the people. If the people turn them out, as they did in al-Anbar, then they become visible and vulnerable to national security forces and the local police. To be sure, the multiethnic nature of the non-Kurdish, non-Anbari regions of Iraq present unique challenges. Certainly, the Sunni-Shiite issues will take time and political skill to resolve. Yet the lessons of Ramadi may have merit, even in the Shiite south. Eighty-five percent of Iraqis claim some tribal affiliation. Some tribes claim both Sunnis and Shiites in their membership; many of these tribes predate Islam. These tribal entities overlap, and in some cases trump, local and national governmental boundaries of authority. I believe that a judicious recognition of these tribal entities is an essential element to stabilizing the nation of Iraq. Again, I don't want to minimize the religious and resource-based issues that face any form of Iraqi federalism, but security measures that employ a tribal affiliation may help to reign in insurgent violence—at least the al-Qaeda brand of insurgent violence—allowing the Iraqis to address other problems. And if al-Qaeda-driven violence is brought to al-Anbar levels across Iraq, then we can address the issue of the number of divisions we can safely bring home.

Continuing forward beyond Iraq, I hope we now have a better understanding of the consequences of invasion. *This* lesson was an expensive one. That understanding begins with comprehensive inventory of the people and culture we've elected to favor with our military presence. We seem to do well in the big wars, the kind we hopefully will never again fight, and the small, below-the-radar wars—those rarely addressed by the media. It's the protracted, intercultural, medium-sized wars that seem to cause us problems—wars like Vietnam and Iraq. These are the conflicts in which maneuver warfare inevitably gives way to insurgency warfare and the people become more important than ground. And the clock starts ticking.

From a conventional perspective, our force has to be better configured for counterinsurgency—militarily, politically, and fiscally. My issues are the military. It would seem that the global, World War II–type conflicts are a thing of the past. If not, our standing conventional force will be asked to fight a holding action while the nation mobilizes. Or we go to the nuclear option. Neither of these is likely; no one, or no nation, wants to deal with a mobilized America or our superior nuclear capability. The most glaring deficiency in our force structure is the lack of cross-cultural awareness and counterinsurgency capability. Here, the lessons of Ramadi most certainly apply. The U.S. Army is charged with the mission of counterinsurgency warfare. It clearly has the talent. Sean MacFarland is a West Pointer and an armor officer. By necessity, he became a superb commander in an ambiguous, almost-desperate counterinsurgent environment. Yet the Army and the Department of Defense have often overlooked this talent when it comes to the promotion of general officers. As I write this the Army colonel-to-brigadier-general promotion list has yet to come out, but it is my understanding the General David Petraeus, who presided over the 2008 promotion board, and Secretary of Defense Robert Gates are keen on promoting these proven counterinsurgency commanders. We'll see. Regarding those priceless cross-cultural warriors like Captain Travis Patriquin, they have to be found, recruited, mentored, and retained—and promoted. Their value in our most probable military scenarios of the future is incalculable.

Our conventional forces must also make it a priority to seek out and properly use our special operations forces. SOF must also look for those opportunities where they can effectively work in the seams of the battlespace in support their conventional brothers. *The Sheriff of Ramadi* illustrated the close working relationship that evolved between the Army and the Navy SEALs. In this work I've focused on the SEAL-Army symbiosis, but the SEALs also worked closely with the Marines, in Ramadi and elsewhere in the Marine AO of al-Anbar province. The Ramadi SEALs I spoke with, while they held their Marine brothers in high regard, reserved their highest praise for the Army. The SEALs and the Army just seemed to reach out to each other. I write this off to the culture of the Marine Corps, which sees itself as an integrated, self-contained expeditionary force. Whatever the reason, the Army seemed to be much more receptive and eager to work with SEALs. One area in which the Marine Corps excelled during the Battle of Ramadi was its effort in supporting the military and police transition teams—the MiTTs and PTTs. The Marines tended to assign its best junior leaders and proven performers to this important duty. Their Army MiTT and PTT counterparts, at least in Ramadi, often seemed to be reservists whose quality varied—some were exceptional and many were not. These transition teams deserve our best officers and NCOs; they have the responsibility for helping the Iraqis do our job so we can go home.

Finally, what can we learn from our special operators—the Navy SEALs—in Ramadi? What can we apply to future SOF-conventional-force operations? Without question, the SEALs were among the most highly trained warriors in Ramadi, which stands to reason. It takes a great deal of time and money to make a battle-ready SEAL. What was unique about the Ramadi task unit was the integration of its SEAL operators and intelligence capabilities into a conventional-force battle plan. This integration was a two-way street. First of all, the conventional command structure, the Army brigade commanders in Ramadi, had to understand what the SEALs could bring to the table, operationally and in the area of intelligence. Then they then had to "direct" the efforts of the SEAL task unit—it was not a brigade asset to command. For their part, the SEALs had to take this direction and put their capabilities at the disposal of the brigade commander. What made this SEAL-conventional-force partnership so unique was that it was a bottom-up alliance based on trust. The Ramadi SEAL task unit commanders asked what they could do to help, and the Army brigade commanders used "their" SEALs to best advantage. In MacFarland's words, "they went into the seams of the battlespace where we couldn't go." The SEAL and Army commanders on the ground worked this out. Is this a lesson or template for future SOF-conventional-force command relationships? Perhaps. In less-contentious situations, there might have been some turf issues. In Ramadi, during the heat of battle, those parochial issues evaporated. The real lesson here is that the guys on the ground, especially when there's an enemy present, will work together to accomplish the mission.

In the past I've been one who's advocated SOF control of battlespace, and even SOF control of conventional assets in that battlespace. Ramadi has caused me to rethink this. When it comes to insurgent battlespace, and that seems to be the likely future scenario, it may simply be a matter of scale. Limited insurgent conflicts, with capable local security forces in place, might be candidates for SOF command and control. Certain parts of Afghanistan may lend themselves to an SOF battlespace commander. An insurgency the size of the one we allowed to metastasize in Iraq, or in a city the size of Ramadi, where the streets are openly contested by an organized insurgency, will probably have to be resolved by conventional forces—infantry and armor. That's why it's so important to recognize insurgent activity early on, before the people fall under the control of the opposition and while the police can still control the streets. That's why it's also important that when an insurgency outgrows the capability of our special operations forces, there are trained conventional forces with competent commanders ready to conduct counterinsurgency warfare. This means conventional commanders who understand what has to be done and are prepared to work with special operations forces to succeed on the insurgent battlefield.

Our SOF components will have to train—and, if necessary, expand—to meet the growing challenges of terrorism and insurgency. I believe they must also be fully prepared to step into the role the Ramadi SEALs pioneered: battlefield support of conventional forces. First the issue of terrorism. My feeling is that terror is a tactic of our current enemy, Islamic extremists. It will probably be the tactic of choice by any future nonstate enemy. Terror may be like illegal drugs—something that we may never be able to eradicate and a menace that requires constant attention. A part of the SOF/SEAL mission will always be to target and kill terrorists. Killing terrorist leaders and forcing terrorist leaders to live a life on the run degrades their organizational and operational activity. For the most part, this mission applies to all SOF components, but is the special province of our special missions units—the ones we all know exist but seldom talk about. This dogged pursuit of these enemies who practice terror, along with political and economic pressure directed at states who sponsor terrorist activity, is probably our best option to manage the terrorist threat—until the terrorists obtain and use a nuclear weapon. Then the gloves come off, and we enter a new era of destabilization and retribution.

Insurgency is the most probable strategy of our enemies. Fortunately, it's the most easily defeated *if* we're prepared to move quickly and professionally with effective counterinsurgent tactics. This can only happen if we acknowledge that the people are the battlefield and if we develop the language and cultural tools to understand and navigate this human terrain. Language skills and cross-cultural understanding have to be front-loaded or we risk another Iraq and another Ramadi. The reclaiming of nations and cities lost to insurgents is just too costly in treasury and in lives. As mentioned above, our conventional forces—and specifically the U.S. Army—must do better at developing counterinsurgent capabilities and counterinsurgent commanders. SOF has to do better as well. As much as special operators in general and SEALs in particular focus on kinetic, direct-action operations, more needs to be done in the area of foreign internal defense—the training of indigenous security forces. If foreign internal defense in the form of combat FID makes this training of local forces more palatable, fine. Local insurgencies have become the weapon of choice for al-Qaeda and its allies. If we don't win the people, then al-Qaeda-inspired insurgents become an ongoing and renewable resource, and we simply can't kill them all. In the final reckoning it will be *their* capability, the capability of the local security forces, that has to be a priority—as it was in Ramadi. And if we're able to intervene quickly and effectively, then perhaps we will get the local police and local security forces on the streets in time to avoid the battle.

But what if we can't? What if the insurgents manage to gain control of the people, through murder and intimidation, ideology, or misinformation? What if, having lost the human terrain, we have to step in and take back the physical terrain? Then we'll have failed again, and the lessons of Ramadi become especially relevant. Then our special operations ground components, like the SEALs in Ramadi, will have to join their conventional brothers on the battlefield.

Index

Abdul, Byron, 155, 156, 169–70, 173, 174, 182
Advanced Special Operations (ASO) units, 50, 98, 219–23
Afghanistan: cultural understanding of, benefits of, 25; deployment rotations in, 15; grooming standards, 87; lives lost in combat action and rescue attempt, 38; marriage into tribal leaders' families by al-Qaeda, 44, 130; Naval Special Warfare group deployment to, 47; SEAL operations in, 16
Africa, 47
Ahmad, 77–79
Alpha Platoon, 202, 203
al-Qaeda. *See* Qaeda in Iraq, al- (AQI)
Ambrose, Stephen, 94
America's First Frogman (Bush), 5
amphibious operations: decline in need for, 6; importance of, 2; during Korea, 6; during World War II, 2–5
Anbar province, al-: attitude of Anbaris toward Iraqi army, 92; coalition force strength, 80; demographics, xvi; geography and culture of, xvi, 26; insurgency in, 26–27, 28, 104–5; insurgency in, escalation of, 231–32; lives lost in, 30; marriage into tribal leaders' families by AQI, 44, 130, 230; occupation force, attitude toward, 230–33; police, role in ending

violence in, 193; responsibility for, 83–84; tribal leader's response to insurgency, 43–44, 71, 80–81; tribal politics in, 26, 43, 132, 145, 225; weapons and ammunition caches, 104; winning of, 228–30
Anbar Salvation Council, 224
Andols, district, Al, 157
Ansar al-Sunnah, 80
AQI. *See* Qaeda in Iraq, al- (AQI)
aqualung, 6, 7
area of operations (AO) Topeka, 66, 81, 84, 101
Asad Marine Base, Al, 38, 84, 141, 189
Awakening movement: AQI efforts to stop, 225; beginning of, 71, 81; council formation, 131–32; operations that paved way for, 121, 130; success in Ramadi through, 143, 225, 229–30; tribal sheikhs' support for, 131–34, 144–45

Baathists, 26–27, 28, 33, 43
Baghdad: embassy in, 188, 191; Green Zone mentality, 191; infrastructure, protection of, xxv, xxvi; insurgency in, xxv, xxvi; intelligence collection and target identification, 45–46; ISOF capabilities, 64; ISOF training by task unit in, 45; occupation of, xxv; press-credential process, 187–88; SEAL operations in, 16–17; security duty in, 70; success in, xxv; task unit deployment to, 44, 70

Garrison, Cally, 83–84, 85
Gates, Robert, 234
Gormley, Bob, 15
Government Center outpost, 29, 66, 80, 101, 129, 144
Green Berets, 34
Grenada operations, 16
Gronski, John, 81, 101
Gulf War operations, 16

Habbaniyah: combat FID, xix; Iraqi army training at, 38–39, 42, 64; task unit deployment to, 38–39, 44, 84, 189; violence and conditions in, 84
Hadithah, 189
Hanson, Jake: background of, 54; battle in Ramadi, coming changes to, 81, 90–91; on Eaton, 60; Fanus capture operation, 76, 77; feelings about leaving Ramadi, 90; informants, treatment of by AQI, 78–79; on McLaughlin, 71; patrol operations, 67–68; Ramadi task unit redeployment to Baghdad, 70; Route Michigan overwatch, 74, 75; security in Ramadi, 58; on snipers, 72, 73; as task unit commander, 53–54; training Iraqi soldiers, 61–62
Hawz district, Al, 100
Hay Al Dhobot district, 66, 67
Hedberg, Rick, 98–100, 118
helicopters: mine-hunting operations, 6; night operations, 187, 193–94; oil embargo enforcement activity, 16; scout training for operations from, 212; swimmer delivery and recovery with, 8
Hell Week, 3, 9, 10
Heller, Jim, 159, 160, 161, 162
HESCO barriers, 58
Hezbollah, 230
Hit, 189
Hite, John, 218–19
Howard, Bud, 74–75
human intelligence, 40–41, 221–22

Hurricane Point Marine base, xv–xvi, 39, 66, 100–101, 107
Hurt, Ned, 202–3, 204
Hussein, Saddam: control methods of, 24–25; presidency of, 24; prisoner release by, 33; UN oil embargo evasion tactics, 16; weapons caches, 104

improvised explosive devices (IEDs): in Anbar province, viii, 30; burial of, 168; Dagger clearance teams, 110; detection and avoidance measures, 51; factory raid, 77–78; radio emitters to defeat detonators, 203; VBIEDs, 177–79
individual augmentees (IAs), 47, 52, 74, 75, 197, 198, 199
informants, former insurgents, 78–79
insurgency: in Anbar province, 26–27, 28, 104–5; in Baghdad, xxv, xxvi; composition of, 27–28; escalation of, 231–32, 236; in Fallujah, 27, 43; in Iraq, xxiii–xxiv, 33–34; Iraqi police, effectiveness of against, 168–69; Islamist agenda of, 27–28, 44, 79–81, 130, 145; overwatch positions, knowledge of, 113–14, 166; in Ramadi, 27, 29–30; in Ramadi, areas controlled by, 66–67, 129–30, 144, 146–47; in Ramadi, escalation of, 42–43, 100–101, 231–32; in Ramadi, reduction in, 196; terror and violence methods, xxiii–xxiv, 42–43; terrorism vs., 86; Tombstone model against, 33–34; treatment of insurgents by SEALs, 77–79; tribal leader's response to, 43–44, 71, 80–81, 132, 233–34; understanding and response to, 232; University of al-Anbar as staging area, 99; urban-warfare skills, 147; in Vietnam, xxiv–xxv, 14. *See also* Qaeda in Iraq, al- (AQI)
intelligence collection and target identification: ASO operations,

and violence tactics, xxiii, 42–43, 44, 79, 86, 104–5, 130, 131, 171, 175, 221, 227; tribal sheikhs as targets, 175, 224–25; tribal sheikhs' pledge to fight, 131–32, 229–30; understanding and response to, 232. *See also* insurgency

Qa'im, Al, 103, 189

Qatana district, 66

Ramadi: area of operations, 66; as capital city, xvi; as capital of AQI, 105; cleanup and reconstruction efforts, 223–24; coalition force strength, 80; counterinsurgency efforts in, 34–35; counterinsurgency success in, xxvi, 31; deterioration of conditions in, 30–31; devastation of buildings in, 203, 207; First Battle of, 30; geography and culture of, 26, 29; glass factory attack by AQI, 70–72; insurgency in, 27, 29–30; insurgency in, areas controlled by, 66–67, 129–30, 144, 146–47; insurgency in, escalation of, 42–43, 100–101, 231–32; lives lost in, 28, 30, 119; Marine Corps operations in, 28; medical engagements, 201, 205–6; preserving peace in, 231; religious ties, 26; security in, 144, 145–46, 182–83, 195–96, 203, 230; tribal leader's response to insurgency, 71, 80–81; tribal politics in, 26, 43–44, 225; violence in, 79–80, 87, 227; violence in, reduction in, 134, 142–43, 189, 195–96, 208

Ramadi, Battle of: battalions and brigades involved in, 107; battle models, 102–3; lives lost in, 124; plan for, 103; police, role in ending, 176–77, 182–83, 193; rules of engagement, 124–25; SEAL support for, 105–7, 115, 128–29, 143–44; Second Battle of, 30; violence and conditions leading

to, 87, 90–91; winning of, xvii–xviii, 133, 193, 222–23, 228–30. *See also* combat outposts (COPs)

Ramadi task unit: attitude toward scouts, 96–97; battle in Ramadi, support for, 105–7, 115; challenges faced by, 144; combined operations with Iraqi soldiers, 127, 143–44; counterinsurgency responsibility of, 141–42; counterinsurgency training, 148; daily activity at, 207; deployment to Ramadi, 44, 45, 49, 53–54, 84, 86, 189, 225; duties of, 54; effectiveness of, 85–86; feelings of incoming SEALs, 90, 150–51; feelings of outgoing SEALs, 89–90, 150; grooming standards, 87–88; Iraqi police, operations with, 144; Iraqi police, training of, 148; mission of, 119–20, 143–44, 147–48, 154; operational turnover, 83–84, 141–42, 146, 150; pacification plans, 84; patrol operations, 42, 67–70, 92–93; predeployment training, 148–50; scout training by, 63–64, 73, 90, 91–92, 119–20, 152–53; Shark Base accommodations and services, 54–57; staff meeting, 207–9; training of Iraqi soldiers, 58–64, 73, 89, 90. *See also* SEAL Squadron Five; SEAL Squadron One; SEAL Squadron Seven; SEAL Squadron Three

Rasha, 149–50

Rawah, 189–90

reputation, importance of, 52, 201

Ricks, Thomas, xvii

Rishawi, Ahmed al-, 225

Rising Wind (Couch), xxi–xxii

Roberts, Ron, 194–96, 201, 206, 207–9

Rolland, Ted, 42

Route Michigan: control of, 66; devastation of buildings along, 203; overwatch operation, 73–75; security around, 80

Ruh, Steve, 187, 202

rules of engagement, 124–25
Ryan, Tim, 144, 146–49, 150, 155–56, 167–68

Saddam Mosque, 74
Salinger, Don, 195
Sattar Abu Risha, Abdul, 131–32, 133, 144, 225
Saudi Arabia, 26, 29
Schwedler, Clark, 142, 183, 184–85
Scouts and Raiders, 3
scuba, 7
Seabees, 47, 50–51, 54–57, 58, 112–13
SEAL Delivery Vehicle (SDV) Teams: mission of, 15–16; Team One, 16, 38; Team Two, 16; UDTs converted to, 15–16
SEAL platoons: command structure, 17, 18; counterinsurgency responsibility of, 141–42; effectiveness of, 85; feelings about returning to Iraq, 151–52; leaders of, duty stations changes for, 142; organization and staffing, 51, 52; reputation, importance of, 52; specialties within, 51–52; training of, 51–52
SEAL squadron commander, 17–18, 48
SEAL Squadron Five: challenges faced by, 144, 148; deployment to Ramadi, 141; medical engagements, 206; officers in, 154–55; operational turnover, 141–42, 146; predeployment training, 148–50
SEAL Squadron One: deployment to Ramadi, 53, 223; operational turnover, 83–84; physical conditioning and training, 88–89; task unit assignments, 44–45
SEAL Squadron Seven: accommodations in Ramadi, 39–40, 54; assault team operations, 195–98; command master chief, 193; deployment rotations, 37; Donkey

Island, Battle of, 216–19; duties of, 58–59, 190; intelligence collection and target identification, 40–42; medical engagements, 206; mixed-team composition, 38; new SEAL officers, deployment with, 189, 201; physical conditioning and training, 215–16; redeployment home, 208–9, 223; task unit assignments, 38–39, 189–90
SEAL Squadron Three: deployment to Ramadi, 81, 86; effectiveness of, 142–43; headquarters relocation, 83–84; operational turnover, 83–84, 146; physical conditioning and training, 88–89; redeployment home, 134; SEAL-Army relations, 117–18
SEAL squadrons: deployment rotations, 37–38, 48, 142; East Coast–West Coast rivalry, 190–91; leaders of, duty stations changes for, 142, 193; Office of Naval Intelligence support for, 45–46; support units for, 45–47; task units in, 18, 48; training of, 37, 48, 51–52
SEAL task unit commanders, 18, 49
SEAL task units: command structure, 18; counterinsurgency efforts from, 35; deployment locations, 38–39, 44, 45, 49, 189–90; Fanus capture operation, 75–77; intelligence collection and target identification, 49–50; Iraqi soldier training by, 38–39; leaders of, duty stations changes for, 142; organization and staffing, 48–52, 84; reputation, importance of, 52, 201; support units for, 48; treatment of insurgents by, 77–79. *See also* Ramadi task unit
SEAL Team Eight, 16, 47
SEAL Team Five: accommodations in Ramadi, 39; deployment with Squadron Seven, 38; location of, 16, 47; responsibilities of, 47
SEAL Team Four, 16, 47

speedball, 215
SSE (sensitive site exploitation), 138, 154
Stallard, Ned: background of, 151; overwatch operations, 162, 163–64, 165–66; overwatch operations, abandonment of, 169; police, operations with, 177–79, 182–83; police training by, 176–77; scout training by, 152; trust of scouts, 153
submarines, 7–8, 11
Sufia district, 94, 170–76, 179–82, 203
suicide bombers, 205, 218, 220–22
Sunnis: in Anbar province, xvi, 26–27; AQI's claim of protection, 230; government, participation in by, 43; as insurgents, 28, 30; patrol of Ramadi by, viii
SURC (Small Unit Riverine Craft), 109
swimmer delivery and recovery, 7, 8
Syria, 22, 26, 29, 71, 130

tactical operations center (TOC), 39–40, 50, 188–89, 195–97
Tall 'Afar battle model, 102–3
Tall 'Afar mafia, 102
Ta'meem district, 67–68, 77, 92–93, 100, 170
Tarawa campaign, 1–2
Teammates: SEALs at War (Enoch), 15
terrorism and terror tactics, 236–37; insurgency vs. terrorism, 86; in Iraq, xxiii–xxiv; in Vietnam, xxiv–xxv
Thailand, 24
Thaylat district, 66
Thomas, Craig: background of, 154; intelligence from police trainees, 175; overwatch operations, 157–62; overwatch operations, abandonment of, 169; police training by, 173; police volunteers, number of, 172; as Sean Smith's replacement, 153; Sufia intelligence operations, 180–81
Tierney, Tad, 189–91

tire, physical conditioning with, 215–16
Tombstone model, 33–34
Topeka area of operations, 66, 81, 84, 101
translators, 199
tribal sheikhs: Awakening movement, support for, 131–34, 144–45; community control by, 26, 43, 80–81; Fanus, delivery of, 77; intelligence from, 77, 174; Iraqi police, support for, 71, 126, 130–31, 132–33, 172–74; marriage into tribal leaders' families by AQI, 44, 130, 230; pledge to fight AQI, 131–33, 230; relationship with Americans, 105, 106, 131–34, 145; resistance to AQI, 104–5, 224, 229–30; response to insurgency, 43–44, 71, 80–81, 132, 233–34; stability in Iraq through, 233–34; tribal interests, 225; tribal politics, 26, 43–44, 132, 145, 225; violence against, 71, 104–5, 130, 131, 224–25; withdrawal of U.S. forces, petition for, 145
Trident division, 46

underwater approaches and recovery, technology to support, 6–8
underwater demolition, 4
Underwater Demolition Teams (UDTs): decommissioning of units, 5–6, 15; evolution of focus of, 15–16; innovative and adaptive mind-set, 8; Korea operations, 6; missions of, 6, 8; team members as SEALs, 9; technology to support underwater approaches and recovery, 6–8; training of, 3, 9–10, 11; Vietnam operations, 13; World War II operations, 3–5
United Nations, 16
University of al-Anbar, 99
unmanned aerial vehicles (UAVs), 196, 197–98

U.S. Air Force special operations forces (SOF), 18

U.S. Army: AO Topeka responsibility for, 66, 84; Army-SOF relations, 116, 118, 120; battlespace control by, xxvii, 18–19; bravery of, 115; coalition force strength, 80; Fallujah, 28–29; Fanus capture operation, 76–77; intelligence operations, 98; lives lost in Fallujah-Ramadi operations, 29; Ramadi, battle to take back, 87; Ramadi operation success and, 19, 143; Ramadi patrol operations, 67–70; SEAL-Army relations, 115–21, 235; special operations forces, 18

U.S. Army battalions: 1-6 mechanized infantry battalion, 107; 1-9 infantry battalion, 153, 171, 204; 1-35 armored battalion, 107; 1-37 armored battalion, 107; 1-37 armored battalion, Bravo Company Bulldogs, 111, 117; 1-506 battalion, 107, 153; 1-506 battalion, attacks on, 100–101; 1-506 battalion, Easy Company, 94, 135; 1-506 battalion, SEAL support for, 93–94, 115–16, 121

U.S. Army Brigade Combat Teams: 1st of the 1st Armored Division, 81, 101, 107, 133, 150, 229; 2nd of the Pennsylvania National Guard, 71, 80, 101

U.S. Army Special Forces: Afghanistan combat action and rescue attempt, lives lost in, 38; Army-SOF relations, 116, 118, 120; command structure, 84; counterinsurgency responsibility of, 34, 141–42; strengths of, 120; as training specialists, 45

U.S. Marine Corps: Anbar province, responsibility for, 66; battlespace control by, xxvii, 18–19; bravery of, 115; coalition force strength, 80; Fallujah operations, 28–29;

Government Center outpost, 29, 66, 80; intelligence operations, 98, 199; lives lost in Fallujah-Ramadi operations, 28, 29; maritime operations, 109; Ramadi operations and, 19, 28, 143; SEAL-Marine relations, 115, 235; sniper training, 121; 3/8 infantry battalion, 107

U.S. Navy: Office of Naval Intelligence support, 45–46; reservists, 74, 75; SEAL-Army relations, 115–21, 235

U.S. Navy SEALs. *See* SEALs

U.S. Navy special operations forces (SOF), 18

VBSS (visit, board, search, and seize) activity, 16

vehicle-borne improvised explosive device (VBIED), 177–79

Vietnam: deployment rotations in, 15; insurgency in, xxiv–xxv, 14; lives lost in, xxiv, 13, 14, 15; local scouts, 12–13; public opinion of war, xx; SEAL operations in, xviii–xix, 11–15; SEAL training for, 14–15; UDTs in, 13

Vietnamese SEAL program, 13

visit, board, search, and seize (VBSS) activity, 16

Wagner, Paul, 91–92, 93

Wall, Chuck: background of, 154–55; intelligence from police trainees, 175–76; overwatch operations, 157–58, 160, 161, 162; police training by, 173; Sufia intelligence operations, 180–82

Warar district, Al, 100

The Warrior Elite (Couch), xv, 11, 218

waterproof firing assemblies, 4

weapons: caches in Anbar province, 104; procurement of, 9; for snipers, 123, 124

Wettack, Don: background of, 151–52; overwatch operations, 162–63,

164; police, operations with, 177–79; police training by, 176; scout training by, 153

Wikul, Pete, 46, 191

Williams, Jack: appreciation for Seabees and engineers, 112–13; background of, 86–87; battle in Ramadi, coming changes to, 90–91; battle in Ramadi, support for, 106, 115, 128–29; Camp Corregidor, support for, 93; character of, 116, 120; deployment to Ramadi, 86; grooming standards, 88; on Hedberg, 118; insurgency vs. terrorism, 86; training of SEALs, 115

Wilson, Adam, 39–40, 41–42

Winters, Sam, 45–46, 83, 84

World War II: amphibious operations, 2–5; frogmen, xix, 1–5, 10, 17; island-hopping campaign, 1–2; occupation after, xxv; Tarawa campaign, 1–2

Zarqawi, Abu Musab al, 27, 29, 43, 76, 80, 105, 130, 141

Zilmer, Richard, 83–84

zone-clearance operations, 100

Dick Couch was born in Mississippi and raised in southern Indiana. He is a 1967 graduate of the U.S. Naval Academy and served with the Navy Underwater Demolition and SEAL teams. While a platoon leader with SEAL Team One in 1970, he led one of the only successful POW rescue operations of the Vietnam War. Upon release from active duty in 1972, he joined the Central Intelligence Agency, where he served as a maritime operations officer. He retired from the Naval Reserve in 1997 with the rank of captain.

Dick began his writing career in 1990 and has published six novels: *SEAL Team One, Pressure Point, Silent Descent, Rising Wind, The Mercenary Option,* and *Covert Action. Pressure Point* was re-released in 2006. *SEAL Team One* was re-released by the Naval Institute Press in 2008.

The Warrior Elite: The Forging of SEAL Class 228, his first nonfiction work, was published in November 2001. *The US Armed Forces Nuclear, Chemical, Biological Survival Manual,* edited by Dick for civilian use, came out in April 2003. *The Finishing School,* a work that details advanced Navy SEAL training, was published in March 2004. *Down Range: Navy SEAL Operations in the War on Terror,* appeared on the shelves in July 2005. Released in March 2007: *Chosen Soldier: The Making of a Special Forces Warrior.* Scheduled for 2009: *My Brother's Keeper* (a novel) and *Inner Warrior* (nonfiction).

Dick is frequently heard on National Public Radio and numerous other radio talk shows and has served as an analyst for Fox TV, MSNBC TV, and ABC radio regarding combat operations in Afghanistan and Iraq. He is a sought-after corporate and motivational speaker. Dick is currently an adjunct professor at the U.S. Naval Academy teaching ethics.

The Naval Institute Press is the book-publishing arm of the U.S. Naval Institute, a private, nonprofit, membership society for sea service professionals and others who share an interest in naval and maritime affairs. Established in 1873 at the U.S. Naval Academy in Annapolis, Maryland, where its offices remain today, the Naval Institute has members worldwide.

Members of the Naval Institute support the education programs of the society and receive the influential monthly magazine *Proceedings* and discounts on fine nautical prints and on ship and aircraft photos. They also have access to the transcripts of the Institute's Oral History Program and get discounted admission to any of the Institute-sponsored seminars offered around the country. Discounts are also available to the colorful bimonthly magazine *Naval History*.

The Naval Institute's book-publishing program, begun in 1898 with basic guides to naval practices, has broadened its scope to include books of more general interest. Now the Naval Institute Press publishes about seventy titles each year, ranging from how-to books on boating and navigation to battle histories, biographies, ship and aircraft guides, and novels. Institute members receive significant discounts on the Press's more than eight hundred books in print.

Full-time students are eligible for special half-price membership rates. Life memberships are also available.

For a free catalog describing Naval Institute Press books currently available, and for further information about joining the U.S. Naval Institute, please write to:

Member Services
U.S. NAVAL INSTITUTE
291 Wood Road
Annapolis, Maryland 21402-5034
Telephone: 800.233.8764
Fax: 410.571.1703
Web address: www.usni.org

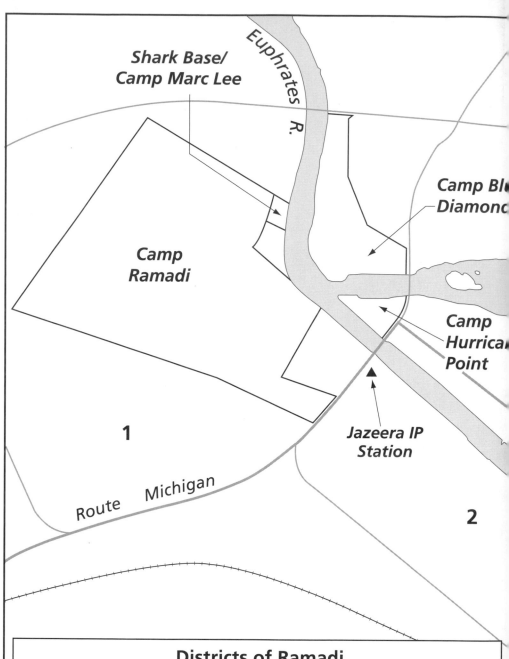

Shark Base/
Camp Marc Lee

Euphrates R.

Camp Bl
Diamond

Camp
Ramadi

Camp
Hurrica
Point

1

Jazeera IP
Station

Route Michigan

2

Districts of Ramadi

1. 5-Kilo District
2. Ta'Meem District
3. Al Warar District
4. Al Hawz District
5. Hay Al Dhobot-1st Officer's District
6. Thaylat District

7. Al Mualemeen District
8. Al Shirikah District
9. Qatana District
10. Al Andols District
11. Hay Al Dhobat Thanya-2nd Officer's District
12. Sina'a Industrial District

13. Al Iskan District aka Police Housing Area
14. Al Mala'ab Large Stadium District
15. Albu Jabar District
16. Sufia District
17. Zeraa Agricultural District